VISUAL QUICKSTART GUIDE

FRONTPAGE 2002

FOR WINDOWS

Nolan Hester

Peachpit Press

Visual QuickStart Guide
FrontPage 2002 for Windows
Nolan Hester

Peachpit Press
1249 Eighth Street
Berkeley, CA 94710
(800) 283-9444
(510) 524-2178
(510) 524-2221 (fax)

Find us on the World Wide Web at: www.peachpit.com
To report errors, please send a note to errata@peachpit.com

Peachpit Press is a division of Pearson Education

Editor: Nancy Davis
Production Coordinator: Connie Jeung-Mills
Production and Composition: David Van Ness
Cover Design: The Visual Group
Indexer: Emily Glossbrenner

ISBN: 0-201-74143-1

0 9 8 7 6 5 4 3 2 1

Printed and bound in the United States of America

To the victims of September 11, 2001.

Special thanks to:
My immensely talented and prodigiously patient editor, Nancy Davis; David Van Ness for being the ever-steady master of all things Quark; Mimi Heft for far more than just a cover; Emily Glossbrenner for the very best indexing—and at lightening speed; Marjorie Baer for encouragement and helping me see Los Angeles in a new light; Nancy Aldrich-Ruenzel for giving me the chance to do this work; and Laika, aka Lou the Wonder Dog. And finally, most especially, to Mary.

TABLE OF CONTENTS

TABLE OF CONTENTS

PART 2:   CREATING BASIC WEB PAGES   87

Chapter 4:   Creating and Formatting Text   89

Chapter 6:   Adding Hyperlinks   135

Index   421

PART I

GETTING STARTED

USING FRONTPAGE 2002

Welcome to FrontPage 2002. Whether you bought it as a stand-alone program or as part of Microsoft Office XP Professional or Developer editions, FrontPage has the tools to make your Web site building quick and easy. FrontPage lets you skip the tedium of creating your Web pages directly in HTML (HyperText Markup Language), the Web's underlying language. Instead you use menus and commands similar to those you already know from Microsoft's other programs, such as Word, Excel, and PowerPoint.

Using FrontPage, you'll find it easy to design your Web site's overall structure, create the necessary pages to flesh out the structure, add multimedia and interactive features to enliven those pages, and, finally, publish the whole thing on the Web by uploading the files to a Web server. Because Office recognizes HTML as easily as its own formats, FrontPage can insert many Office documents directly into your new Web pages.

Whether you're working for a one-person business or an international firm, FrontPage includes all the tools and functions you need to build Web sites to post on the Internet or on private intranets.

What's New

Compared with FrontPage 2000, which made a huge leap past the clunkiness of FrontPage 98, the changes in FrontPage 2002 may seem only incremental. But the more time you spend in FrontPage 2002, the clearer it becomes that the newest version is significantly smoother and more powerful than FrontPage 2000. Those changes are highlighted throughout the book, but here's a partial list:

◆ In a new feature straight out of PowerPoint, FrontPage can create basic vector-based shapes and text effects (**Figures 1.1** and **1.2**). Those effects will display correctly in version 5 or later Web browsers, and shapes created in other Office applications can be pasted directly into FrontPage. For more information, see *Adding and Editing Drawings* on page 197.

◆ An optional task pane gives you quick access to your most-used commands, such as creating a new page or inserting clip art. This same feature has been added to Office XP. For more information, see *Using the task pane* on page 22.

◆ The main window now displays a set of page tabs, which let you quickly switch among all your open FrontPage pages as you work. For more information, see *The FrontPage Main Window* on page 17.

◆ Link Bars replace the sometimes confusing-to-implement Navigation Bars of FrontPage 2000. You'll find it much easier to customize Link Bars and build drop-down menus of your most-used links.

Figure 1.1 PowerPoint fans rejoice: FrontPage now mimics its cousin program's ability to insert vector-based shapes.

Figure 1.2 Text effects, such as shadows, can now be applied within FrontPage—and display correctly in version 5 or later Web browsers.

◆ The new Database Interface Wizard may affect your Web intranet more than any other change in FrontPage 2002. The wizard makes it possible to display corporate-sized database results on FrontPage-created Web sites—and grant specific users the ability to edit that data from within a Web browser. For more information, see *Adding Database Connections* on page 317.

◆ You can now insert into your pages various items from MSNBC, such as headlines or stock quotes, and they will be updated automatically as they change on MSNBC. For more information, see *Adding Web Components* on page 236.

WHAT'S NEW

Important Changes

Sometimes it's the little changes, not the flashy new features, that make the biggest difference in your daily use of a program. Here are the changes most likely to affect your work:

♦ Continuing the trend begun with the 2000 versions of FrontPage and Office, FrontPage 2002 is even more tightly bound to the look and functions of the simultaneously released Office XP. Both programs, for example, now sport a task pane for common tasks. Both now also use floating toolbars that fade away when not being used. For more information, see *FrontPage Basics* on page 15.

♦ The folder list and navigation panes have been streamlined to make it easier to control how pages link to one another. For more information, see *FrontPage Basics* on page 15.

♦ You now have more control over table formats with tools for automatically filling cells and applying custom effects (**Figure 1.3**). For more information, see *Creating Tables* on page 250.

Figure 1.3 The Tables toolbar now lets you apply custom formats, as well as automatically fill in empty cells.

◆ User-level security offers finer control over who can access pages—a feature requested by many FrontPage 2000 users. For more information, see *Installing and Configuring FrontPage* on page 409.

◆ Using a set of revamped panes, you now can update your remote Web site by drag-and-dropping locally generated pages. For more information, see *Publishing to the Web* on page 394.

◆ You now can take a folder of images and automatically create an entire gallery of quick-to-download thumbnail versions of each image. In the previous version of FrontPage, you could only create thumbnails one image a time. For more information, see *To create a thumbnail photo gallery* on page 185.

IMPORTANT CHANGES

Using This Book

The key to this book, like all of Peachpit's Visual QuickStart Guides, is that word *visual*. As much as possible, I've used illustrations with succinct captions to explain how FrontPage works. Ideally, you should be able to quickly find what you need by scanning the table of contents, page tabs, illustrations, or captions. Once you find a relevant topic, the text provides the essential details and tips.

This book's written with the assumption that you're familiar with Windows' basic operation and understand the general concept of how the World Wide Web works. If you're looking for under-the-hood Web server details, this isn't your book. Instead, we take things step by step and whenever a potentially confusing step or concept arises, I'll try to steer you through any rough spots and wrong turns. As the cover says, I focus on getting you "up and running in no time."

Throughout the book, you'll find these symbols and typographic cues to speed you along in learning FrontPage:

Tips: Signified by a ✔ in the margin, tips highlight shortcuts for performing common tasks or ways you can use your new FrontPage skills to solve common problems.

Italic words: When *italicized* words appear in the book's text, you'll find the very same words on the FrontPage screen itself when you reach that step in the program. The italicized term might appear as a button or tab label, the name of a text window or an option button in a dialog box, or as one of several choices in a drop-down menu. Whatever the context, the italics are meant to help you

Figure 1.4 Sometimes the original dialog boxes or deep menus (left) will be faded out in the middle to save space on the page (right).

quickly find the item in what can sometimes be a crowded screen. If the step includes an accompanying illustration, use it to help you find the item being discussed. Two examples: Click the *Browse* button to navigate to the file you want to use. Click the drop-down menu and select *asp* from the choices.

Code font: When a word or words appears in `code font`, it's used to indicate the literal text you need to type into FrontPage. Because FrontPage does its best to shield you from the tedium coding, you won't see this very much in the book. An example: After *font family:* type `Verdana, Arial, Helvetica, sans serif`; as the name for your connection. *`Italicized code font`* indicates code items where you are expected to replace the italicized word with a word related to your own files or documents. An example: Type *`yourConnection`* as the name for your connection.

Menu commands and keyboard shortcuts: Menu-based commands are shown as: File > New > Task. Keyboard-based shortcuts (when available) are shown in parentheses after the first step in which they can be used. For example: (Ctrl K) means that to insert an image you should press the Ctrl and K keys at the same time.

Fades in figures: Sometimes a FrontPage dialog box or menu is so deep that it can be hard to fit on the page with all the other figures—and still leave it large enough to read. In those cases, I fade out the middle or end of the figure to save some space (**Figure 1.4**). Nothing critical to understanding the step is ever left out. And it sure beats running teeny, tiny figures.

Updates and Feedback

For FrontPage updates and patches, make a point of checking Microsoft's web site from time to time: www.microsoft.com

This book also has a companion site where you'll find examples from the book, tips and tricks based on real-world tasks, and corrections for inadvertent mistakes. So drop by www.peachpit.com/vqs/frontpage2002 when you can.

Finally, I and Peachpit's editors have done everything possible to make this book error free and clear as glass. Please write me at frontpage@waywest.net if you spot a mistake—or have a suggestion. Readers of the previous edition offered lots of tips, which I've used throughout this new edition. With your help, the *next* edition will be even better. Like a Web site, a book's never really done.

Web Planning Tips

Despite all the hoopla about the Web being an entirely new medium, it revolves around a pretty old phenomenon: our eyeballs. Yep, we *look* at Web sites. We don't taste or smell them. And we don't test drive them. That means we depend on *visual* cues for how to use a site. By following the basic visual principles explained in the next few pages, you'll be more than halfway toward making your Web site a pleasure to use.

By the way, there are plenty of great books out there devoted solely to designing Web sites. If you want to dive deeper, here are five great jumping-off points.

The Non-Designer's Web Book: An Easy Guide to Creating, Designing, and Posting Your Own Web Site by Robin Williams and John Tollett (Peachpit Press).

Here's a pair of books that together distill lifetimes of design wisdom into timeless advice for every Web designer: *Hot Wired Style: Principles for Building Smart Web Sites* by Jeffrey Veen (Wired Books); and *Web Style Guide: Basic Design Principles for Creating Web Sites* by Patrick J. Lynch and Sarah Horton (Yale University Press).

Love or hate. People rarely have middle-ground reactions to Piquin peppers, Neil Young, and these two opinionated books: *Creating Killer Web Sites: The Art of Third-Generation Site Design* by David Siegel (Hayden Books); and *Designing Web Usability: The Practice of Simplicity* by Jakob Nielsen (New Riders). Both are worth savoring, along with those peppers and Mr. Young.

Keep it clean

Clutter kills. Sites that go a thousand directions at once leave visitors confused or, worse, irritated. Imagine if parking garages were laid out like some Web sites: We'd all still be trying to find the entrance. Make it simple, make it obvious. A rule of thumb: If you have to explain how a site works, it's not working.

Clutter comes in many guises. Everyone, for example, has encountered Web sites with what I call fake front doors. Instead of offering a home page with links to products and staff, the site's first page serves up an absolutely gorgeous graphic or layered animation. It swirls and whirls—as your hard drive churns and churns—until finally there appears the equivalent of the old "Click Here" link: "Discover the power of XYZ Widgets" or "Want to find out more?" So you click one more time and finally come to the company's *real* front door—a home page where you can start looking for the information you need.

Don't make your visitors knock twice to get in the door. And for gosh sakes, don't make them beg. If you want to orient visitors with a series of images, make them small and make them snappy to download. Most importantly, strip away every bit of clutter for the cleanest possible site.

Keep it lean

The Web's too slow. It was too slow last year; it'll still be too slow next year. Wish as we might for connections speedy enough to handle full-motion video, CD-quality sound, and Java applets galore, most folks are still using telephone modems to reach the Web. As palm-sized organizers and email-capable cell phones proliferate, more and more people will be using the Web with less rather than more bandwidth.

Even a state-of-the-art inhouse intranet with fast computers and fast pipes can't entirely escape the bandwidth bogeyman. Most likely the on-the-road sales force will be tapping into that intranet via a dial-up connection for sales data or product listings.

See what I mean—the Web's too slow and the speed limit will remain a problem for some years to come. Don't fight—and never ignore—such limits. Instead use them to guide you in building your site. As architect and multimedia trailblazer Charles Eames put it four decades ago: "Design largely depends on constraints."

Make it easy

Nobody has to tell you how to read a newspaper or a magazine for two reasons: You already know the "rules" and even if you didn't they're pretty obvious. Big headlines mean a story's more important than one with a small headline. Items grouped together suggest that they're related. Front page stories carry more urgency than those inside the section. Size, proximity, and placement are hallmarks of the print medium's centuries-old "interface." Because the Web's so new, there's a temptation to think that means it has no rules. But trust your eyeballs; the visual touchstones of size, proximity, and placement are fairly constant even when the medium's new.

Just as the red light is the first on a traffic signal, give visual weight to the most important item on each Web page. That, of course, means you have to decide what's most—and least—important on each page and the site overall. So before you start working on that amazing animated graphic for your home page, make sure you're clear about your site's intended message and about who will be using the site.

Just as you wouldn't put sports stories in a newspaper's food section, you shouldn't build a Web site with your tech-support advice buried in the marketing section. Obvious, you say, but lots of Web sites fail to put related items together. Save your Web visitor some work by grouping similar items.

WEB PLANNING TIPS

In planning a Web site, deciding what to put where (placement) is perhaps the hardest guideline for which to find the right balance. If a site's too "deep," visitors will have to click down layer after layer to find the information they need (**Figure 1.5**). The risk is that they'll never find what they're looking for. On the other hand, you can create a site that's too "shallow" with a home page that has so many links that it becomes a confusing mess (**Figure 1.6**).

Ideally, a visitor to your site should be able to find what they're seeking in two or three mouse clicks (**Figure 1.7**). That's easy to say, but hard to achieve. Fortunately, FrontPage's navigation view makes it easy to shuffle your pages around until you strike a happy medium where almost all the site's information can be reached in no more than four mouse clicks.

As you learn how to use FrontPage's various tools in the chapters ahead, remember: keep it clean, keep it lean, and make it easy.

Figure 1.5 In this Web site structure, a key function—ordering products—is buried too "deep" for visitors to easily find it.

Figure 1.6 If you create a Web site structure that's too "shallow," you risk overwhelming visitors with a home page crammed with links that give equal emphasis to everything.

Figure 1.7 With a balanced Web site structure, the home page features only the most important links, items are grouped in logical categories, and everything can be reached in two or three clicks.

FRONTPAGE BASICS

This chapter gives you a quick overview of Microsoft FrontPage's main features and the basic tasks of opening, closing, and saving Web pages and sites. Each of the items covered, whether it's FrontPage's views, menus, or toolbars, is explained in more detail later in the book. Starting here gives you an overall feel for the program's organization and functions, letting you dive in deeper when you're ready.

❶ *Application menu (click to activate)*

Restore
Move
Size
Minimize
Maximize
Close Alt+F4

❷ *Web site name*
Selected Web page name
Page selection tabs

❹ *Close application window*
Maximize window
Minimize window

❸ *Search FrontPage Help*

❺ *Menu bar*
Standard toolbar
Formatting toolbar

❻ *Views Bar*

❼ *Page view tabs*

❽ *Drawing toolbar (with AutoShapes)*

❾ *Download progress indicator*

❿ *Estimated download time (click to change connection speed)*

14.4
28.8
56K
ISDN
T1
T3

Figure 2.1 FrontPage's main window opens in the *Normal* view by default. To change the page view, click the *HTML* or *Preview* tabs.

The FrontPage Main Window

By default, the FrontPage 2002 main window opens in the *Normal* page view setting (**Figure 2.1**). The only major changes from FrontPage 2000's window are the addition of page selection tabs ❷, a text window for searching FrontPage's Help ❸, and a new Drawing toolbar ❸.

❶ **Application menu box:** Clicking the FrontPage icon triggers a pop-up box of choices for sizing the main window: Restore, Move, Size, Minimize, Maximize, and Close.

❷ **Web site, selected Web page name, page selection tabs:** The Web site name is set when a new Web is created (see page 43). You set an individual page's name when you first create it. Click any page selection tab to select and display that Web page in the main window.

❸ **Search FrontPage Help:** By typing a question or keyword in the text window, and pressing (Return), you'll be presented with a choice of topical answers. Click to select one and FrontPage's Help will take you directly to the answer. For more information, see *To use FrontPage's Help* on page 36.

❹ **Window control buttons:** Clicking the three buttons will (left to right): collapse the window into the taskbar (minimize), expand the window to full screen (maximize), or close that window.

❺ **Menu bar and toolbars:** By default, FrontPage displays the Menu bar, Standard toolbar, and Formatting toolbar. To change which bars appear, choose View > Toolbars and toggle on/off your choices.

❻ **Views Bar:** By default, FrontPage opens to the Page view. Click any of the other five icons to toggle to another view: *Folders* to arrange files and folders; *Reports* to assess the files, links, and pictures of an open Web site; *Navigation* to see and edit a Web site's structure; *Hyperlinks* to see the links to and from each page in a Web site; and *Tasks* to see, create, or edit a To-do list for the Web site.

❼ **Page view tabs:** By default, FrontPage opens in the *Normal* view, which lets you edit the open Web page. Click *HTML* view to see or edit a page's coding; click *Preview* to see how the page will look in a Web browser. *Preview* will not appear if you don't have Microsoft's Web browser, Internet Explorer, installed on your machine. (Internet Explorer doesn't need to be running, just installed.)

❽ **Drawing toolbar:** New in FrontPage 2002 and on by default, the Drawing toolbar offers quick access to the new vector-based shapes and text effects. For more information, see *Using the Toolbars* on page 24.

❾ **Download progress indicator:** The icon spins while FrontPage is opening a Web page; it stops once all the page's related files have opened.

❿ **Estimated download time:** By default, FrontPage is set to show how many seconds the current page will take to download over a 28.8 bps modem connection. You can click to change the connection speed, though 28.8 probably reflects the average dial-up user's modem rate.

Starting and Quitting FrontPage

To launch FrontPage

1. Click the Start button in the Windows taskbar, and if you installed FrontPage as part of Office XP, point your cursor to Programs, then Office, and click the Microsoft FrontPage icon (top right, **Figure 2.2**). If you installed FrontPage as a stand-alone program, click Start, point your cursor to Programs, and click the Microsoft FrontPage icon (bottom left, **Figure 2.2**).

2. Once FrontPage launches, you'll be presented with a blank main window (**Figure 2.3**), at which point you can create a new page or Web site, or open an existing page or Web site.

To quit FrontPage

◆ After saving your work (Ctrl S), choose File > Exit (Alt F4) (**Figure 2.4**).

Figure 2.2 If FrontPage came as part of Office XP, click the *Start* button, and then choose *Programs, Office,* and *Microsoft FrontPage* (top). If you installed FrontPage as a stand-alone program, click *Start,* and choose *Programs* and *Microsoft FrontPage* (bottom).

Figure 2.3 When FrontPage launches, it displays a blank main window.

Figure 2.4 To quit FrontPage, choose File > Exit (Alt F4).

STARTING AND QUITTING FRONTPAGE

Figure 2.5 Clicking the *HTML* tab lets you inspect or edit the current page's HTML coding.

Figure 2.6 Clicking the *Preview* tab gives you a rough sense of how the current page will appear within a Web browser.

Figure 2.7 Some effects, such as slide shows, may not appear using the Preview tab (left) but will preview correctly with the Preview in Browser command (right).

Using Normal, HTML, and Preview Views

In page view, you can choose from three different views by clicking the tabs: Normal (the default), HTML, or Preview. The Normal page view lets you directly edit the current Web page—without seeing any of the underlying HTML code (**Figure 2.1**). The HTML view, naturally, shows all the coding and allows you to change the code directly (**Figure 2.5**). Preview view lets you get a better idea of how the page will look within a Web browser (**Figure 2.6**).

✔ Tips

- Instead of clicking the tabs to change your page view, you also can press Ctrl Page Up or Ctrl Page Down to cycle forward or backward from *Normal* to *HTML* to *Preview*.

- In theory, the Preview tab should work just like the Preview in Browser command (File > Preview in Browser). In practice, some items (scrolling text) will appear the same with either approach. However, other effects (animation slide shows) may not appear using the Preview tab but will preview correctly with the command (**Figure 2.7**). To be sure, always use File > Preview in Browser.

Using the Views icons

FrontPage offers six different ways to see and edit your Web pages or sites, depending on which icon you click in the Views Bar (**Figure 2.8**). By default, FrontPage displays the page view (**Figure 2.9**). The other choices let you quickly see the folders, reports, navigation structure, hyperlinks, or tasks related to the current Web page or site. Each view displays a different set of information about your site and pages (**Figures 2.10–2.14**).

Figure 2.8 Click any of the six icons to quickly change your view of the current Web page or site.

Figure 2.9 By default, FrontPage displays the Page view when you first open a Web site.

Figure 2.10 Clicking the *Folders* icon in the Views Bar gives you a folder-level view of the current Web site.

Figure 2.11 Clicking the *Reports* icon in the Views Bar gives you an analytical overview of the current Web site.

Figure 2.12 Clicking the *Navigation* icon in the Views Bar shows you the current Web site's overall structure. This is great for roughing out a site before you start building individual Web pages.

Figure 2.13 Clicking the *Hyperlinks* icon in the Views Bar shows the links to and from the current Web page.

Figure 2.14 Clicking the *Tasks* icon in the Views Bar lets you create a To-do list for the Web site and track the status of those tasks.

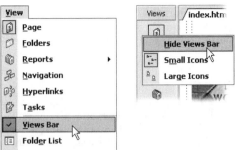

Figure 2.15 The Views Bar can be toggled on or off by choosing View > Views Bar (left) or right-clicking the Views Bar and choosing *Hide Views Bar* (right).

Figure 2.16
To quickly see your Web site's folder structure—no matter which view you're in—click the Folder List icon in the Standard toolbar. To hide the folders, click the icon again.

Figure 2.17 Use the Folder List/Navigation tabs to quickly switch your view (left) or by clicking the Folder List icon in the Standard toolbar (right).

To switch views

1. Make sure the Views Bar is visible in FrontPage's left pane. If it is not, choose View > Views Bar (left, **Figure 2.15**).

2. Click any of the six icons in the Views Bar.

3. FrontPage's right pane will switch to reflect your choice.

✔ Tips

■ If you want maximum work space for your pages, you can hide the Views Bar by choosing View > Views Bar, and unchecking the Views Bar or by right-clicking the Views Bar and choosing *Hide Views Bar* (**Figure 2.15**). To toggle the Views Bar back on, repeat either procedure.

■ No matter which view you're using, you can quickly see your site's folder structure by clicking the Folder List icon in the Standard toolbar (**Figure 2.16**). Click the icon again to hide the folders. Or choose View > Folder List to toggle the folders on and off.

■ If the Folder List already is visible, you can quickly switch to navigation view by clicking the *Navigation* tab at the bottom of the *Folder List* pane or by clicking the Folder List icon in the Standard toolbar and selecting *Navigation Pane* (**Figure 2.17**).

Using the task pane

The task pane, a new feature for FrontPage 2002 based on Office XP, makes it easier to perform common tasks, such as creating new pages or using page templates. The pane offers one of three views: *New Page or Web*, *Clipboard*, or *Search* and automatically displays the last view used.

Despite the similar names, FrontPage's task pane has nothing to do with its task view. (The task pane applies only to the current Web page; while the task view works across the entire Web site.) Unfortunately, FrontPage's Help doesn't include any information on the task pane—adding to the confusion.

To use the task pane

1. Choose View > Task Pane (**Figure 2.18**).

2. When the task pane appears on the main window's right side, use the arrows or triangle at the top of the pane to choose among its three views (**Figure 2.19**).

3. Once the desired pane view appears, click any icon in the pane to activate that action (**Figure 2.20**).

✔ Tips

- The task pane's clipboard is a great place to store images, hyperlinks, or any other item you use often (left, **Figure 2.21**).

- For more information on using the task pane's search options, see page 166 (right, **Figure 2.21**).

Figure 2.18 To display the task pane, use the View menu.

Figure 2.19 Use the arrows or triangle at the top of the task pane to choose among its three views.

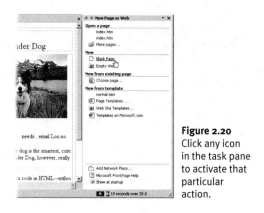

Figure 2.20 Click any icon in the task pane to activate that particular action.

Figure 2.21 The task pane's Clipboard view (left) makes a great place to store images, hyperlinks, or other items you use often, while its Basic Search view (right) helps you find items in the page or site.

Figure 2.22 Choose Tools > Options to have the task pane appear by default.

Figure 2.23 To separate the task pane from the main window, click its top bar and drag it elsewhere on your desktop.

To start the task pane automatically

1. Choose Tools > Options (left, **Figure 2.22**).

2. When the Options dialog box appears, click the General tab, and check *Startup Task Pane* (right, **Figure 2.22**).

3. Click *OK* to close the dialog box. Once you restart FrontPage, the task pane will appear automatically along the main window's right side.

To move the task pane to the desktop

◆ To move the task pane out of FrontPage's main window, click your cursor on the top of the pane and drag the pane to a new spot on the desktop, where it will then appear with its own title (**Figure 2.23**).

To close the task pane

◆ Choose View > Task Pane and release your cursor or click the X in the top-right corner of the task pane. The task pane will close.

Using the Toolbars

By default, the Standard and Formatting toolbars (**Figures 2.24** and **2.25**) appear at the top of FrontPage's main window and the Drawing toolbar appears at the bottom of the window. But depending on which Web tasks you're doing at the moment, displaying one or more of FrontPage's nine other toolbars can be particularly handy (**Figures 2.26–2.35**). Like all of FrontPage's toolbars, they can be customized to your heart's desire. Or you can create your own custom toolbar. For details, see *To customize an existing toolbar* and *To create a new toolbar* on pages 30 and 31.

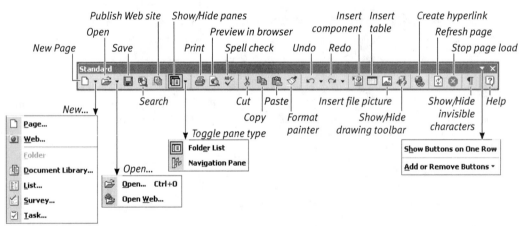

Figure 2.24 Icons in the Standard toolbar, which by default appears just below the menu bar, trigger FrontPage's most commonly used commands.

Figure 2.25 Icons in the Formatting toolbar, which appears by default, generally correspond to text appearance commands in the Format menu.

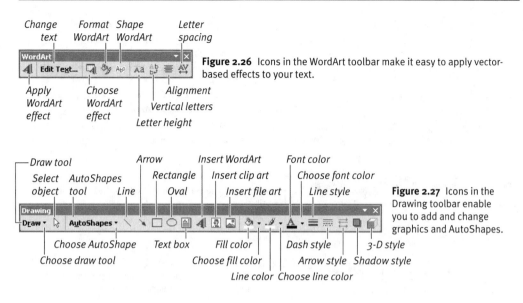

Change text
Format WordArt
Shape WordArt
Letter spacing

Figure 2.26 Icons in the WordArt toolbar make it easy to apply vector-based effects to your text.

Apply WordArt effect
Choose WordArt effect
Vertical letters
Alignment
Letter height

Draw tool
Select object
AutoShapes tool
Line
Arrow
Rectangle
Oval
Insert WordArt
Insert clip art
Insert file art
Font color
Choose font color
Line style

Figure 2.27 Icons in the Drawing toolbar enable you to add and change graphics and AutoShapes.

Choose AutoShape
Choose draw tool
Text box
Fill color
Choose fill color
Dash style
Arrow style
Line color
Choose line color
3-D style
Shadow style

Enlarge canvas

Figure 2.28 Icons in the Drawing Canvas toolbar let you control the size of the canvas when working with vector-based images.

Fit canvas to drawings
Scale canvas up or down

Choose event
Choose effect

Figure 2.29 The drop-down menus in the DHTML Effects (Dynamic HTML) toolbar let you set up formatting effects that are triggered by the Web user's actions. For details, see page 354.

Effect setting
Highlight effect

Toggle view: portrait/landscape
Include in navigation bars

Figure 2.30 The drop-down menu and icons in the Navigation toolbar, which only works in the navigation view, control your view of the current Web site's structure. For details, see page 56.

Zoom view
Add external link
View subtree only

Create thumbnail
Position absolutely
Rotate left
Rotate right
More contrast
Less contrast
Crop
Format picture
Set transparent color
Add/remove buttons
Create hotspots
Add text
Select

Insert picture
Bring forward
Send back
Flip vertical
Flip horizontal
Brighter
Dimmer
Line style
Set color
Resample picture
Bevel border
Restore picture

Figure 2.31 The Pictures toolbar's icons help you edit aspects of any selected graphic. For details, see page 161.

Figure 2.32 The icons and text boxes in the Positioning toolbar help you control the absolute and relative positioning of the selected page element. For details, see page 193.

Figure 2.33 The drop-down menus and icons in the Reporting toolbar, used only in the Reports view, help you check the current Web site's files, functions, and hyperlinks. For details, see page 359.

Figure 2.34 The Style toolbar has no buttons and opens the Style dialog box. For details, see page 339.

Insert rows
Delete cells
Merge cells
Align top
Align bottom
Spread columns evenly
Apply fill color
Choose fill color
AutoFormat
Fill down
Fill right

Erase
Draw table
Insert columns
Split cells
Center
Autofill
Spread rows evenly
Apply AutoFormat Combo
Choose AutoFormat Combo

Figure 2.35 Icons in the Tables toolbar control the major aspects of creating and adjusting tables in your Web pages.

USING THE TOOLBARS

Figure 2.36 To turn on or off any toolbar, choose View > Toolbars and make a choice from the drop-down menu.

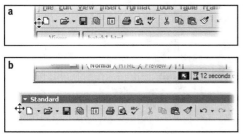

Figure 2.37 To move a docked toolbar, click anywhere in the bar (a) and drag it onto the desktop (b).

To turn on/off toolbars

1. Choose View > Toolbars and select a toolbar from the drop-down menu to turn on or off (**Figure 2.36**). Checked toolbars are already on; unchecked ones are off.

2. Release your cursor on the selected toolbar and it will appear (or disappear) above or below FrontPage's main window.

Rearranging the toolbars

FrontPage lets you move any of its toolbars to where they're most convenient for your work. Sometimes it's easiest to have your activated toolbars "docked," that is, running horizontally across the top or bottom of FrontPage's main window. For some tasks, however, you may prefer to have a toolbar sitting out on the desktop itself. FrontPage also lets you resize the toolbars to fit your workspace.

To move toolbars to the desktop

◆ To move a docked toolbar (those running across FrontPage's main window), click your cursor on the toolbar and drag the toolbar to a new spot on the desktop, where it will then appear with its own title (**Figure 2.37**).

To dock toolbars in the main window

◆ To move a freestanding toolbar into a docked position, click on the toolbar and drag it to the zone just above or below FrontPage's main window. As your cursor approaches the docking area, the freestanding toolbar will snap into place (**Figure 2.38**).

To resize freestanding toolbars

◆ To shrink a *freestanding* toolbar, click its outer edge and drag the cursor toward the toolbar's center. To expand the toolbar, drag the cursor away from the toolbar's center (**Figure 2.39**).

Figure 2.38 To dock a freestanding toolbar, click and drag it to FrontPage's main window (a). As your cursor approaches the docking area (b), the freestanding toolbar will "snap" into place (c).

Figure 2.39 To resize a toolbar, click on its edge and while holding down the cursor, drag it horizontally or vertically.

Figure 2.40 To add or remove toolbar buttons, click the triangle at the end of the toolbar and the *Add or Remove Buttons* drop-down menu will appear.

Figure 2.41 When you move the cursor over the *Add or Remove Buttons* menu, a drop-down menu will appear showing all the toolbar's available buttons.

Figure 2.42 Click the item you want to remove or add to the selected toolbar. When you're done, click anywhere outside the drop-down menu to trigger the change.

Figure 2.43 To reset the toolbar to its original condition, click the triangle at the end of the toolbar, move to the *Add or Remove Buttons* drop-down menu, and click *Reset Toolbar*.

Customizing the toolbars

FrontPage lets you add or remove toolbar buttons. You also can customize toolbars by adding extra buttons to existing toolbars or by creating new, blank toolbars from scratch and adding only the buttons you need.

To add or remove toolbar buttons

1. Click the triangle at the end of the toolbar you want to customize and the *Add or Remove Buttons* drop-down menu will appear (**Figure 2.40**).

2. Move the cursor over the *Add or Remove Buttons* drop-down menu, click *Standard*, and another drop-down menu will appear showing all of the toolbar's current buttons, marked by checks (**Figure 2.41**).

3. Click the item you want to remove and the check will disappear (**Figure 2.42**).

4. Continue unchecking (removing) or checking (adding) items until you're satisfied. Then click anywhere outside the drop-down menu and the toolbar will reflect your changes.

✔ Tip

■ It's all too easy to accidentally remove an entire menu. To quickly undo your button changes, you can reset a toolbar to its original condition. Just click the triangle at the end of the toolbar, and choose Add or Remove Buttons > Standard > Reset Toolbar (**Figure 2.43**). The toolbar's original buttons will reappear.

To customize an existing toolbar

1. If you want to add buttons not immediately available in a toolbar's add/remove drop-down menu, choose Add or Remove Buttons > Customize (**Figure 2.44**).

2. When the Customize dialog box appears, make sure the *Commands* tab is selected.

3. Click one of the menu categories in the left pane, then click the command in the right pane that you want to add to your toolbar (**Figure 2.45**).

4. With the command still highlighted, drag your cursor to the spot in the toolbar where you want the button to appear (**Figure 2.46**).

5. Release the cursor and the command button will be inserted into the toolbar.

Figure 2.44 To add buttons not already available in a toolbar's add/remove drop-down menu, select *Customize*.

Figure 2.45 Click a category in the left pane, then, in the right pane, click the command you want to add to your toolbar.

Figure 2.46 Once you choose a command, drag it to the toolbar you're customizing.

Figure 2.47 To create a new toolbar, choose Tools > Customize.

Figure 2.48 In the Customize dialog box, click the *Toolbars* tab, and then click *New*.

Figure 2.49 Give your new toolbar a descriptive name and click *OK*.

Figure 2.50 Click and drag commands from the right pane onto your new toolbar. When you've finished, click *Close*.

To create a new toolbar

1. Choose Tools > Customize (**Figure 2.47**).

2. When the Customize dialog box appears, click the *Toolbars* tab, and then click *New* (**Figure 2.48**).

3. When the New Toolbar dialog box appears, type in a descriptive name for your new toolbar, and click *OK* (**Figure 2.49**). The new toolbar will appear in the Customize dialog box's list of available toolbars. The toolbar itself also will appear on the desktop, but since it doesn't have any icons yet, it'll be tiny and hard to spot.

4. To add icons to your new toolbar, click the Customize dialog box's *Commands* tab.

5. Choose a command category in the left pane, then click on a command icon in the right pane, drag it to your new toolbar, and release your cursor. The icon will be placed in your new toolbar.

6. As you continue selecting and adding icons, your new toolbar will become large enough to resize. When you have finished adding commands icons, click *Close* (**Figure 2.50**). Your new toolbar will appear as a freestanding toolbar, but remember that you can always dock it in the main window. For details, see *To dock toolbars in the main window* on page 28.

✔ Tip

- By now you may realize there are three ways to get to the Customize dialog box: 1) View > Toolbars > Customize, 2) Tools > Customize, and 3) the *Add or Remove Buttons* drop-down menu that appears when you click the triangle at the right end of any toolbar. They all work identically.

To delete a toolbar

1. If you want to get rid of a toolbar (instead of just hiding it from view), choose View > Toolbars > Customize (**Figure 2.51**).

2. When the Customize dialog box appears, click in the list on the name of the toolbar you want removed, and click *Delete* (**Figure 2.52**).

3. When the alert dialog box appears, click *OK*. The toolbar will be removed from the list in the Customize dialog box.

Figure 2.51 To delete a toolbar, choose View > Toolbars > Customize.

Figure 2.52 When the Customize dialog box appears, click the toolbar you want removed, and click *Delete*.

Figure 2.53 The File menu controls application-wide actions such as creating, opening, closing, saving, publishing, and importing Web pages or sites.

Figure 2.54 Most of the Edit menu's commands are common to all programs. The fifth section lets you control file access when more than one person is working on a Web site.

Figure 2.55 The View menu lets you show or hide all six of FrontPage's views, plus the toolbars.

The Menus

The menus that appear across the top of FrontPage's main window remain the same no matter what you're doing. However, some of the menus, such as Frames, can be used only while viewing or editing Web pages containing frames.

The File menu

Commands found in the File menu involve application-wide actions: creating, opening, closing, saving, publishing, and importing Web pages or sites (**Figure 2.53**). The File menu also lets you set up print settings, change FrontPage's general properties, and quit the program.

The Edit menu

Most of the Edit menu's commands operate just as they do in other programs—except the fifth section of the menu (**Figure 2.54**). That section lets you set up a Check In/Check Out system to avoid file version conflicts when more than one person is working on a Web site. For details, see *Managing Web Site Workflow* on page 359.

The View menu

Most of the commands found in the View menu duplicate those triggered by clicking the icons in the Views Bar (**Figure 2.55**). The menu's Toolbars choice lets you turn on or off any of FrontPage's 12 toolbars.

THE MENUS

The Insert menu

As the name suggests, this enables you to insert into Web pages everything from line breaks, dates, and hyperlinks to Java applets and Office XP or Office 2000 components, such as charts and spreadsheets (**Figure 2.56**).

The Format menu

Commands found in the Format menu control the appearance of your text, HTML tags, and what FrontPage calls themes, which establish your Web site's overall graphic look (**Figure 2.57**).

The Tools menu

The Tools menu gives you control over many of FrontPage's overall settings (**Figure 2.58**). It also leads to FrontPage's dictionary and thesaurus.

Figure 2.56 The Insert menu lets you place into your Web pages everything from line breaks, dates, and hyperlinks to Java applets and Office components.

Figure 2.57 The Format menu controls text appearance and generally corresponds to the Formatting toolbar icons.

Figure 2.58 The Tools menu controls many of FrontPage's overall settings, plus the dictionary and thesaurus.

Figure 2.59 The Table menu controls major aspects of creating and adjusting tables in your Web pages and generally corresponds to the Table toolbar icons.

Figure 2.60 The Frames menu controls formatting of frame-based pages and is not accessible when viewing a non-frame page.

Figure 2.61 Use the Window menu to jump to any open FrontPage window.

Figure 2.62 Use the Help menu to reach the FrontPage help system.

The Table menu

Whether it's adding tables to a page or tweaking the arrangement of individual rows and columns, you'll find the most commonly used commands in the Table menu (**Figure 2.59**).

The Frames menu

Commands found in the Frames menu are accessible only when you're viewing a page containing HTML frames (**Figure 2.60**). Frame-based pages are created with the New Page command ([Ctrl][N]). For details, see page 274.

The Window menu

FrontPage lets you open multiple Web pages and sites simultaneously. The Window menu lets you quickly switch from one window to another (**Figure 2.61**). This also can be done by clicking the page tabs in FrontPage's main window.

The Help menu

Common to any Windows program, the Help menu gives you direct access to FrontPage's help system (**Figure 2.62**).

THE MENUS

To use FrontPage's Help

1. Choose Help > Microsoft FrontPage Help ($\boxed{F1}$) (**Figure 2.63**).

2. When the Microsoft FrontPage Help dialog box appears, click one of the three tabs—*Contents*, *Answer Wizard*, or *Index*—depending on your question (**Figures 2.64–2.66**). Whether you click the icons in the *Contents* tab or click *Search* in the *Answer Wizard* or *Index* tabs, the results will appear in the right pane.

Figure 2.63 To start FrontPage's Help feature, choose Help > Microsoft FrontPage Help.

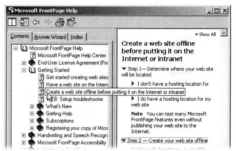

Figure 2.64 The *Contents* tab presents a topical overview of FrontPage—great for broad conceptual questions. Click the left pane's icons to have the information displayed in the right pane.

Figure 2.65 The *Answer Wizard* tab lets you type in a sentence-style question, which is sometimes the best approach if you're not sure exactly what to ask.

Figure 2.66 Use the *Index* tab to find a specific term or phrase. First enter the phrase in text box 1, then click *Search*. Fine-tune your request based on the initial results in box 2 (keywords) or box 3 (topics). Double-clicking the entry in either box will display the full text in the right pane. Click *Clear* to start a new search.

Figure 2.67 Get quick help by typing a question into the text window, choosing an option from the drop-down list (left) and selecting an item from the Help window (right).

✔ Tips

■ Which part of FrontPage's Help System you use depends on your question: *Contents* presents a topical overview of the program, which is handy for broad conceptual questions. If you're not sure even what to ask, *Answer Wizard* lets you type in a sentence-style question. *Index* shows every help entry—great for when you have a precise question about a particular problem or feature.

■ The fastest way to use Help is to type a question into the Help text window, press Enter, and then click one of the options in the drop-down menu. FrontPage will immediately jump to that entry in the index (**Figure 2.67**).

Creating, Opening, Saving, and Closing Web Pages

To build a Web page, you can take three routes: Create a new page from scratch and save it. Create a new page based on a template. Or open an existing page, alter it, and then save it using the Save As command to give it a new name. For more information on templates, see *Using Templates and Themes* on page 77.

To create a new blank Web page

1. Choose File > New > Page or Web, or click the New Page icon ([Ctrl][N]) (**Figure 2.68**).

2. If you chose File > New > Page or Web in step 1, a task pane will appear down the right side of the main window. Click the *Blank Page* icon (**Figure 2.69**) to create an entirely blank page (**Figure 2.70**). If you clicked the New Page icon in step 1, the blank page will appear immediately.

✔ Tip

- You also can create a new page based on one of FrontPage's dozens of templates. For more information, see *Using Templates and Themes* on page 77.

Figure 2.68 To open a new Web page, choose File > New > Page or Web, or click the New Page icon ([Ctrl][N]).

Figure 2.69 If you're using the task pane, click the *Blank Page* icon to create a new Web page.

Figure 2.70 When you create a new Web page, FrontPage will open a blank page with a generic title.

Figure 2.71 To open an existing Web page, choose File > Open or click the Open icon ($\boxed{\text{Ctrl}}\boxed{\text{O}}$).

Figure 2.72 When the Open File dialog box appears, navigate to the file you want, and double-click it.

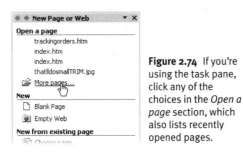

Figure 2.73 Once opened, the existing Web page appears in FrontPage's main window.

To open an existing Web page

1. Choose File > Open or click the Open icon ($\boxed{\text{Ctrl}}\boxed{\text{O}}$) (**Figure 2.71**).

2. When the Open File dialog box appears, navigate to the file you want to open and either double-click it, or type its name into the File name box and click *Open* (**Figure 2.72**).

3. The Web page appears in FrontPage's main window (**Figure 2.73**).

✔ Tips

- To narrow or widen your search for a Web page in the Open File dialog box, use the *Files of type* drop-down menu.

- If the task pane is open, you also can click any of the choices in the *Open a page* section, which includes a list of recently opened Web pages (**Figure 2.74**).

Figure 2.74 If you're using the task pane, click any of the choices in the *Open a page* section, which also lists recently opened pages.

To save a Web page

1. Choose File > Save As (**Figure 2.75**).

2. When the Save As dialog box appears, use the folder-level icon to navigate to where you want to save the page (top, **Figure 2.76**).

3. While still in the Save As dialog box, click the *Change* button to choose a title for your page (bottom, **Figure 2.76**). When the Set Page Title dialog box appears, type the name you want Web browsers to display as the Web page's title and click *OK* (**Figure 2.77**). For details, see the Tip below.

4. By default, the file name also will be based on the page's first line of text. If that's not what you want it called, type into the *File name* text box a distinctive name. Be sure to end it with the .htm suffix, then click *Save* (**Figure 2.78**). The file will be saved with the name you gave it.

✔ Tip

■ If you don't choose a title for your Web page when saving the page, FrontPage will generate one based on the page's first line of text—which will get picked up by Web browsers (**Figure 2.79**).

Figure 2.75 Choose File > Save As to save a Web page.

Figure 2.76 Use the folder-level icon to navigate to where you want to save the page (top), then set a title for your Web page, by clicking the *Change* button (bottom).

Figure 2.77 In the Set Page Title dialog box, enter the name you want Web browsers to display as the Web page's title, then click *OK*.

Figure 2.78 Give the page a distinctive file name with an .htm suffix and click *Save*.

Figure 2.79 Change your page's title when you save it or Web browsers will use the file's first bit of text as the title (top), when you really want a more descriptive title (bottom).

Figure 2.80 To save a Web page under another name, choose File > Save As.

Figure 2.81 To close a Web page, choose File > Close or click the X in the top-right corner of the page.

To save a Web page under another name

1. Choose File > Save As (**Figure 2.80**).

2. When the Save As dialog box opens, navigate to where you want the file saved, then click the *Change* button to give the page a new title (**Figure 2.76**). When the Set Page Title dialog box appears, type the name you want Web browsers to display as the Web page's title and click *OK* (**Figure 2.77**).

3. Enter a distinctive name into the File name field and click *Save*. The file will be saved with the new name.

To close a Web page

◆ Assuming you have already saved the page, choose File > Close ([Ctrl][F4]) or click the X in the top-right corner of the page (**Figure 2.81**). FrontPage remains running, leaving you free to open another Web page or move on to other tasks.

SAVING, CLOSING A WEB PAGE

41

Printing Web Pages

While FrontPage doesn't let you print out an entire Web site at once, you can easily print out individual Web pages.

To print a Web page

1. If you have not already done so, check your printer's settings by choosing File > Page Setup and make any adjustments.

2. If you want to see a preview of the current Web page, choose File > Print Preview.

3. FrontPage's main window displays the preview and includes buttons to inspect each page, see two pages at a time, or zoom in and out on the pages (**Figure 2.82**). If you're satisfied with the preview, click the *Print* button. Or click *Close* and then choose File > Print (Ctrl P) (**Figure 2.83**).

Figure 2.82 FrontPage's print preview window lets you see two pages at a time or zoom in for a closer look.

Figure 2.83 To print the current Web page, choose File > Print.

Figure 2.84 To create a new Web site Choose File > New > Page or Web or click the New icon and choose *Web* from the drop-down menu.

Figure 2.85 If you're using the task pane, click the *Empty Web* icon.

Figure 2.86 If you want to store the Web site somewhere other than the folder listed in the *Specify the location of the new web* text window, click *Browse* and navigate to your preferred folder.

Creating, Opening, and Closing Web Sites

Any collection of related, linked Web pages—or even a single home page—is considered a Web *site*. FrontPage automatically organizes any documents and graphics you create for your site. As long as you work within FrontPage, you can move your pages around and FrontPage will maintain the hyperlinks among the pages and files—saving you from the plague of broken links.

To create a new blank Web site

1. Choose File > New > Page or Web or click the New icon and choose *Web* from the drop-down menu (**Figure 2.84**).

2. If you chose File > New > Page or Web in step 1, a task pane will appear on the right side of the main window. Click the *Empty Web* icon (**Figure 2.85**).

3. When the Web Site Templates dialog box appears (**Figure 2.86**), the *Empty Web* icon will automatically be selected. If you want to store the Web site somewhere other than the folder listed in the *Specify the location of the new web* text window, click *Browse* and navigate to your preferred folder.

(continued)

4. When the Web Site Templates dialog box reappears, click *OK* and the Create New Web dialog box will appear briefly (**Figure 2.87**). FrontPage's main window will appear completely blank (**Figure 2.88**), which may leave you wondering if you have done something wrong. Click the *Navigation* icon in the *Views Bar*, then click the New Page icon to automatically create a blank home page (**Figure 2.89**). You're ready to begin adding pages to the Web site or content to individual pages. For details on structuring your Web site, see page 48.

✔ Tips

■ In step 2, you can click *OK* instead of *Browse* if you have previously created a Web site and want the new site to be stored in the same spot. Be aware, however, that FrontPage automatically bases the names of new sites on the previous site. If you're not careful, you'll wind up with *MySite1*, *MySite2*, *MySite3*. It quickly can become hard to tell which site is which, so clicking *Browse* is often the best way to keep your sanity.

■ In step 3, once you have created your first Web site, FrontPage automatically highlights the icon for that same site type the next time you create a Web site.

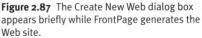

Figure 2.87 The Create New Web dialog box appears briefly while FrontPage generates the Web site.

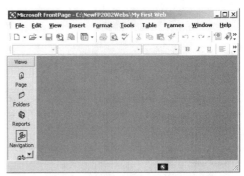

Figure 2.88 When you first create a new Web site, FrontPage's main window will appear completely blank.

Figure 2.89 To change the view first seen in Figure 2.88, click *Navigation* in the *Views Bar*, and then click the New Page icon to automatically create a blank home page.

Figure 2.90 To create a template-based Web site, click the *Web Site Templates* icon in the task pane.

Figure 2.91 When the Web Site Templates dialog box appears, click a template or wizard, and click *OK*.

Figure 2.92 When the home page of the template-based Web site appears, you're ready to begin adding content.

To create a template-based Web site

1. Choose File > New > Page or Web.

2. When the task pane appears on the right side of the main window, click the *Web Site Templates* icon (**Figure 2.90**).

3. When the Web Site Templates dialog box appears (**Figure 2.91**), click on a template or wizard to use in creating your new Web site. If you want to store the Web site somewhere other than the folder listed in the *Specify the location of the new web* text window, click *Browse* and navigate to your preferred folder.

4. Click *OK* and the Create New Web dialog box will appear briefly. When the home page of the template-based Web site appears (**Figure 2.92**), you're ready to begin adding content to any of the site's pages. For details on structuring your Web site, see page 48.

To open an existing Web site

1. Choose File > Open Web (**Figure 2.93**).

2. When the Open Web dialog box appears, navigate to where you stored your existing Web site on your local hard drive or internal network (**Figure 2.94**). Click *Open*.

3. When the Web opens, click the *Folders* icon to see all the Web site's files or click the *Navigation* icon to see its structure (**Figures 2.95** and **2.96**). You're ready to begin adding pages to the site's structure or content to individual pages.

✔ Tip

■ You also can open and download a Web site posted on the Internet.

To close a Web site

◆ Choose File > Close Web (**Figure 2.97**). The current Web site closes.

Figure 2.93 Choose File > Open Web to open an existing Web site.

Figure 2.94 When the Open Web dialog box appears, navigate to an existing Web site and click *Open*.

Figure 2.95 Click the *Folders* icon to see all of a Web site's files.

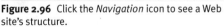

Figure 2.96 Click the *Navigation* icon to see a Web site's structure.

Figure 2.97 Choose File > Close Web to close a Web site.

CREATING A WEB SITE

As explained in Chapter 1, giving some upfront thought to your Web site's purpose and audience will save you a lot of time and headaches once you actually begin creating your site. Assuming you've done your planning, this chapter walks you through the actual creation of your site.

FrontPage's navigation view offers some great tools to help you quickly create a site—and restructure it if you change your mind midway through. Because FrontPage preserves the links among pages even as you restructure the site, it's easy to experiment with various options until you're satisfied.

To create pages within a Web site structure

1. Once you open a Web site (see page 43), switch to navigation view by clicking the Navigation icon in the Views Bar (**Figure 3.1**).

2. Within the navigation pane, click on the page to which you want to add a page. The selected page will change from yellow to blue.

3. Right-click and choose *New > Page* from the shortcut menu (**Figure 3.2**). You also can add a new page by pressing Ctrl N. The new page will appear with a generic name (**Figure 3.3**).

4. Continue adding pages until you've roughed out as much of the Web site as you want (**Figure 3.4**). You're now ready to title, rename, and rearrange your Web site's new pages.

✔ Tips

■ To give yourself more screen space to work with, you may want to hide the *Folder List* pane by choosing View > Folder List, clicking the Folders icon in the toolbar, or clicking the *X* in the *Folder List* pane (**Figure 3.5**).

■ While **Figure 3.2** shows a page being added to the Home Page, you can use the same steps to add a page to *any* other page you select, as in **Figure 3.4**.

Figure 3.1 Click the Navigation icon in the Views Bar to switch to navigation view.

Figure 3.2 To add a new page to your Web structure, right-click and choose *New > Page* from the shortcut menu (or press Ctrl N).

Figure 3.3 The new page, with a generic name, will appear attached to the selected page.

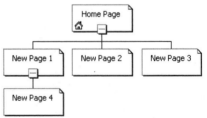

Figure 3.4 By using the New Page command repeatedly, you can quickly rough out a Web site structure.

Figure 3.5 Hide site folders and files by choosing View > Folder List (left), clicking the Folders icon in the toolbar (middle), or clicking the X in the Folder List pane (right).

Figure 3.6 To give each new page a distinctive title, press (Tab) to move to the desired page. When the name becomes highlighted, type in a new title, then press (Enter).

Figure 3.7 Press (Tab) or (Enter) to move from page to page and continue giving each a distinct title.

Figure 3.8 You also can retitle any page by right-clicking it and choosing *Rename* from the shortcut menu.

Figure 3.9 To check what a file's really named, right-click within the page and choose *Properties* (left) or *Page Properties* (right) from the shortcut menu.

Figure 3.10 The Properties (top) or Page Properties (bottom) dialog boxes let you compare the file name (in the *Filename* or *Location* boxes) with the title (in the *Title* box).

To give a new page a title

1. To give each new page a distinctive title (see *Tips* below) while in navigation view, press (Tab) to move to the desired page. The name of the page will become highlighted (**Figure 3.6**).

2. Type in a new name and press (Enter) or press (Tab) to apply the change and move to the next page you want to retitle (**Figure 3.7**).

✔ Tips

- You also can retitle any page by right-clicking it and choosing *Rename* from the shortcut menu (**Figure 3.8**).

- Contrary to what you might expect, changing the name of a page while in navigation view doesn't rename the page file—just the page's *title*. As long as you remain in the navigation pane, even selecting *Rename* in the shortcut menu only changes the page's title—not its file name. Confusing? You bet. To really change the page's file name, see *To rename a Web page*, on the next page.

- If you ever get confused, FrontPage offers two quick ways to compare a Web page's title to its file name. If you're in navigation view, right-click the page icon, and choose *Properties* from the short cut menu (left, **Figure 3.9**). If you're in page view, right-click anywhere in the page and choose *Page Properties* from the shortcut menu (right, **Figure 3.9**). When the properties dialog box opens, compare the file name in the *Filename* or *Location* text boxes with the name in the *Title* text window (**Figure 3.10**). If the title's not what you intended it to be called, type a new title into the *Title* window. If the file name's not correct, see *To rename a Web page* on the next page.

GIVING A NEW PAGE A TITLE

To rename a Web page

1. Make sure you are in page view and that the *Folder List* is visible by choosing View > Folder List or by clicking the Folders icon (**Figure 3.5**).

2. Click inside the *Folder List* pane on the file you want to rename (**Figure 3.11**).

3. With the file highlighted, type in a new name. Make sure to end it with .htm and press (Enter). The file's name changes in the *Folder List* pane and also appears at the top of the right pane (**Figure 3.12**). Choose File > Save ((Ctrl)(S)).

✔ Tip

■ As long as you are in page view (not navigation view), you can actually change the name of a page file by right-clicking it in the *Folder List* and choosing *Rename* from the shortcut menu (**Figure 3.13**).

Figure 3.11 To rename a Web page, click *inside* the *Folder List* pane on the file you want to rename.

Figure 3.12 Once you rename a file, the new name appears in the *Folder List* pane and at the top of the right pane.

Figure 3.13 To change the name of a file, right-click it in the Folder List and choose *Rename* from the shortcut menu.

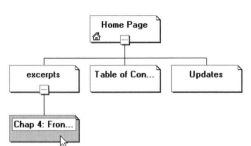

Figure 3.14 To move a page, first click inside the Navigation pane and the page will change color.

Figure 3.15 As you drag the selected page, a gray line will indicate possible new page destinations.

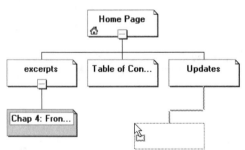

Figure 3.16 Continue dragging the page until the line connects to your intended destination.

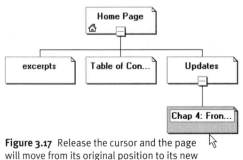

Figure 3.17 Release the cursor and the page will move from its original position to its new place in the Web site's structure.

Rearranging a Web Site's Structure

The ability to let you quickly restructure your Web site while preserving links between pages is one of FrontPage's best features. Such rearranging is done in the navigation view, where FrontPage presents an easy to understand set of linked boxes, much like an organization chart. This is very handy when you're roughing out a new site and want to experiment with different structures. Move a page—or a whole group of pages—and see if you like it. If not, you can easily move it again. Most importantly, not a single hyperlink will be broken in the process.

To rearrange a single page

1. If you're not already in navigation view, click the Navigation icon in the Views Bar.

2. Click inside the right-hand pane on the page you want to move. The page will turn from yellow to blue (**Figure 3.14**).

3. As you drag the page, FrontPage will draw a gray line to possible new destinations for the page (**Figure 3.15**). Continue dragging the page until the line connects to your intended destination (**Figure 3.16**).

4. Release the cursor and the page will move from its original position to its new place in the Web site's structure (**Figure 3.17**).

✔ Tips

- To move a page up a level, click and drag the page until a gray line connects it to the same level as its parent page. Release the cursor and the page will move up a level (**Figure 3.18**).

- To move a page to a site's top level, click and drag the page until a gray line connects it to the uppermost page. Release the cursor and the selected page will move to the top level.

- You can save any changes to the overall navigation structure within the navigation view by right-clicking on a blank spot in the main window and choosing *Apply Changes* from the shortcut menu (**Figure 3.19**).

Figure 3.18 To move a page up a level, click and drag the page until a gray line connects it to the same level as its parent page (top). Release the cursor and the page will move to the new spot (bottom).

Figure 3.19 Save changes to the structure by right-clicking on a blank spot in the main window and choosing *Apply Changes*.

REARRANGING A WEB SITE'S STRUCTURE

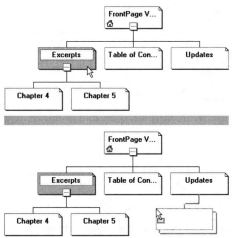

Figure 3.20 To rearrange a group of pages, click the top page of the subtree you want to move and drag it to a new destination.

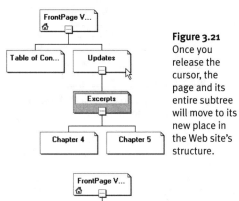

Figure 3.21 Once you release the cursor, the page and its entire subtree will move to its new place in the Web site's structure.

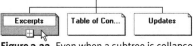

Figure 3.22 Even when a subtree is collapsed (indicated by a ⊞ icon), you can move it by clicking and dragging the visible page.

Figure 3.23 When you release the cursor, the page and its hidden subtree will move to the new spot in the site structure.

To rearrange groups of pages

1. If you're not already in navigation view, click the Navigation icon in the Views Bar.

2. Click inside the right-hand pane on the top page of the subtree of pages you want to move. The page will turn from yellow to blue.

3. Drag the top page of the subtree to a new destination. As you drag the page, FrontPage will draw a gray line to possible new destinations for the page and its subtree (**Figure 3.20**).

4. Release the cursor, and the page along with its entire subtree, will move from its original position to its new place in the Web site's structure (**Figure 3.21**).

✔ Tip

■ You can move a subtree even when it's collapsed (indicated by a ⊞ icon on the visible page) by dragging the visible page to the desired place in the site structure (**Figures 3.22** and **3.23**). For details on collapsing and expanding site subtrees, see *Controlling Your View of the Site Structure* on page 56.

REARRANGING A WEB SITE'S STRUCTURE

Adding or Excluding Pages in the Site Structure

It may not always be practical to create new Web pages by building them within the navigation view. Inevitably you will wind up with some free-standing Web pages that you will want to incorporate into your Web site's navigational structure. There also will be times you want to remove a page from your structure.

To add an existing page to a Web site structure

1. Switch to navigation view, make sure the *Folder List* is visible, and select in the *Folder List* the file (Web page) you want to add to the site's structure (top, **Figure 3.24**).

2. Drag the file into the main window and, as you position it, a dotted line will connect to the nearest page (bottom, **Figure 3.24**). Without releasing the cursor, reposition the file so that the dotted line connects to the desired part of the Web site diagram.

3. Release the cursor and the page will be added to the Web site structure (**Figure 3.25**).

✔ Tip

■ Once you add a page to the structure, its position within the navigation diagram can be changed any time.

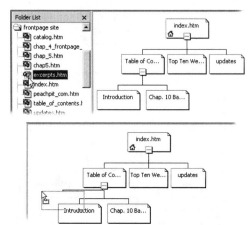

Figure 3.24 To add an existing page to the site structure, select the file in the *Folder List* (top), and drag it into place in the main window (bottom).

Figure 3.25 Release your cursor and the page will be added to the Web site structure.

Figure 3.26 To remove an existing page from the site structure, right-click the page and choose *Delete* from the shortcut menu.

Figure 3.27 Make sure the option button labeled *Remove page from the navigation structure* is checked before you click *OK*.

To remove an existing page from a Web site structure

1. Make sure you are in navigation view, right-click on the page you want to remove, and choose *Delete* from the shortcut menu (**Figure 3.26**).

2. When the Delete Page dialog box appears, make sure the option button labeled *Remove page from the navigation structure* is checked and click *OK* (**Figure 3.27**). The page will be removed from the Web site's navigation structure, while remaining in the site's *Folder List* (**Figure 3.28**).

✔ Tip

- Don't be thrown off by that word *Delete*. Fear not: The *Remove page* choice is always selected in the Delete Page dialog box, which means the page is just removed from the navigation structure and not actually deleted.

Figure 3.28 The page will be removed from the Web site's navigation structure, while remaining in the site's *Folder List*.

Controlling Your View of the Site Structure

When you're first setting up a Web site's structure, you'll spend a lot of time in navigation view. For that very reason, FrontPage gives you lots of choices when using the navigation view. You can look at the entire structure or just a portion. You can zoom in or out when viewing the site, or flip the view from vertical to horizontal. Whether you view the site vertically or horizontally simply depends on which makes more sense for you—there's no right or wrong.

To collapse the site structure

◆ While in navigation view, click a page's ⊟ icon to hide every page below it (**Figure 3.29**). All pages below the icon will disappear from view (**Figure 3.30**).

To expand the site structure

◆ While in navigation view, click a page's ⊞ icon to show every page below it (**Figure 3.30**). Any pages hidden below the page will reappear (**Figure 3.29**).

✔ Tip

■ If the Navigation toolbar is active, you can expand or collapse the structure by clicking the toolbar's subtree icon (**Figure 3.31**).

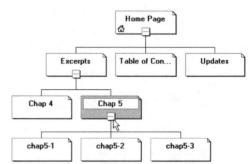

Figure 3.29 To collapse the site structure, click a page's ⊟ icon to hide the pages below it.

Figure 3.30 Pages with a ⊞ icon indicate that there are more pages hidden from view.

Figure 3.31 To quickly expand or collapse the site structure, click the Navigation toolbar's subtree icon.

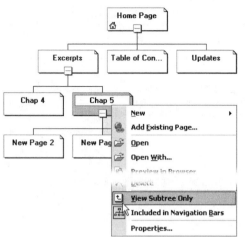

Figure 3.32 To view only the subtree of a selected page, right-click and choose *View Subtree Only* from the shortcut menu.

To view only a subtree

1. While in navigation view, click the page on which you want to focus.

2. With the page still selected, right-click and choose *View Subtree Only* from the shortcut menu (**Figure 3.32**). All the pages *above* the selected page's level will be hidden (**Figure 3.33**).

To expand a subtree

◆ While in navigation view, click the arrow extending from the subtree's top-level page (**Figure 3.34**). The entire site's structure will appear (**Figure 3.35**).

Figure 3.33 When you choose *View Subtree Only*, all the pages above the selected page will be hidden.

Figure 3.34 To expand a subtree, click the arrow extending from the subtree's top-level page.

Figure 3.35 After clicking the subtree icon, the entire site's structure will appear.

To change the site structure view

◆ While in navigation view, right-click anywhere in the right pane and choose *Portrait/Landscape* from the shortcut menu (**Figure 3.36**). Depending on your current view, the site's structure will switch from portrait (vertical) to landscape (horizontal) or vice versa (**Figure 3.37**). To return the orientation to its original position, choose *Portrait/Landscape* again.

✔ Tip

■ If the Navigation toolbar is active, you can toggle your view of the structure by clicking the Portrait/Landscape icon (**Figure 3.38**).

Figure 3.36 To change the navigation view, right-click anywhere in the right pane and choose *Portrait/Landscape* from the shortcut menu.

Figure 3.37 After changing the view, the structure appears in landscape mode.

Figure 3.38 To quickly toggle your view of the site's structure, click the Navigation toolbar's Portrait/Landscape icon.

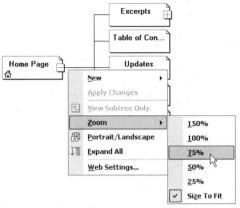

Figure 3.39 To zoom the navigation view in or out, right-click in the navigation pane, point to *Zoom*, and choose a percentage or *Size To Fit* in the shortcut menu.

Figure 3.40 To quickly zoom in or out on the site's structure, click the Navigation toolbar's drop-down menu.

To zoom in or out on the site structure

◆ Right-click on a blank spot in the navigation pane, point to *Zoom*, and choose a percentage or *Size To Fit* your monitor view in the shortcut menu (**Figure 3.39**). The view will change to reflect your choice.

✔ Tip

■ If the Navigation toolbar is active, you can zoom in or out using the preset percentages on the toolbar's drop-down menu (**Figure 3.40**).

Using Link Bars and Shared Borders

What had been called navigation bars in the previous version of FrontPage have been redubbed link bars in FrontPage 2002. More important than the name change, link bars are easier to use and less confusing than the old navigation bars.

Use link bars whenever you need to create a consistent set of hyperlinks for a group of pages or an entire Web site. Link bars offer several advantages over individual hyper-links. You create them once and then apply them to any number of pages. They also offer a great way to create site-wide navigational links to let users quickly jump to your site's Home page or other main pages.

You have two choices in creating link bars: build them manually and place them on certain pages or let FrontPage generate them based on your site's navigation structure. For example, FrontPage can generate hyper-links to any page *above* the selected page (known as a *parent* page), to all pages on the same level as the selected page, or to any page *below* its level (a *child* page). In all cases, FrontPage will update the link bars whenever you change the site's structure.

You even can put more than one link bar on a page, creating several distinct levels of navigation. For example, one bar's links could point to a site's top-level topic pages and another bar could point to previous and next pages on the same level. You also can create custom link bars for special-case links on single pages. For details, see *To create a custom link bar* on page 71.

Before you add link bars, first create your Web site's basic structure. If you haven't already roughed out that structure, see page 48. It's a matter of work style whether you create link bars as part of roughing out your

Web site's structure (when the pages are still mostly empty) or after you have added content to the pages. Some folks, myself included, find that having to consider site-wide links upfront makes for a more cohesive site design. Other people find this approach completely backward and plain frustrating. If you're one of them, skip ahead to the next few chapters and come back after you have built out your pages and want to link them together.

Shared borders offer a great way to handle site-wide information that may need regular updating, such as company logos, copyright notices, or contact numbers. With shared borders, you can change that type of information in one place and it's automatically updated on every page. While many sites use frames for the same purpose, frames have the drawback of being hard to bookmark and navigate. Shared borders accomplish the same thing with less hassle.

You can even combine shared borders with link bars. That, however, has its own limits since the links remain relative to each page and may not be consistent enough for use in site-wide shared borders. To work around that problem you can turn *off* the shared borders for individual pages or create multiple sets of custom links. For details, see *To turn off shared borders for a single page* on page 76 and *To create a custom link bar* on page 71.

For the most benefits with the fewest headaches, however, try to avoid combining link bars and shared borders. Another way to help users find their way around large Web sites is to create a table of contents or site map. For more information, see *Adding a Web site table of contents* on page 245.

To create a navigation-based link bar

1. Assuming you've already roughed out your site's structure, make sure you are in page view by clicking the Page icon in the Views Bar.

2. Click in the current page where you want the link bar to appear and choose Insert > Navigation (**Figure 3.41**).

3. When the Insert Web Component dialog box appears, click *Bar based on navigation structure* in the list labeled *Choose a bar type* (*Link Bars* will already be selected in the *Component type* list), and click *Next* (**Figure 3.42**).

4. Use the dialog box's scroll bar to find the bar style you want to use and click *Next* (**Figure 3.43**).

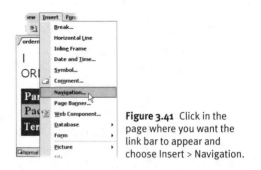

Figure 3.41 Click in the page where you want the link bar to appear and choose Insert > Navigation.

Figure 3.42 When the Insert Web Component dialog box appears, click *Bar based on navigation structure* in the right-hand list.

Figure 3.43 Use the scroll bar to choose one of FrontPage's many pre-built link bar styles.

Figure 3.44 Use the *Choose an orientation* pane to have the links run across or down the page.

Figure 3.45 Use Link Bar Properties dialog box's *General* tab to control which pages are included in your link bar.

Figure 3.46 A navigation-based link bar appears across the top of the page.

5. Use the *Choose an orientation* pane to have the links run across or down the page and click *Finish* (**Figure 3.44**).

6. When the Link Bar Properties dialog box appears, the *General* tab will already be activated. Choose one of the six option buttons to control which pages will be linked to the current page (**Figure 3.45**). Check one or both of the *Additional pages* boxes if you also want links to the *Home page* or *Parent page*. Based on your choices, the squares in the site diagram will change to show which pages relative to the current page will be linked. For details, see *Navigation-based link bar options* on page 64.

7. Click *OK* and the link bar will be inserted into the current page (**Figure 3.46**).

✔ Tip

■ You will need to repeat these steps on every page on which you want the navigation link bar to appear.

Navigation-based link bar options

The Link Bar Properties dialog box gives you
precise control over which pages are included
in your link bar (**Figure 3.45**). It also lets you
control the appearance of those links.

- **Hyperlinks to add to a page:** Found
  under the dialog box's *General* tab, this
  section gives you six choices for which
  pages will be linked. The pages highlighted in the dialog box's site tree diagram change to reflect your choice
  (**Figure 3.47**). The tree doesn't actually
  show your particular site but simply
  displays which links will be activated
  relative to your current page. You can
  add two other links by clicking the
  Additional pages choices (**Figure 3.48**).
  In the legend below the tree, the *Page
  link bar will appear on* symbol refers to
  your current page.

- **Style, Orientation and appearance:**
  Use the dialog box's *Style* tab to further
  refine your link bar (**Figure 3.49**). While
  graphic styles dominate the top of the
  Choose a style window, if you scroll almost
  to the bottom, you'll find some choices for
  displaying the links in HTML text.

Figure 3.47 The *General* tab's *Hyperlinks to add to
page* includes a diagram to show which pages will
be hyperlinked to the current page.

Figure 3.48 Besides the six main hyperlink
choices, the Link Bar Properties dialog box
also lets you include links to the site's *Home
page*, your page's *Parent page*, or to both.

Figure 3.49 In addition to controlling which
pages are linked, the Link Bar Properties
dialog box's *Style* tab lets you dictate how the
links look.

Figure 3.50 To change the default navigation labels, right-click in the main window and choose *Web Settings* from the shortcut menu.

Figure 3.51 Click the *Navigation* tab in the Web Settings dialog box to reach the default navigation labels.

Figure 3.52 Change any of the default labels by typing your own labels into each text box and clicking *OK*. The new labels will be applied to the current Web site only.

Changing the default labels for navigation-based link bars

When you apply navigation-based link bars to pages, FrontPage uses a set of labels by default: *Home* for the *Home page*, *Up* for *Parent level* pages, and *Back* or *Next* for the previous or next page. Most times, those labels will suit your purposes. However, if you occasionally want more specific labels—*Customer Service* instead of *Home* or *Return to last page* instead of *Back*—FrontPage lets you customize to your heart's content.

To change navigation-based link bar labels

1. Click the Navigation icon in the Views Bar to switch to the navigation view.

2. Right-click on any blank spot in the main window and choose *Web Settings* (**Figure 3.50**).

3. When the Web Settings dialog box appears, click the *Navigation* tab (**Figure 3.51**).

4. Change any or all of the default navigation labels (*Home*, *Up*, *Back*, and *Next*) by typing your own labels into each text box (**Figure 3.52**). Click *OK* and these labels will be used when you add site-wide link bars.

✔ Tips

- Your custom navigation labels will be used only in the current Web site, so they won't mess up custom or default labels in your other Web sites.

- If you change your mind about using custom navigation labels, return to the *Navigation* tab in the Web Settings dialog box, click *Default*, and then *OK*. The original *Home*, *Up*, *Back*, and *Next* labels will replace the custom labels.

To exclude a single page from a navigation-based link bar

◆ In navigation view, right-click the page you do not want included in the link bar, and choose *Included in Navigation Bars* from the shortcut menu (**Figure 3.53**). The action works like an on-off toggle and, so, the selected page will be *excluded* from the link bar. Its exclusion is denoted by the page turning gray in navigation view (**Figure 3.54**).

Figure 3.53 To exclude a single page from a link bar, right-click that page and choose *Included in Navigation Bars*.

Figure 3.54 Pages excluded from a navigation-based link bar appear dark gray in navigation view.

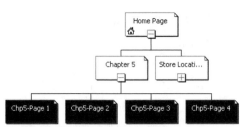

Figure 3.55 Add the same-level pages to the site's structure before creating your back/next link bar.

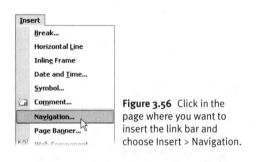

Figure 3.56 Click in the page where you want to insert the link bar and choose Insert > Navigation.

Figure 3.57 When the Insert Web Component dialog box appears, click *Bar with back and next links* in the right-hand list.

Figure 3.58 Use the scroll bar to choose a pre-built link bar style.

Creating back/next and custom link bars

You might think that a link bar that displays back and next buttons would work similarly to a navigation-based link bar since both presumably depend on the relative structure of the rest of the site. In truth, the process of creating a back/next link bar is virtually identical to how you create a custom link bar.

To create a back/next link bar

1. Assuming you've already roughed out some same-level pages on your site's structure (**Figure 3.55**), switch to page view by clicking the Page icon in the Views Bar.

2. Click in the page where you want to insert the link bar and choose Insert > Navigation (**Figure 3.56**).

3. When the Insert Web Component dialog box appears, click *Bar with back and next links* in the list labeled *Choose a bar type* (*Link Bars* will already be selected in the *Component type* list), and click *Next* (**Figure 3.57**).

4. If your site uses a pre-built graphic theme, click *Use Page's Theme* in the *Choose a bar style* window, or scroll down and select the bar style you want to use, then click *Next* (**Figure 3.58**).

(continued)

5. Use the *Choose an orientation* pane to have the links run across or down the page and click *Finish* (**Figure 3.59**).

6. When the Create New Link Bar dialog box appears, type an easy to remember *Name* in the text window and click *OK* (top, **Figure 3.60**). That name will then appear in the *Choose existing* window of the Link Bar Properties dialog box (bottom, **Figure 3.60**).

7. Click the *Add link* button to begin building the list of pages you want to be part of the particular set of back/next links (**Figure 3.61**).

Figure 3.59 Use the *Choose an orientation* pane to have the links run across or down the page and click *Finish*.

Figure 3.60 Type a *Name* in the text window (top), click *OK*, and it will appear in the *Choose existing* window of the Link Bar Properties dialog box (bottom).

Figure 3.61 Use the *Add link* button to build a list of pages you want to be part of that set of back/next links.

Figure 3.62 Select the current page as the first link for your link bar (top) and give it an easy to recognize label in the *Text to display* window (bottom).

Figure 3.63 A link to this first page will be added to what will become a list of *Links*.

Figure 3.64 Once you have built a list of page links, click *OK*.

8. When the Add to Link Bar dialog box appears, begin by selecting the current page that's open (top, **Figure 3.62**). Type into the *Text to display* window an easy to recognize name for this page link (it doesn't have to be the page's title but that will make things simpler for you as your site grows), and click *OK* (bottom, **Figure 3.62**). A link to this first page will be added to what will become a list of *Links* in the Link Bar Properties dialog box (**Figure 3.63**)

9. Repeat step 8 for each page you want added to the list of back/next list of links for this particular link bar (**Figure 3.64**).

(continued)

10. After you finish building the list of links for this particular back/next link bar, you need to insert the link bar on every page on which you want it to appear by repeating steps 2–5. When the *General* tab of the Link Bar Properties dialog box appears, make sure that the link bar name appearing in the *Choose existing* text window is the same one you created in step 6 for the first page, then click *OK*. The *Back* and *Next* links will be inserted on each page. You'll know when you've reached the last of the pages for this back/next link bar because only the *Back* link will appear on the page (**Figure 3.65**).

11. Save the insertion of the link bar on all the pages by choosing File > Save All, and switch to your browser (Ctrl Shift B). Open the first page in your series, and click the *Next* link. By clicking each *Next* button, you'll be able to move through each of the pages in your series (**Figure 3.66**).

✔ Tips

- In step 8, FrontPage by default opens the *Current Folder*, since in most cases that's where the page you want will be stored. To look elsewhere, choose another icon in the *Link to* or *Look in* columns (**Figure 3.67**).

- In **Figure 3.65**, you'll notice that the link bar includes *+add link*. This comment text will not appear in the user's Web browser and is simply there to remind you that you can add another link to the bar at any time by right-clicking it and choosing *Link Bar Properties* from the shortcut menu. For more information, see *Changing link bar properties* on page 73.

- Also in step 10, you can use any existing link bars by clicking the *Choose existing* drop-down menu.

Figure 3.65 The last page in a series of pages with back/next link bars will display only the *Back* link.

Figure 3.66 The completed back/next link enables a Web browser to move through a series of same-level pages.

Figure 3.67 Use the *Link to* and *Look in* buttons to build links to pages not in the current Web folder.

Figure 3.68 When the Insert Web Component dialog box appears, click *Bar with custom links* in the right-hand list.

Figure 3.69 Use the scroll bar to choose a pre-built link bar style.

Figure 3.70 Use the *Choose an orientation* pane to have the links run across or down the page and click *Finish*.

To create a custom link bar

1. Switch to page view by clicking the Page icon in the Views Bar, click in the page where you want to insert the link bar, and choose Insert > Navigation (**Figure 3.56**).

2. When the Insert Web Component dialog box appears, click *Bar with custom links* in the list labeled *Choose a bar type* (*Link Bars* will already be selected in the *Component type* list), and click *Next* (**Figure 3.68**).

3. If your site uses a pre-built graphic theme, click *Use Page's Theme* in the *Choose a bar style* window, or scroll down and select the bar style you want to use, and then click *Next* (**Figure 3.69**).

4. Use the *Choose an orientation* pane to have the links run across or down the page and click *Finish* (**Figure 3.70**).

5. When the Link Bar Properties dialog box appears, click *Create New* (since you're creating a new custom link bar) and give your custom link bar an easy to remember *Name* in the text window of the Create New Link Bar dialog box. Click *OK* and the Link Bar Properties dialog box will reappear displaying the name of your new link bar.

(continued)

USING LINK BARS AND SHARED BORDERS

6. Click the *Add link* button and use the Add to Link Bar dialog box to navigate to the pages you want used in building your custom link bar. Use the dialog box's *Text to display* window to create new labels for each link (**Figure 3.71**).

7. Once you have finished building the custom link list, click *OK* (**Figure 3.72**). The link bar will be displayed in the selected page (**Figure 3.73**). Save the changes to the page by choosing File > Save ([Ctrl][S]).

✔ Tip

■ Since you are building a custom set of links using pages from potentially anywhere on the Web, each page's *original* title or file name may have little to do with your list of links. For that reason, pay particular attention to giving each link a label that makes sense in its *new* context (**Figure 3.71**).

Figure 3.71 Use the Add to Link Bar dialog box's *Text to display* window to create labels for each custom link.

Figure 3.72 Once you finish building the custom link list, click *OK*.

Figure 3.73 Custom link bars offer choices not found in navigation-based link bars.

Figure 3.74 To edit a back/next or custom link bar, right-click the bar and choose *Link Bar Properties*.

Figure 3.75 Use the *General* tab's buttons to add, remove, modify, and move up or down your links.

Changing link bar properties

FrontPage automatically updates the hyperlinks used by the link bars whenever you rearrange your Web site's structure. But you'll have to manually edit a link bar's properties if you want to change a link bar's graphics, orientation, which pages are used in the links, how the links are labeled, or the order in which the links are listed. You can change these properties at any time. The process varies depending on whether you are changing navigation-based, back/next, or custom link bars. FrontPage also gives you the option of changing the default labels used on navigation-based and back/next link bars.

To edit a back/next or custom link bar

1. Make sure you are in page view, then right-click the link bar you want to change and choose *Link Bar Properties* from the shortcut menu (**Figure 3.74**).

2. When the Link Bar Properties dialog box appears, the *General* tab will already be selected (**Figure 3.75**). To add another page link to the list of *Links*, click the *Add link* button; to delete a page link, click *Remove link*.

(continued)

3. To change the name of the link or the page it points to, click *Modify link* and use the Modify Link dialog box when it appears to navigate to a new page or change the link label's name, then click *OK* (**Figure 3.76**). To reorder the list of links, select a link and use the *Move up* or *Move down* buttons to change the order in the *Links* window. Check *Home page* or *Parent page* if you want those links included as well.

4. If those are all the changes you need to make, click *OK* and the Link Bar Properties dialog box will close and the changes will be applied. To change the link bar's appearance, click the *Style* tab in the Link Bar Properties dialog box (**Figure 3.77**). When you're done, click *OK* and the changes will be applied.

Figure 3.76 Use the Modify Link dialog box to use another page for an existing link.

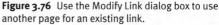

Figure 3.77 The *Style* tab lets you change a link bar's graphical style, along with its orientation or appearance.

Figure 3.78 To create site-wide link bars, first define the areas common to every page by choosing Format > Shared Borders. The same action also lets you turn off borders for single pages.

Figure 3.79 In the Shared Borders dialog box, check any or all of the four boxes: *Top, Left, Right,* and *Bottom*.

Figure 3.80 Use the Border Properties dialog box to set the shared area's *Border* or *Color*.

Figure 3.81 Similar to print-based headers or footers, you can use this page's top and bottom shared border areas for site-wide text or graphics.

To add shared borders

1. Make sure you've already opened the Web site for which you want to set borders, then choose Format > Shared Borders (**Figure 3.78**).

2. When the Shared Borders dialog box appears, choose the *All pages* or *Current page* radio button (**Figure 3.79**). By default, the *Top* and *Left* boxes are already checked, but you can check any or all of the four boxes: *Top, Left, Right,* and *Bottom*. (Do not check the *Include navigation buttons* boxes unless you want link bars included in the shared border areas.) A dashed line will appear within the dialog box showing where shared border areas will appear. For details on the choices, see the *Tip* below.

3. If you want to apply a border or color to the shared border, click the *Border Properties* button and use the drop-down menus in the Border Properties dialog box to set the *Border* or *Color* (**Figure 3.80**). (To use a picture for the border, you must first move it to the current Web's folder.)

4. Once you've made your choices, click *OK* to close the dialog box, then click *OK* again to close the Shared Borders dialog box. The shared borders will be added to the selected pages. You can then add text or graphics to the shared area (**Figure 3.81**).

✔ Tip

■ Only the *Top, Left and Right* choices in the Shared Borders dialog box let you show hyperlinks to other pages—and only if you also check *Include navigation buttons*, even if you only want text links (**Figure 3.79**). The *Bottom* choice can contain text, graphics, or invisible comments but not hyperlinks. For details, see *Adding Hyperlinks* on page 135.

To turn off shared borders for a single page

1. Make sure you are in page view, and choose Format > Shared Borders (**Figure 3.78**).

2. When the Shared Borders dialog box appears, click the *Current page* radio button and uncheck any other boxes (**Figure 3.82**). Click *OK* and the selected page appears without any shared borders (**Figure 3.83**).

Figure 3.82 To turn off a page's shared border, choose the *Current page* button, uncheck all other boxes, and click *OK*.

Figure 3.83 The same page as in Figure 3.81 after the shared borders have been turned off.

Figure 3.84 To create a page from a template, click the *Page Templates* icon in the task pane.

Figure 3.85 The Page Templates dialog box's *General* tab offers a variety of page templates. Choose one and click *OK*.

Figure 3.86 Once a template opens, you can begin replacing headings, text, and graphics with your own.

Using Templates and Themes

FrontPage's built-in templates and themes can save you tons of time in producing great-looking pages. Use the templates for building pages and sites, then use the themes to apply graphic touches to a single page or a whole site. To make creation of some of the more complicated templates easier, FrontPage has included several program "wizards" to guide you step-by-step through the process.

To create a page from a template

1. Choose File > New > Page or Web and a task pane will appear down the right side of the main window. Click the *Page Templates* icon in the *New from template* section (**Figure 3.84**).

2. When the Page Templates dialog box appears with the *General* tab already selected, choose a template for your page, and click the *OK* button (**Figure 3.85**). For help creating form pages, open the *Form Page Wizard* and follow its instructions. For more information on forms, see page 289. (For details on the *Frames Pages* and *Style Sheets* tabs, see pages 274 and 343.)

3. Once the template opens, you can select headings and text, replacing them with your own text (**Figure 3.86**). For details on creating and formatting text, see page 89.

(continued)

4. To replace a picture, right-click on it and choose *Picture Properties* from the shortcut menu (Alt Enter) (**Figure 3.87**).

5. When the Picture Properties dialog box appears, click the *General* tab, and then click *Browse* to navigate to the graphic you want to use instead (**Figure 3.88**). To insert the new graphic, click *OK*. For more on using graphics, see *Adding and Editing Images* on page 161.

6. The new graphic will appear in the template (**Figure 3.89**). To save the page, choose File > Save (Ctrl S), navigate to the folder where you want to save it, then click *Save* (**Figure 3.90**).

Figure 3.87
To replace a template's picture, right-click on the picture and choose *Picture Properties* from the shortcut menu.

Figure 3.88
When the Picture Properties dialog box appears, click *Browse* to navigate to your replacement graphic.

Lou the Wonder Dog

Web Tricks
Adding Smells
Animalation
Hiding Scripts
Drop Cats
Laying Out

Resources
Byte
M-Bone
smalldog.com

Relaxing at Carson Pass

Everyone thinks their dog is the smartest, cutest, best canine in the world. Lou the Wonder Dog, however, really is the smartest dog I've ever had.

For example, Lou can code in HTML--without using FrontPage. Incredible but true. What's her secret? Visual QuickStart Guides from Peachpit Press.

Figure 3.89 Once you've replaced a template's heads, text, and graphics with your own, choose File > Save (Ctrl S).

Figure 3.90
Navigate to the folder where you want to save the modified template, then click *Save*.

Figure 3.91
To create a Web site from a template, click the *Web Site Templates* icon in the task pane.

Figure 3.92 Choose a Web site template in the Web Site Templates dialog box, specify where you want it saved, and click *OK*.

Figure 3.93 Use the navigation view and *Folder List* to see the overall structure and all the pages of your new template-based Web site.

Figure 3.94 Open a page in the template-based Web site and begin substituting your own copy, heads, properties, and graphics. Be sure to save your work with File > Save (Ctrl S).

To create a Web site from a template

1. Choose File > New > Page or Web and a task pane will appear down the right side of the main window. Click the *Web Site Templates* icon in the *New from template* section (**Figure 3.91**).

2. When the Web Site Templates dialog box appears, click on one of the Web site templates (**Figure 3.92**). Be sure to specify in the pathname text box where you want the site saved, then click *OK* and the Web site will be created.

3. Switch to navigation view and choose View > Folder to see the Web site's overall structure and all its pages (**Figure 3.93**).

4. Double-click on any page in the site to open it and begin substituting your own copy, heads, properties, and graphics (**Figure 3.94**).

5. Save the page by choosing File > Save (Ctrl S). Continue editing other pages in your new template-based Web site until you're done, saving each in turn.

✔ Tips

■ You can add a multi-page template to an existing Web site. In the Web Site Templates dialog box (**Figure 3.92**), just be sure to choose the *Add to current Web* checkbox. This enables you, for example, to add a customer support or discussion area to an existing corporate Web site.

■ For help creating a Web discussion board or importing an existing Web site, use the FrontPage wizards listed in the Web Site Templates dialog box (**Figure 3.92**).

■ For even more templates, click *Templates on Microsoft.com* in **Figure 3.91** and you'll be connected to a trove of online templates.

To apply a theme to a page or Web site

1. Open a page or Web site to which you want to apply a theme and choose Format > Theme (**Figure 3.95**).

2. If the page or site does not already have a theme, the sample area will be blank when the Themes dialog box opens (**Figure 3.96**).

3. In the dialog box's upper-left corner, choose one of the two radio buttons to apply a theme to *All pages* or to *Selected page(s)*. By default, it's set to *All pages*, which makes sense since themes mainly are used to give your site a uniform look.

4. Choose a theme by clicking on it in the left-hand list and you'll see a sample of it in the right-hand window (**Figure 3.97**).

Figure 3.95
Open a page or Web site where you want to apply or change a theme and choose Format > Theme.

Figure 3.96 If a page or site doesn't already have a theme, the Themes dialog box's sample window will be blank. Choose either *All pages* or *Selected page(s)* in the upper left to control how widely a theme is applied.

Figure 3.97 Choose a theme in the left-hand list and you'll see a sample of it in the right-hand window.

Figure 3.98 The Themes dialog box contains four checkboxes in the lower left—*Vivid colors*, *Active graphics*, *Background picture*, or *Apply using CSS*—that will punch up your pages even more.

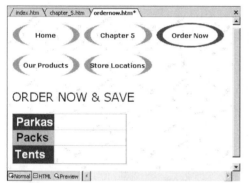

Figure 3.99 A formerly drab page (**Figure 3.62**) after applying FrontPage's Citrus Punch theme.

5. You can tweak the theme by choosing any of the four checkboxes in the lower-left corner: *Vivid colors*, *Active graphics*, *Background picture*, or *Apply using CSS* (if you're using Cascading Style Sheets). Each effect (except CSS) can be previewed in the right-hand sample window (**Figure 3.98**).

6. Once you've selected a theme and tweaked it to your satisfaction, click *OK* in the Themes dialog box and it will be applied to your page or site (**Figure 3.99**). If you want to change the theme even more, see *To modify a theme* on the next page.

✔ Tip

- Even though the Themes dialog box seems to suggest that you can apply a theme to several pages at a time (**Figure 3.96**), you really only have two choices: apply a theme to the single page you have open or to the entire Web site. If you want to apply a theme to just, say, four of your site's pages, you'll have to open each page, one at a time, and then apply the theme to each in turn.

USING TEMPLATES AND THEMES

To modify a theme

1. Open a page or Web site that uses a theme you want to change, make sure you're in page view, and choose Format > Theme (**Figure 3.95**).

2. When the Themes dialog box appears, the current theme will automatically appear in the right-hand sample window. If you want to modify it, click on it in the left-hand column, and click *Modify* at the bottom center of the dialog box (**Figure 3.100**).

3. Just above the *Modify* button, three buttons will appear: *Colors*, *Graphics*, and *Text* (**Figure 3.101**). Click one of the three (you can come back and modify the other two later if you want).

Figure 3.100 Click the *Modify* button at the bottom of the Themes dialog box to customize any theme.

Figure 3.101 FrontPage lets you modify three aspects of a theme: its *Colors*, *Graphics*, or *Text*.

Figure 3.102 The *Color Schemes* tab in the Modify Theme dialog box lets you pick overall combinations and whether you want those colors *Normal* or *Vivid*. The other two tabs set colors for individual items.

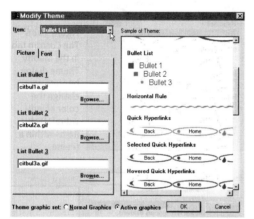

Figure 3.103 The graphics version of the Modify Theme dialog box lets you replace the graphic items used in existing themes.

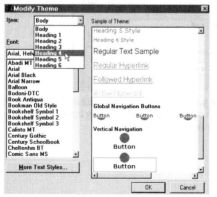

Figure 3.104 The text version of the Modify Theme dialog box lets you change the fonts associated with each HTML item.

4. Depending on your choice, the Modify Theme dialog box that appears will display options for changing your theme colors, graphics, or text (**Figures 3.102–3.104**). For details on the options, see *Theme options*. Make your changes and click *OK*.

5. When the Themes dialog box reappears, you can apply your changes to the existing theme or save them as a new theme. Click *Save* to change the existing theme; *Save As* for a new theme.

6. Finally, click *OK* and the theme modifications will be applied to the selected Web page or site.

Theme options

FrontPage gives you a tremendous amount of control in customizing its built-in themes. Follow the steps in *To modify a theme* to reach the Modify Theme dialog box and its various options (**Figures 3.102–3.104**).

◆ **Colors:** Click any of the three tabs to change aspects of a theme's color. The *Color Schemes* tab lets you apply the color combinations of another theme to the current theme (**Figure 3.102**). The *Color Wheel* tab lets you change the hue and brightness of the current color scheme (**Figure 3.105**). The *Custom* tab lets you change the color of individual HTML items, such as all your Level 1 headings or your active hyperlinks (**Figure 3.106**). Choose the *Vivid colors* radio button at the bottom of the dialog box if you want to give the color combinations a bit more punch.

◆ **Graphics:** The graphics version of the Modify Theme dialog box lets you replace various graphics in existing themes with your own graphics or other clip art (**Figure 3.103**). Use the dialog box's drop-down menu to pick an item or category of items that you want to change, such as all the bullets used in a theme (**Figure 3.107**). Then click *Browse* to navigate to the new graphic you want to use. Choose the *Active graphics* radio button at the bottom of the Modify Theme dialog box if you want to animate buttons when, for example, a user mouses over them. Preview the before, during, and after versions of the animations in the sample window. Just remember to use this option with restraint.

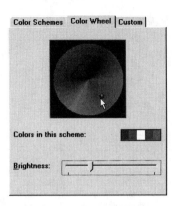

Figure 3.105
The *Color Wheel* tab in the Modify Theme dialog box lets you change the hue and brightness of a selected color combination.

Figure 3.106
The *Custom* tab in the Modify Theme dialog box lets you change the color of individual HTML items within a theme.

Figure 3.107 Use the drop-down list in the graphics version of the Modify Theme dialog box to change an item or category of items.

Figure 3.108 The Style dialog box—reached from the Modify Theme dialog box—lets you change the fonts used in any HTML tag.

◆ **Text:** As you might guess, the text version of the Modify Theme dialog box lets you change the fonts associated with each HTML item, including the text used within such graphics as buttons (**Figure 3.104**). Use the dialog box's drop-down menu to pick your body text or one of your headings. Click the *More Text Styles* button to change even more HTML items (**Figure 3.108**). The *List* drop-down menu will actually let you see all the HTML tags, but think first whether you really want to start changing fonts that widely.

✔ Tip

■ The choices available to you in the various Modify Theme dialog boxes are affected by which boxes you checked in the Themes dialog box (see step 5 in *To apply a theme to a page or Web site*). If you find yourself unable to turn on an option in one of the Modify Theme dialog boxes, go back to the Themes dialog box and change your checkbox choices.

PART 2

CREATING BASIC WEB PAGES

CREATING AND FORMATTING TEXT

The whole point of a program like FrontPage is to spare you the tedium of coding in HTML. For that reason, creating and formatting text with FrontPage is very much like using any word processing program: You type away and the formatting is handled behind the scene. Likewise, most of the standard techniques you use in word processing programs—selecting, moving, cutting, and copying text—work similarly in FrontPage.

Entering and Editing Text

Entering text in FrontPage works almost identically to typing in a word processing program. When your typing reaches the right edge of the document window, the text automatically wraps to the next line. Similarly, you use the cursor to select text, which then can be moved, copied, or pasted elsewhere.

To enter text on a Web page

1. If you're not already in page view, click the Page icon in the Views Bar (**Figure 4.1**). Also make sure the Normal tab at the bottom of the page is active (**Figure 4.2**).

2. Make sure the Folder List is visible by choosing View > Folder List or by clicking the Folder icon (**Figure 4.3**).

3. Select the page on which you want to enter text by double-clicking its listing in the Folder List pane.

4. Within the right pane, click your cursor where you want to enter text on the page. A blinking vertical bar will mark the text insertion spot (**Figure 4.4**).

5. Start typing and the text will appear on the page at the insertion spot (**Figure 4.5**).

Figure 4.1 Before working with text, switch to page view by clicking the Page icon in the Views Bar.

Figure 4.2 Whenever you're working with text, make sure the *Normal* tab is active.

Figure 4.3 It's easier to jump from file to file with the Folder List visible. Choose View > Folder List or click the Folder icon.

Figure 4.4 Click inside the right pane to begin adding text to a Web page.

Figure 4.5 Because the HTML code is hidden, entering text in FrontPage is quite similar to using a standard word processor.

```
chap_4.htm
```
What could be simpler? You type and text appears. It's not rocket|

Figure 4.6 Click where you want to insert text and a blinking vertical bar will appear.

```
chap_4.htm
```
What could be simpler? You type and text appears. It's not rocket,

Figure 4.7 Begin typing at the vertical bar and the text will be inserted.

To move the text cursor

1. Use your mouse or the arrow keys to move the cursor to where you want to insert text. An I-beam will mark the cursor's screen location (**Figure 4.6**).

2. Click at the insertion point and the blinking vertical bar will move to that spot (**Figure 4.7**). You're ready to begin typing at the new spot.

✔ Tips

- To jump from word to word, press Ctrl→ or Ctrl←.

- To jump from paragraph to paragraph, press Ctrl↓ or Ctrl↑.

To select text

1. Position your cursor at the beginning or end of the text you want to select.

2. Click and drag your cursor to select the text, which will become highlighted (**Figure 4.8**).

3. You now can copy the selected text (Ctrl C) or cut it to the clipboard (Ctrl X) for pasting elsewhere (Ctrl V).

To delete text

1. Position your cursor at the beginning or end of the text you want to select.

2. Click and drag your cursor to select the text, which will become highlighted (**Figure 4.8**).

3. Press ←Backspace or Delete and the text will be deleted (**Figure 4.9**).

Figure 4.8 Click and drag the cursor to highlight and select text for editing.

---

chap_4.htm ✕

What could be simpler?
You type and text appears. It's not rocket, well it's not a cliche that's for sure.

FrontPage |s completely painless.

Figure 4.9 Press ←Backspace or Delete and any highlighted text will be deleted.

Table 4.1

Shortcuts for selecting text	
TO SELECT	PRESS
Character to right of cursor	Delete
Character to left of cursor	←Backspace
Single word	Double-click
Word to right of cursor	Shift Ctrl →
Word to left of cursor	Shift Ctrl ←
From cursor to end of line	Shift End
From cursor to beginning of line	Shift Home
From cursor to line down	Shift ↓
From cursor to line up	Shift ↑
Entire paragraph	Alt click
To end of paragraph	Ctrl Shift ↓
To beginning of paragraph	Ctrl Shift ↑
Paragraph below cursor	Shift Ctrl ↓
Paragraph above cursor	Shift Ctrl ↑
To end of next screen	Shift Page Down
To beginning of previous screen	Shift Page Up

Table 4.2

Shortcuts for deleting text	
TO DELETE	PRESS
Character to right of cursor	Delete
Character to left of cursor	←Backspace
Word to right of cursor	Ctrl Delete
Word to left of cursor	Ctrl ←Backspace

chap_4.htm   ×

What could be simpler?
You type and text appears. It's not rocket, well
it's not a cliche that's for sure.

FrontPage makes even brain surgery seem
like a breeze. And, best of all, it's completely
painless.

Figure 4.10 To move text, first select with your
cursor.

chap_4.htm   ×

What could be simpler?
You type and text appears. It's not rocket, well
it's not a cliche that's for sure.

FrontPage makes even brain surgery seem

Figure 4.11 Once you've highlighted the text,
drag your cursor to the text's new location.

chap_4.htm   ×

What brain could be simpler?
You type and text appears. It's not rocket, well
it's not a cliche that's for sure.

FrontPage makes even surgery seem like a
breeze. And, best of all, it's completely

Figure 4.12 Release your cursor where you
want the text inserted and it will move from its
previous spot.

Figure 4.13 To cut text, choose Edit > Cut (Ctrl X). To
paste text, choose Edit > Paste (Ctrl V).

Figure 4.14 FrontPage's Standard toolbar includes icons for cutting, copying,
or pasting any text you select.

To move text

1. Select the text you want to move
   (**Figure 4.10**).

2. Click and drag the highlighted text to its
   new location (**Figure 4.11**).

3. Release the cursor and the text will be
   moved to the new spot (**Figure 4.12**).

✔ Tips

- You also can select the text, cut it to the
  clipboard ((Ctrl X)), click where you want
  to move it, and paste it in place ((Ctrl V))
  (**Figure 4.13**).

- If the Standard toolbar is active, you also
  can click the Cut, Copy, or Paste icons
  (**Figure 4.14**).

MOVING TEXT

To undo an action

◆ Choose Edit > Undo or press Ctrl Z. The previous action will be undone.

To redo an action

◆ Choose Edit > Redo or press Ctrl Y. The previous action will be reapplied.

✔ Tips

■ Both the *Undo* and *Redo* choices under the Edit menu change, depending on the previous action (**Figure 4.15**).

■ If the Standard toolbar is active, you also can click the Undo or Redo icons, which include drop-down menus listing the most recent actions (**Figure 4.16**).

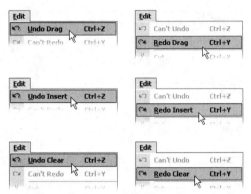

Figure 4.15 The *Undo* (left) and *Redo* (right) choices under the Edit menu change, based on the previous action.

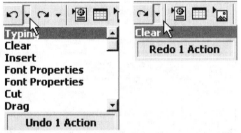

Figure 4.16 The Standard toolbar contains Undo and Redo icons, which include drop-down menus showing the most recent actions.

Figure 4.17 To add a line break to text, choose Insert > Break.

Figure 4.18 In the Break dialog box, *Normal line break* will be selected by default. Click *OK* and the break will be inserted.

```
chap_4.htm

What could be simpler?
You type and text appears. It's not rocket, well it's not a cliche that's for
sure
```

Figure 4.19 Once a line break is inserted, the text will break to the next line—without you having to enter the HTML code.

To add a line break to text

1. Within the right pane, click your cursor where you want the text to break to a new line.

2. Choose Insert > Break (**Figure 4.17**).

3. When the Break dialog box appears, *Normal line break* will be selected by default (**Figure 4.18**). Click *OK* (or press Enter) and a line break will be inserted (**Figure 4.19**). For details on the box's margin-related choices, see *Formatting Paragraphs, Lists, and Headings* on page 119.

✔ Tips

- You also can insert a line break by typing Shift Enter.

- To remove a line break, place the cursor on the beginning of the line before the break and press ←Backspace. The break will be removed.

To add a paragraph

1. Within the right pane, click your cursor where you want the paragraph to appear in the text (**Figure 4.20**).

2. Press [Enter] and a paragraph will be inserted into the text (**Figure 4.21**).

Showing line break and paragraph marks

Just as with word processing programs, you have the option of displaying normally hidden symbols that mark the location of line breaks and paragraph within the text.

To show/hide break and paragraph marks

◆ Click the Show All icon in the Standard toolbar (**Figure 4.22**). The text will display all line break and paragraph return marks (**Figure 4.23**). To hide the marks, click the Show All icon again.

---

chap_4.htm

What could be simpler?
You type and text appears. It's not rocket, well it's not a cliche that's for sure. FrontPage makes even brain surgery seem like a breeze. And, best of all, it's completely painless.

Figure 4.20 Click your cursor where you want a paragraph to appear.

chap_4.htm

What could be simpler?
You type and text appears. It's not rocket, well it's not a cliche that's for sure.

FrontPage makes even brain surgery seem like a breeze. And, best of all, it's completely painless.

Figure 4.21 Press [Enter] and a paragraph will be inserted into the text.

Figure 4.22
To show/hide line break and paragraph marks, click the Show All icon in the Standard toolbar.

chap_4.htm   ×

What brain brain be simpler? ↵
You type and text appears. It's not rocket, well it's not a cliche that's for sure. ¶

FrontPage makes even surgery seem like a breeze. And, best of all, it's completely painless.¶

Figure 4.23 The Show All icon lets you see normally hidden symbols that mark line breaks and paragraphs.

Finding and Replacing Text

Besides the standard find and replace functions you'd expect, FrontPage also lets you search the HTML, which means you can find words, phrases, or even bits of code that may not be visible in the Normal view.

To find text on a single page

1. If you're not already in page view, click the Page icon in the Views Bar and make sure the *Normal* tab is selected.

2. Make the Folder List visible by choosing View > Folder List or clicking the Folder icon.

3. Choose Edit > Find ((Ctrl)(F)) (**Figure 4.24**).

4. When the *Find* tab of the Find and Replace dialog box appears, type in the word or phrase you're seeking and choose *Current Page* (**Figure 4.25**).

5. By default, FrontPage will search in *All* directions, though you can use the drop-down menu to select *Up* or *Down*. Use the checkboxes if you want the search to *Match case* or *Find whole word only*. Click *Find Next* and the first instance of the word or phrase will be found (**Figure 4.26**).

6. The *Find* tab of the Find and Replace dialog box will remain visible, allowing you to continue clicking *Find Next* until you find the instance you're looking for.

7. When you're done searching, click *Cancel* or the Close button in the dialog box's upper-right corner.

Figure 4.24 To find text on a single page or across an entire Web site, choose Edit > Find.

Figure 4.25 In the Find and Replace dialog box, type in the word or phrase you're seeking and choose *Current Page*. Check any other search criteria and click *Find Next*.

Figure 4.26 The Find and Replace dialog box remains visible even after the first instance of the word or phrase is found. Click *Find Next* again to continue searching.

Figure 4.27 To search an entire Web site, choose *All pages*, set your other criteria, and click *Find In Web*.

To find text across a Web site

1. If you're not already in page view, click the Page icon in the Views Bar and make sure the *Normal* tab is selected.

2. Make the Folder List visible by choosing View > Folder List or clicking the Folder icon.

3. Choose Edit > Find ([Ctrl][F]) (**Figure 4.24**).

4. When the *Find* tab of the Find and Replace dialog box appears, type in the word or phrase you're seeking and choose *All pages* (**Figure 4.27**).

5. By default, FrontPage will search in *All* directions, though you can use the drop-down menu to select *Up* or *Down*. Use the checkboxes if you want the search to *Match case* or *Find whole word only*. Click *Find In Web*.

6. FrontPage will search through all the pages of the current Web site and list the pages containing the search phrase and how many times it appears on those pages (**Figure 4.28**).

7. Double-click on the page listing you'd like to search in detail, and you'll be taken to the first instance of the search phrase on that page. A basic Find and Replace dialog box also will appear in which you can click *Find Next* to continue searching the page (**Figure 4.29**).

8. The next instance of the search phrase on that page will appear. To keep searching, click *Find Next* again and the next instance will appear (**Figure 4.30**).

Figure 4.28 After searching the Web site, FrontPage will list every page with the phrase and how many times it appears. Double-click a page listing to search it.

Figure 4.29 A standard Find dialog box will appear. Click *Find Next* to continue searching the individual page.

Figure 4.30 To keep searching, continue clicking *Find Next*. To search another Web page, click the *Back to List* button and you'll be returned to the list of pages containing the search phrase.

FINDING AND REPLACING TEXT, HTML

Figure 4.31 To see other pages, click the Find and Replace dialog box's *Back to List* button and you'll be returned to the original search results dialog box.

9. If you want to see instances of the search phrase on one of the other pages initially listed, click the Find and Replace dialog box's *Back To List* button and you'll be returned to the original search results dialog box (**Figure 4.31**).

10. Double-click any other page in the list and instances of the search phrase on that page will appear.

11. When you're done, click *Cancel* or the Close button in the dialog box's upper-right corner.

FINDING AND REPLACING TEXT, HTML

To search the site's HTML code

1. If you're not already in page view, click the Page icon in the Views Bar and make sure the *Normal* tab is selected.

2. Choose Edit > Find ([Ctrl][F]) (**Figure 4.24**).

3. When the *Find* tab of the Find and Replace dialog box appears, type in the word or phrase you're seeking, choose *All pages*, and set your other search criteria. Then check the *Find in HTML* box and click *Find in Web* (**Figure 4.32**). FrontPage will list every page where the search phrase appears (**Figure 4.33**).

4. Double-click an individual page listing and you'll be taken to the first instance of the search phrase—even if it's in normally invisible HTML coding (**Figure 4.34**).

5. Continue to search that page by clicking *Find Next* or return to other page listings by clicking *Back To List*. When you're done, click *Cancel* or the Close button in the Find and Replace dialog box's upper-right corner.

✔ Tip

■ If you know the basics of HTML coding, this option offers a quick way to fix or replace coding across an entire Web site. If you don't understand HTML, this option can get you into deep trouble—fast.

Figure 4.32 To search the Web site's HTML code, type in what you're seeking and choose *All pages*. Then check the *Find in HTML* box and click *Find in Web*.

Figure 4.33 FrontPage will list every page where the search phrase exists—even pages containing invisible HTML coding.

Figure 4.34 Here's an example where FrontPage has found the search phrase in an HTML hyperlink.

Figure 4.35 To replace text on a single page or the entire site, choose Edit > Replace ([Ctrl][H]).

Figure 4.36 To replace text or HTML on a single page, type in the word, phrase, or code you're seeking, choose *Current Page* and click *Find Next*.

Figure 4.37 Once you begin the search, FrontPage will display the first instance of the text or code. Click *Replace*.

To replace text or HTML on a single page

1. If you're not already in page view, click the Page icon in the Views Bar and make sure the *Normal* tab is selected.

2. Make the Folder List visible by choosing View > Folder List or clicking the Folder icon.

3. Choose Edit > Replace ([Ctrl][H]) (**Figure 4.35**).

4. When the *Replace* tab of the Find and Replace dialog box appears, type in the word, phrase, or code you're seeking in the *Find what* window, the text or code you want to replace it with in the *Replace with* window, choose *Current Page*, and set your other search criteria, such as *Find in HTML* (**Figure 4.36**).

5. Click *Find Next* and the first instance of the text or code will be found (**Figure 4.37**).

6. Click *Replace* and FrontPage will make the fix and immediately move to the next instance of the text or code.

(continued)

FINDING AND REPLACING TEXT, HTML

7. Continue clicking the *Find Next* and *Replace* buttons until an alert dialog box tells you that FrontPage has finished searching the page. Click *OK* (**Figure 4.38**).

8. When the Find and Replace dialog box reappears, click *Cancel* or the Close button in its upper-right corner.

✔ Tip

■ If you're absolutely sure you want to replace every instance of a search phrase, click *Replace All* in the *Replace* tab of the Find and Replace dialog box and the search-and-replace process for the entire page will occur automatically (**Figure 4.39**).

Figure 4.38 An alert dialog box appears once FrontPage has finished searching the page. Click *OK* to see the list of other pages containing the text or code you searched for.

Figure 4.39 To automatically replace every instance of the search phrase, click *Replace All* in the Replace dialog box.

Figure 4.40 To search and replace across an entire Web site, type in the text or code you're seeking, choose *All pages,* and click *Find In Web.*

Figure 4.41 FrontPage will list all the pages in the Web site containing the search phrase and how many times it appears in each page. To see any page, double-click its listing.

Figure 4.42 Once you double-click a page listing, FrontPage jumps to the page and displays the first instance of the search phrase. To fix it, click *Replace.*

To replace text or HTML across a Web site

1. If you're not already in page view, click the Page icon in the Views Bar and make sure the *Normal* tab is selected.

2. Make the Folder List visible by choosing View > Folder List or clicking the Folder icon.

3. Choose Edit > Replace ([Ctrl][H]) (**Figure 4.35**).

4. When the *Replace* tab of the Find and Replace dialog box appears, type in the text or code you're seeking in the *Find what* window, the text or code you want to replace it with in the *Replace with* window, choose *All pages,* and set your other search criteria, such as *Find in HTML.* Click *Find In Web* (**Figure 4.40**).

5. FrontPage will search through all the pages of the current Web site and list the pages containing the search phrase and how many times it appears in those pages (**Figure 4.41**).

6. Double-click any of the pages listed and you'll be taken to that page's first instance of the text or code you'd like to replace (**Figure 4.42**).

(continued)

FINDING AND REPLACING TEXT, HTML

7. Click *Replace* and FrontPage will fix the search phrase and immediately move to the next instance of the phrase (**Figure 4.43**).

8. When FrontPage has searched and replaced every instance of the phrase on the page, a dialog box will appear asking whether you want to save your changes and close the page (**Figure 4.44**). Click *Back To List* to save and close the page and you'll be returned to the original search results dialog box. The *Replace* tab of the Find and Replace dialog box marks the page you just searched and replaced as *Edited* (**Figure 4.45**).

9. Double-click any other page in the list and that page's instances of the search phrase will appear. Repeat steps 7–9.

10. When you're done, click *Cancel* or the Close button in the dialog box's upper-right.

Figure 4.43 After each replace, FrontPage immediately moves to the next instance of the phrase.

Figure 4.44 After it has replaced every instance of the phrase on a page, FrontPage asks whether you want to save your changes and close the page. Click *Back To List*.

Figure 4.45 Once the fixes on a page have been saved, the Find and Replace dialog box will mark the page as *Edited*. Double-click any other listing to search that page.

Figure 4.46 To begin spell checking, choose Tools > Spelling (F7) or, if the Standard toolbar is active, click the Spelling icon.

Figure 4.47 When FrontPage finds a suspected error, the Spelling dialog box will display the word and offer suggested spellings.

Figure 4.48 When FrontPage finishes checking the page, it displays an alert dialog box. Click *OK*.

Checking Spelling

FrontPage lets you check the spelling on a single page or across an entire Web site. It even lets you check spelling as you type, though that particular option drives a lot of people crazy. I prefer running the spell check after I've built a page. By the way, FrontPage lets you change the dictionary language from the default U.S. English to more than two dozen other languages.

To check spelling on a single page

1. If you're not already in page view, click the Page icon in the Views Bar and make sure the *Normal* tab is selected.

2. Choose Tools > Spelling (F7) or if the Standard toolbar is active, click the Spelling icon (**Figure 4.46**).

3. FrontPage will begin checking the current page. When it finds a suspected error, the Spelling dialog box will display the word and offer a suggested spelling (**Figure 4.47**).

4. If you want to use the suggested word, click *Change* or *Change All* if you want every instance on the page fixed. If you know the word's spelled correctly—perhaps it's a trademark that FrontPage doesn't recognize—check *Ignore* or *Ignore All*. You also can add terms like trademarks to FrontPage's dictionary by clicking *Add*. If the suggested word isn't correct, you can type in your own spelling and click *Change* or *Change All*.

5. FrontPage will continue checking the page and display an alert dialog box when it's done. Click *OK* and you're done (**Figure 4.48**).

To check spelling across a Web site

1. Switch to folder view by clicking the Folders icon in the Views Bar.

2. Choose Tools > Spelling or if the Standard toolbar is active, click the Spelling icon (**Figure 4.49**).

3. When the Spelling dialog box appears, make sure that the *Entire web* radio button is selected (**Figure 4.50**). Click *Start* and FrontPage will begin checking the entire Web site. FrontPage will search the current Web site and list pages containing suspected misspellings and how many misspellings appear on each page (**Figure 4.51**).

4. Double-click any of the pages listed and you'll be taken to that page's first instance of the suspected misspelling. FrontPage also will show suggested spellings for the word.

5. Just as in spell checking a single page, you may click *Change* or *Change All*, *Ignore* or *Ignore All*, or you can type in your own spelling and click *Change* or *Change All*.

Figure 4.49 To check spelling across a Web site, switch to folder view and then choose Tools > Spelling.

Figure 4.50 Check *Entire web* in the Spelling dialog box and click *Start* to spell check every page.

Figure 4.51 FrontPage will search the current Web site and list pages containing suspected misspellings. To see a page, double-click its listing.

Figure 4.52 When FrontPage has fixed all the misspellings on a page, a dialog box will appear asking whether you want to continue checking the next page.

Figure 4.53 When FrontPage has fixed all the misspellings on the site, a dialog box will appear asking whether you want to close the page and return to the list. Click *Back To List*.

6. When FrontPage has fixed all the misspellings on the first page, a dialog box will appear asking whether you want to check for errors on the other pages (**Figure 4.52**). Click *Next Page* and FrontPage will automatically open and check the next page in the list. If you want to limit the spelling check to certain pages, click *Back To List* where you can jump to another page.

7. When FrontPage has fixed all the misspellings on the site, a dialog box will appear asking whether you want to close the page and return to the list (**Figure 4.53**). Click *Back To List* and you'll be returned to the list of pages with suspected misspellings. The pages you have spell checked will be marked as *Edited*.

8. When you're done, click *Cancel* or the Close button in the dialog box's upper-right corner.

To check spelling as you type

1. Choose Tools > Page Options (**Figure 4.54**).

2. When the Page Options dialog box appears, click the *General* tab and check the box marked *Check spelling as you type* (**Figure 4.55**).

3. Click *OK* and FrontPage will automatically check your spelling.

✔ Tip

■ Instead of having FrontPage check your spelling as you type, it's probably best to check *Hide spelling errors in all documents* in the Page Options dialog box. Otherwise, FrontPage will underline any word it doesn't recognize—which can make for an awful lot of red underlines (**Figure 4.56**).

To change the dictionary language

1. Choose Tools > Page Options (**Figure 4.54**).

2. When the Page Options dialog box appears, use the *Default spelling language* drop-down menu to pick a language other than U.S. English (**Figure 4.55**). When you're done, click *OK*.

Figure 4.54 To check spelling as you type, choose Tools > Page Options.

Figure 4.55 The Page Options dialog box lets you control whether FrontPage checks and shows spelling errors as you type. It also lets you set your dictionary's language.

The beauty of a DeBabelizer BatchLists is twofold. First, no matter what you do to the BatchList itself, your original files are left alone and, so, remain safe. Secondly, you can set the BatchList's order, which determines the order of actions applied to it, *independently* of where the files reside or how they're named.

Figure 4.56 The drawback of showing spelling errors as you type: Any word FrontPage doesn't recognize gets underlined, which makes for a messy page.

Formatting Text

If you're hand coding in HTML, making a word appear in bold face involves a surprising amount of rigmarole. In FrontPage, applying character styles works similarly to how it's done in word-processing programs: make a selection, click an icon, and you're done. The Formatting toolbar, which is on by default, includes everything you'll need for the most common text changes (**Figure 4.57**). Still more text formatting choices are available in the Font dialog box (details on page 115).

Figure 4.57 The Formatting toolbar includes icons for applying most text changes.

To change the font face

1. Make sure you're in page view by clicking the Page icon in the Views Bar.

2. Select the text you want to change (**Figure 4.58**).

3. Click the arrow just to the right of the Formatting toolbar's font window and scroll through the drop-down menu until you find a font you want (**Figure 4.59**).

4. Click on the font you want and it will be applied to the selected text (**Figure 4.60**).

✔ Tip

■ You also can change highlighted text by right-clicking in the page and choosing *Font* ([Alt][Enter]) from the shortcut menu (**Figure 4.61**). When the Font dialog box appears, choose the font from the scrolling Font window, then click *OK* (**Figure 4.62**). For details on the Font dialog box, see *Font options* on page 115.

Figure 4.58 Select the text whose font you want to change.

Figure 4.59 To change the font face, click the arrow for the Formatting toolbar's font window and scroll through the drop-down menu for the font you want.

Figure 4.60 Once you click on the font, the change is applied to the selected text.

Figure 4.61 You can reach the Font dialog box any time, by selecting text, right-clicking in the page, and choosing *Font* ([Alt][Enter]) from the shortcut menu.

Figure 4.62 The Font dialog box offers extensive control over the appearance and formatting of any highlighted text.

Figure 4.63 Select the text whose size you want to change, click the arrow for the Formatting toolbar's Font Size window, and scroll through the drop-down menu for the size you want.

Everyone thinks their
cutest, best canine in the
Dog, however, really is the
ever had. I

Figure 4.64 Once you click on the size, the change is applied to the selected text.

To change the font size

1. Make sure you're in page view by clicking the Page icon in the Views Bar.

2. Select the text you want to change.

3. In the Formatting toolbar, click the arrow just to the right of the Font Size window and choose a size from the drop-down menu (**Figure 4.63**).

4. Release the cursor and the new size will be applied to the selected text (**Figure 4.64**).

✔ Tip

■ You also can change the text's font size by right-clicking the page and choosing *Font* ([Alt][Enter]) from the shortcut menu (**Figure 4.61**). Within the Font dialog box, click the *Size* drop-down menu, make your choice, and click *OK* (**Figure 4.62**). For details see *Font options* on page 115.

CHANGING FONT SIZE

To change the font style

1. If you're not already in page view, click the Page icon in the Views Bar and make sure the *Normal* tab is selected.

2. Select the text you want to change (**Figure 4.65**).

3. Click one of the three style icons (*Bold*, *Italic*, or *Underline*) in the Formatting toolbar (**Figure 4.66**).

4. The style is applied to the selection (**Figure 4.67**).

Everyone thinks their dog is the smartest, cutest, best canine in the world. Lou the Wonder Dog, however, really is the smartest dog I've ever had.

For example, Lou can code in HTML--without using FrontPage.

Figure 4.65 Select the text whose style you want to change.

Figure 4.66 Click one of the three style icons in the Formatting toolbar.

Everyone thinks their dog is the smartest, cutest, best canine in the world. Lou the Wonder Dog, however, really is the *smartest* dog I've ever had.

For example, Lou can code in HTML--without using FrontPage.

Figure 4.67 Once you click one of the style icons, the change is applied to the selected text.

Figure 4.68 Select the text whose color you want to change.

Figure 4.69 Click the arrow next to the Font Color icon and choose a color from the drop-down menu.

Figure 4.70 Once you release the cursor, the color change is applied to the selected text.

To change the font color

1. Make sure you're in page view by clicking the Page icon in the Views Bar.

2. Select the text you want to change (**Figure 4.68**).

3. Click the arrow just to the right of the Font Color icon and choose a color from the drop-down menu (**Figure 4.69**).

4. Release the cursor and the color will be applied to the selected text (**Figure 4.70**).

✔ Tip

■ You also can change the text's color by right-clicking the page and choosing *Font* ([Alt] [Enter]) from the shortcut menu (**Figure 4.61**). Within the Font dialog box, click the *Color* drop-down menu, make your choice, and click *OK* (**Figure 4.62**). For details see *Font options* on page 115.

To change text alignment

1. Make sure you're in page view by clicking the Page icon in the Views Bar.

2. Select the text you want to change (**Figure 4.71**).

3. In the Formatting toolbar, click one of the four alignment icons (**Figure 4.72**).

4. Release the cursor and the text will be aligned based on which icon you clicked (**Figure 4.73**).

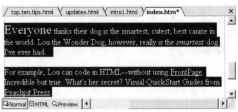

Figure 4.71 Select the text whose alignment you want to change.

Figure 4.72 Click one of the four alignment icons in the Formatting toolbar.

Figure 4.73 Once you click one of the alignment icons, the change is applied to the selected text.

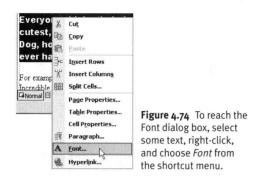

Figure 4.74 To reach the Font dialog box, select some text, right-click, and choose *Font* from the shortcut menu.

Figure 4.75 The Font dialog box's *Font* tab lets you change the selected text's font, font style, size, and text color.

Figure 4.76 The *Character Spacing* tab lets you change the selected text's horizontal spacing and vertical positioning.

Font options

To open the Font dialog box, select some text, right-click, and choose *Font* from the shortcut menu (**Figures 4.74** and **4.75**). The dialog box's *Font* tab ❶ is active by default and lets you change the font, font style, size ❷, and text color ❸. It also lets you apply text effects ❹ not available within the Formatting toolbar. Check a box and you can see its effect within the *Preview* window ❺.

Clicking the Font dialog box's *Character Spacing* tab ❻ displays the *Spacing* ❼ and *Position* ❽ drop-down menus, which let you adjust the horizontal spacing and vertical positioning of the text you've selected (**Figure 4.76**). The *Preview* window ❾ lets you see the effects of various spacing and positioning combinations. For details on spacing and positions, see the next page.

To change character spacing

1. Make sure you're in page view by clicking the Page icon in the Views Bar.

2. Select the text you want to change.

3. Right-click and choose *Font* from the shortcut menu (**Figure 4.74**).

4. When the Font dialog box appears (**Figure 4.76**), click the *Character Spacing* tab.

5. Use the *Spacing* drop-down menu to quickly choose whether you want the text's horizontal spacing to be *Expanded*, *Normal*, or *Condensed*. The results will be displayed in the *Preview* window. To fine tune the horizontal spacing, use the arrows of the adjacent *By* window to adjust the spacing in either direction (**Figure 4.77**).

6. When you're done, click *OK* and the spacing will be applied to the selected text.

To change character positioning

1. Make sure you're in page view by clicking the Page icon in the Views Bar.

2. Select the text you want to change.

3. Right-click and choose *Font* from the shortcut menu (**Figure 4.74**).

4. When the Font dialog box appears (**Figure 4.76**), click the *Character Spacing* tab.

5. Use the *Position* drop-down menu to quickly adjust the text's vertical alignment. The results will be displayed in the Preview window (**Figure 4.78**).

6. When you're done, click *OK* and the spacing will be applied to the selected text.

Figure 4.77 Within the Font dialog box, use the *Spacing* drop-down menu to control whether the text is *Expanded*, *Normal*, or *Condensed*. The adjacent *By* window lets you fine tune the spacing.

Figure 4.78 Within the Font dialog box, use the *Position* drop-down menu to control the text's vertical alignment.

Figure 4.79 To remove all text formatting, select the text and choose Format > Remove Formatting (Ctrl Shift Z).

To remove text formatting

1. Make sure you're in page view by clicking the Page icon in the Views Bar.

2. Select the text whose formatting you want to remove.

3. Choose Format > Remove Formatting (Ctrl Shift Z) (**Figure 4.79**). All of the text's formatting will be removed, reverting back to its default settings.

REMOVING TEXT FORMATTING

Using Symbols and Special Characters

The advantage of having FrontPage automatically handle your HTML coding becomes particularly obvious when you need to add special characters to your Web pages. Whether it's a copyright symbol, a formula operator, a Euro sign, or a Cyrillic character, FrontPage can handle it and spare you the headache of remembering the HTML equivalent.

To add a symbol or special character

1. Click in the page where you want the symbol or special character to appear.

2. Choose Insert > Symbol (**Figure 4.80**).

3. When the Symbol dialog box appears, click the *Subset* drop-down menu and choose which symbol or language subset you want to use (**Figure 4.81**). Release your cursor once you have scrolled to the desired subset and its characters will appear in the dialog box's main window.

4. Find the particular symbol you need by using the main window's scroll bar, select it, and click *Insert* (**Figure 4.82**). The character will be inserted into your Web page.

✔ Tip

■ The Symbol dialog box's *Recently used symbols* window can save you a ton of time if you use particular characters over and over (**Figure 4.81**). After you have inserted a particular character into a page once, it will be added to the *Recently used symbols* window—where it will be immediately available the next time you need it. The window can store up to 16 recent characters.

Figure 4.80 To add a symbol or special character to a page, choose Insert > Symbol.

Figure 4.81 Use the Symbol dialog box's *Subset* drop-down menu to find a particular subset of characters.

Figure 4.82 Select the desired symbol in the dialog box's main window and click *Insert*.

FORMATTING PARAGRAPHS, LISTS, AND HEADINGS

While graphics give your Web pages pizzazz, it's the paragraphs, lists, and headings that handle the real workload of setting your pages' visual hierarchy. FrontPage lets you easily set and control all three, primarily with the Formatting toolbar (**Figure 5.1**). If those controls, however, don't provide exactly what you need—or you want to create a custom style and use it repeatedly—consider using style sheets. See *Building Style Sheets and Dynamic Effects* on page 335.

Figure 5.1 The drop-down menus and buttons in the Formatting toolbar control your paragraphs, lists, and headings.

Using Paragraphs

FrontPage lets you change the appearance of your paragraphs by adjusting their alignment, indentation, the spacing above and below the paragraph, and line spacing (leading).

To align a paragraph

1. Make sure you're in page view by clicking the Page icon in the Views Bar.

2. Click anywhere in the paragraph you want to realign and choose one of the four alignment buttons in the Formatting toolbar (**Figure 5.2**). (By default, paragraphs are aligned to the left.) The new alignment will be applied (**Figure 5.3**).

Align Left (Ctrl+L) — Justify
Center (Ctrl+E) — Align Right (Ctrl+R)

Figure 5.2 To align a paragraph, click one of the four alignment buttons in the Formatting toolbar.

chp5-page_1.htm*

5: Formatting Paragraphs, Lists, and Headings

While graphics give your Web pages pizzaz, it's the paragraphs, lists, and headings that handle the real work of setting your page's visual hierarchy. FrontPage lets you easily set and control all three, primarily with the Formatting toolbar (Figure 5.1).

If those controls, however, don't provide exactly what you need—or you want to create a custom style and use it repeatedly—consider using style sheets. See *Building Style Sheets and Dynamic Effects* on page 000.

Normal   HTML   Preview

chp5-page_1.htm*

5: Formatting Paragraphs, Lists, and Headings

While graphics give your Web pages pizzaz, it's the paragraphs, lists, and headings that handle the real work of setting your page's visual hierarchy. FrontPage lets you easily set and control all three, primarily with the Formatting toolbar (Figure 5.1).

If those controls, however, don't provide exactly what you need—or you want to create a custom style and use it repeatedly—consider using style sheets. See *Building Style Sheets and Dynamic Effects* on page 000.

Normal   HTML   Preview

Figure 5.3 The paragraph was aligned to the left (top) until being reformatted to align on the right (bottom).

Figure 5.4 To change a paragraph's indentation, click the Increase Indent or Decrease Indent button.

Figure 5.5 After applying the indent, the paragraph will shift to reflect your choice.

Figure 5.6 To indent a paragraph even more, keep clicking the Increase Indent button.

Figure 5.7 You can see the normally hidden HTML tags as you work by choosing choose View > Reveal Tags. Repeat the command to hide them again.

Indenting paragraphs

FrontPage gives you several ways to indent paragraphs. The quickest way involves using the buttons in the Formatting toolbar; the more precise method requires setting custom indentations within the Paragraph dialog box.

To indent paragraphs

1. Be sure you're in page view, then click anywhere in the paragraph you want to indent.

2. Click the Increase Indent button or the Decrease Indent button in the Formatting toolbar (**Figure 5.4**). The indenting will be applied (**Figure 5.5**).

3. If you want to indent the paragraph even more, continue clicking the Increase Indent button until you're satisfied with the result (**Figure 5.6**).

✔ Tips

- The indent buttons affect both margins of the selected text *equally* (**Figure 5.6**). To set *different* indents for each margin, see *To customize paragraph indents* on the next page.

- As with all Web editors, FrontPage uses HTML tags to format your text. But to keep the document from getting cluttered, FrontPage ordinarily hides the coding from sight. To see the tags at any point, choose View > Reveal Tags ([Ctrl][I]) (**Figure 5.7**). Repeat the command to hide the tags again.

USING PARAGRAPHS

121

To customize paragraph indents

1. Be sure you're in page view, then right-click anywhere in the paragraph whose style you want to change and choose *Paragraph* from the shortcut menu (**Figure 5.8**).

2. When the Paragraph dialog box appears, use the *Indentation* section's arrows to set the indentation (in points) *Before text* and *After text* (**Figure 5.9**).

3. Click *OK* and your custom indentation will be applied (**Figure 5.10**).

Figure 5.8 To modify the Normal paragraph style, right-click anywhere in the paragraph and choose *Paragraph* from the shortcut menu.

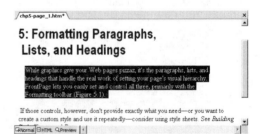

Figure 5.9 Use the Paragraph dialog box's pop-up menus and arrows to simultaneously change multiple aspects of a paragraph. The *Preview* area at the bottom shows how the changes will look.

Figure 5.10 Custom indentation of 15 points on the left, 60 points on the right applied to the highlighted paragraph.

Paragraph styling

The easiest way to change several aspects of a paragraph at once is to modify FrontPage's *Normal* style. Normal style by default uses the Times New Roman font with single line spacing, left-aligned, with no indentations. Or you can use the built-in *Formatted* style, which uses Courier monospaced in a typewriter-like style that requires you to manually enter any line returns. It looks clunky but before fancy HTML came along, it was often the only way to make text wrap exactly.

To modify the Normal paragraph style

1. Be sure you're in page view. Right-click anywhere in the paragraph whose style you want to change and choose *Paragraph* from the shortcut menu (**Figure 5.8**).

2. When the Paragraph dialog box appears, use the pop-up menus and arrows to set your paragraph's alignment, indentation, indentation for the paragraph's first line only, the amount of blank space you want before and after the paragraph, and the line spacing within the paragraph (**Figure 5.9**). The *Preview* area at the bottom of the dialog box lets you see how the indents and spacing will be applied.

3. Once you're satisfied with the changes, click *OK* and the styling will be applied to the selected paragraph.

✔ Tip

■ The Paragraph dialog box includes the option to change the spacing between words (**Figure 5.9**). Unfortunately, FrontPage can't show how the word spacing will appear. You'll have to switch to your Web browser to see the effect—and most browsers don't support the feature. You're better off skipping the word spacing feature entirely.

To apply the Formatted paragraph style

1. Be sure you're in page view and click where you want the Formatted style to begin.

2. Use the Style drop-down list in the Formatting toolbar to choose *Formatted* (**Figure 5.11**).

3. Begin typing, using the spacebar to align and wrap the text (**Figure 5.12**).

4. When you're ready to switch back to the Normal format, use the Style drop-down list in the Formatting toolbar to choose *Normal* (**Figure 5.13**).

Figure 5.11 To apply the *Formatted* paragraph style, use the Style drop-down list.

Figure 5.12 The Formatted style looks terrible, but lets you align these inventory numbers.

Figure 5.13 Use the Style drop-down list to switch back to the Normal format.

Figure 5.14 To quickly create a bulleted list, click the Bullets button in the Formatting toolbar.

Figure 5.15 You also can create a bulleted list using the Style drop-down menu.

Figure 5.16 Nothing fancy: the default bullet style.

Figure 5.17 To apply bullets to several paragraphs at once, just select them and click the Bullets button.

Using Lists

FrontPage lets you create a variety of list styles, which can be broken into two general groups: unordered lists and ordered lists. Unordered lists, also known as unnumbered or bulleted lists, are great for presenting a series of items that have no particular order, such as a list of supplies. Use ordered or numbered lists whenever you want to present a list of items in sequence. While FrontPage will create directory and menu lists, they're not supported by most browsers, so it's best to avoid using them.

Creating unordered lists

By default, FrontPage uses solid, round bullets. However, you can use any of the bullets within FrontPage's built-in themes—or create custom bullets. For details, see *Customizing lists* on page 128.

To create a bulleted list

1. Be sure you're in page view. Click anywhere in the line or paragraph that you want to begin with a bullet.

2. Click the Bullets button in the Formatting toolbar (**Figure 5.14**). Or use the Style drop-down list in the Formatting toolbar to choose *Bulleted List* (**Figure 5.15**). A bullet will be added to the line or paragraph (**Figure 5.16**).

3. To continue adding bullets to the list, press (Enter). Once you're done building the list, press (Enter) twice and FrontPage will switch to regular body type.

✔ Tips

- To apply bullets to several paragraphs at once, just select them and click the Bullets button (**Figure 5.17**).

- To remove bullets, click anywhere in the bulleted line or paragraph and click the Bullets button once more.

USING LISTS

125

Creating definition lists

Definition lists are handy for glossaries and other dictionary-style information because the format puts a word or term on a single line with the definition indented immediately below it. Though you can type in all the terms and definitions and then format them, it's generally easier to switch to the Defined Term format and begin typing since all the formatting will be handled automatically.

To create a definition list

1. Place your cursor where you want the first definition to appear.

2. Use the Style drop-down list in the Formatting toolbar to choose *Defined Term* (**Figure 5.18**).

3. Release the cursor and type in your first term. Then press (Enter) and the cursor will jump to the next line, automatically add an indent, and switch to the Definition format (**Figure 5.19**).

4. Type in your definition. If you want to add more terms, press (Enter) again and FrontPage will jump to a new line and switch back to the Defined Term format.

5. Once you're done adding terms, press (Enter) *twice* and FrontPage will switch back to the normal body text (**Figure 5.20**).

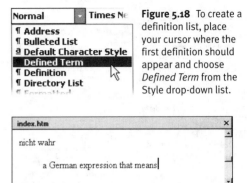

Figure 5.18 To create a definition list, place your cursor where the first definition should appear and choose *Defined Term* from the Style drop-down list.

Figure 5.19 After you type in your first term and press (Enter), the cursor will jump to the next line, automatically add an indent, and switch to the Definition format.

Figure 5.20 Once you're done adding terms, press (Enter) *twice* and FrontPage will switch back to the normal body text.

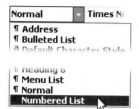

Figure 5.21 To create a numbered list, select your text and click the Numbering button in the Formatting toolbar.

Figure 5.22 You also can number text by using the Style drop-down list and choosing *Numbered List*.

Figure 5.23 Once numbering is applied, press Enter to continue adding items to the list.

Figure 5.24 If you reformat a previously numbered item to regular text, FrontPage automatically renumbers the remaining text into *two* sequences.

Creating ordered lists

Use ordered lists whenever you want to present a list of items in sequence. Though ordered lists usually are numbered, FrontPage also lets you use letters (A, B, C,...). For details, see *Customizing lists* on the next page.

To create a numbered list

1. Be sure you're in page view. Select the lines or paragraphs you want numbered.

2. Click the Numbering button in the Formatting toolbar (**Figure 5.21**). Or use the Style drop-down list in the Formatting toolbar to choose *Numbered List* (**Figure 5.22**). In either case, the selected lines or paragraphs will be numbered in sequence (**Figure 5.23**).

3. To continue adding numbered items to the list, press Enter. Once you're done building the list, press Enter twice and FrontPage will switch to regular body type.

✔ Tips

■ To remove numbers, click anywhere in the numbered line or paragraph and click the Numbering button once more. The remaining items will be renumbered and even broken into two sequences if necessary (**Figure 5.24**).

■ Instead of numbering items after you've written them, you can number them as you type. Just place your cursor where you want the first item in the list to appear, click the Numbering button, and the number 1 will appear. Begin typing, pressing Enter whenever you want the next number to begin.

USING LISTS

Customizing lists

As usual, FrontPage offers you several choices for customizing your lists. Your sources of bullets for unordered lists are particularly wide: You can use FrontPage's built-in themes, the clip art that comes with FrontPage, or any graphic of your own. To use the bullets built into FrontPage's themes, see *To apply a theme to a page or Web site* on page 80.

To customize lists

1. Click anywhere in the page and choose Format > Bullets and Numbering (**Figure 5.25**). If you are changing an existing list, just right-click in the list and choose *List Properties* from the shortcut menu (**Figure 5.26**).

2. Depending on what you clicked in step 1, either the Bullets and Numbering or List Properties dialog box will appear (**Figures 5.27** and **5.28**). Choose one of the tabs, which can include: *Picture Bullets*, *Plain Bullets*, *Numbers*, or *Other*.

3. Make your choices and click *OK* to apply the change to your page. For details, see *List options* on the next page.

Figure 5.25 To customize your bullets or numbers, click anywhere in the page and choose Format > Bullets and Numbering.

Figure 5.26 To customize an existing list, right-click in the list and choose *List Properties* from the shortcut menu.

Figure 5.27 The Bullets and Numbering dialog box lets you insert your own pictures as graphical bullets.

Figure 5.28 The List Properties dialog box gives you complete control over customizing bullets, numbers, and lists.

Figure 5.29 To use your own graphic as a bullet, navigate to the file and then click *OK*.

Figure 5.30 The *Numbers* tab of the List Properties dialog box gives you five numbering/lettering styles plus a blank option.

List options

Follow the steps in *To customize lists* to reach the Bullets and Numbering or List Properties dialog box (**Figures 5.27** and **5.28**). Both boxes offer the Picture Bullets, Plain Bullets, and Numbers tabs; Other appears only in the List Properties box:

◆ **Picture Bullets:** This tab lets you use your own graphics as bullets—even if you're also using one of FrontPage's built-in themes. To turn off the theme's bullets, click *Specify picture*, then click *Browse* and navigate to the graphic file you want to use (**Figure 5.29**). Click *OK* and the selected graphic will be used for your bullets.

◆ **Plain Bullets:** This tab lets you choose one of three plain bullet styles (**Figure 5.28**). The fourth, upper-left choice offers a somewhat roundabout option for canceling the bullets entirely. Once you've made your choice, click *OK* to apply the plain bullet style.

◆ **Numbers:** This tab lets you choose five numbering/lettering styles (**Figure 5.30**). Again, the upper-left choice lets you cancel numbering. Use the *Start at* arrows if you want to start the numbering at, say, 4 or the fifth letter, E. Once you've made your choice, click *OK* to apply.

(continued)

USING LISTS

◆ **Other:** This tab lets you quickly switch the style of an entire list to any of the other styles in the text window (**Figure 5.31**). Once you've made your choice, click *OK* to apply.

✔ Tip

■ Every tab of the List Properties dialog box includes checkboxes for *Enable Collapsible Outlines* and *Initially Collapsed*. These features are available only if you're using Dynamic HTML (DHTML) and are recognized only by version 4 or later browsers. For details, see *Building Style Sheets and Dynamic Effects* on page 335.

Figure 5.31 The *Other* tab of the List Properties dialog box lets you change an entire list to another style.

```
index.htm                                    ×
Geologic Time

    I.   Cenozoic|
    II.  Mesozoic
    III. Paleozoic
    IV.  Precambrian
Normal  HTML  Preview  ◄          ►
```

Figure 5.32 To create a nested list, click in a bulleted or numbered list right where you want the subdivision to start.

```
index.htm                                    ×
Geologic Time

    I.   Cenozoic
         I.  Quaternary|
    II.  Mesozoic
    III. Paleozoic
    IV.  Precambrian
Normal  HTML  Preview  ◄          ►
```

Figure 5.33 By default, the nested subdivision's numbering or lettering matches the level above it.

Figure 5.34 To change a *subdivision's* numbering or lettering scheme, right-click and choose *List Item Properties*.

```
index.htm                                    ×
Geologic Time

    I.   Cenozoic
         A.  Quaternary
    II.  Mesozoic
    III. Paleozoic
    IV.  Precambrian
Normal  HTML  Preview  ◄          ►
```

Figure 5.35 The nested item, *Quaternary*, now has a letter instead of a number.

Nested lists

Nested lists, sometimes called multilevel lists, enable you to create subdivisions within an overall list. They also lend themselves to customizing, such as using numbers at one level and letters at another.

To create a nested list

1. First create a bulleted or numbered list, then click in that list just before the place you want to insert a nested subdivision (**Figure 5.32**).

2. Press Enter and click the Increase Indent button *twice* (**Figure 5.4**).

3. When a new, blank line is inserted into the list, begin typing your first nested item. By default, it will be numbered or lettered just like the level above it (**Figure 5.33**).

4. If you want to change the *subdivision's* numbering or lettering scheme, right-click and choose *List Item Properties* from the shortcut menu (**Figure 5.34**).

5. When the List Item Properties dialog box appears, choose a numbering or lettering style, click *OK*, and the style will be applied to the nested item only (**Figure 5.35**).

(continued)

USING LISTS

6. To add another item at this same nested level, press (Enter) and it will be numbered or lettered in the same style you chose in step 5. Continue adding items at that level until you're done.

7. If you want to nest still another level in the list, repeat steps 1–6 (**Figure 5.36**).

8. When you're done building the nested list, press (Enter) twice to switch back to regular body type.

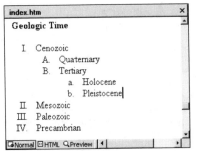

Figure 5.36 FrontPage lets you nest items within already nested items, changing the numbering or lettering style at each level.

✔ Tip

■ In step 4, be sure to choose *List Item Properties* not *List Properties* (**Figure 5.34**). *List Item Properties* controls the nested list items; *List Properties* controls the overall list in which the item nests.

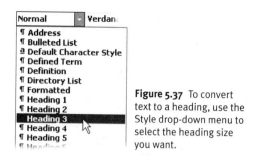

Figure 5.37 To convert text to a heading, use the Style drop-down menu to select the heading size you want.

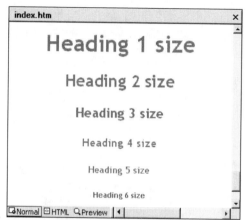

Figure 5.38 Sizes range from Heading 1, the largest, to Heading 6, the smallest.

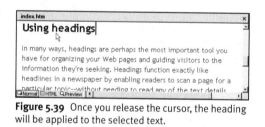

Figure 5.39 Once you release the cursor, the heading will be applied to the selected text.

Using Headings

In some ways, headings are your most important tool for guiding visitors through your Web pages. Headings function exactly like headlines in a newspaper by enabling readers to scan a page for a particular topic—without needing to read any of the text details. As with a newspaper, big headings should be used for your most important topics and smaller headings for less important items. It's simple—but vital—in bringing visual order to your pages. While this section just deals with heading sizes, remember you also can change heading font, color, and style. For details, see *Formatting Text* on page 109.

To add headings

1. Click anywhere in the line of text you want to make into a heading.

2. Click on the Style drop-down menu in the Formatting toolbar and select the heading size you want to apply (**Figure 5.37**). Heading 1 is the largest; Heading 6 the smallest (**Figure 5.38**).

3. Release your cursor and the heading will be applied (**Figure 5.39**).

✔ Tip

■ While you can apply a heading to as much as a full paragraph of text, generally it's easier to read a heading if you use no more than two short lines of text. In fact, the fewer words the better.

USING HEADINGS

To change a heading size

1. Click anywhere in the heading to select it.

2. Click on the Style drop-down menu in the Formatting toolbar and select a new heading size.

3. Release your cursor and the new heading size will be applied.

ADDING HYPERLINKS

The Web's essential beauty springs from the user's ability to jump from file to file anywhere in the world. Hyperlinks make that possible. Hyperlinks, or simply links, come in several varieties: links to other files around the globe, links to other spots within the document already on your screen, links to send email, and links embedded in pictures. Microsoft FrontPage makes it easy to create them all.

Text links are explained on the next page; image links are covered separately on page 152. It's also worth remembering that *Creating a Web Site* on page 47 discusses how to automatically link entire pages as you build or reorganize your site.

Absolute and Relative Links

Fundamental to using links is understanding the difference between what are called absolute and relative hyperlinks. An absolute link shows a file's full Web address (http://www.peachpit.com/books/catalog/K5914.htm) while a relative link just includes the file name and the folder it's stored in (/My Webs2/formatting.htm). You *must* use an absolute link any time you create a link to a Web page or file *not* on your own Web site, sometimes called an external link. Relative links *should* be used to link to files within your own Web site.

The advantage of relative links is that you can rearrange your Web site and files without breaking any links, which stymies Web browsers. Precisely because your home page has an absolute address, a Web browser can bounce from relative link to relative link within your Web site even if you move expensivepart.htm from www.yoursite.com/parts/ to www.yoursite.com/supplies/. Rearranging your site is inevitable. You'll outgrow the original structure, find a better way to do it, or whatever. Follow the steps in *To link to a page in your Web site* and FrontPage will automatically create relative links—saving you the work of *manually* updating all those links later on.

Figure 6.1 Switch to page view by clicking the Page icon in the Views Bar.

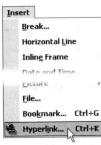

Figure 6.2 To create a link, choose Insert > Hyperlink (left) or click the Hyperlink button in the Standard toolbar (right).

Figure 6.3 To quickly create a link, right-click your selection and choose *Hyperlink* from the shortcut menu.

Figure 6.4 In the Insert Hyperlink dialog box, the text you selected in step 2 appears in the *Text to display* window.

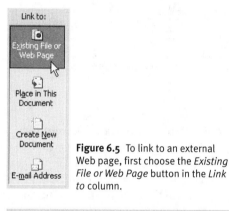

Figure 6.5 To link to an external Web page, first choose the *Existing File or Web Page* button in the *Link to* column.

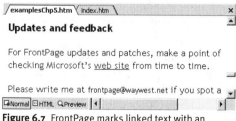

Figure 6.6 If you don't know a site's URL, find it by clicking the Web browser button to navigate to the desired Web page.

Updates and feedback

For FrontPage updates and patches, make a point of checking Microsoft's web site from time to time.

Please write me at frontpage@waywest.net if you spot a

Figure 6.7 FrontPage marks linked text with an underline.

To link to an external Web page

1. Make sure you're in page view by clicking the Page icon in the Views Bar (**Figure 6.1**).

2. Select the text you want to link.

3. Choose Insert > Hyperlink or click the Hyperlink button in the Standard toolbar (**Figure 6.2**). You also can right-click in the page and choose *Hyperlink* from the shortcut menu (Ctrl K) (**Figure 6.3**).

4. When the Insert Hyperlink dialog box appears (**Figure 6.4**), the text you selected in step 2 will appear in the *Text to display* window, where you can change it if you like.

5. Choose the first *Link to* button, *Existing File or Web Page* (**Figure 6.5**). For details on the *Link to* choices, see *Insert Hyperlink options* on page 138.

6. If you know the site's URL, type it directly into the *Address* text window and skip to step 9. If you don't know the URL, click the Web browser button to navigate to the desired Web page (**Figure 6.6**). For details, see *Insert Hyperlink options* on page 138.

7. When your default Web browser launches, use it to navigate to the external Web page to which you want to link.

8. Once you reach the external Web page you're seeking, switch back to the Insert Hyperlink dialog box and the URL will be automatically pasted into the *Address* text window.

9. Click *OK* to close the dialog box and your selection will be linked—indicated by the underline in the Web page (**Figure 6.7**).

ADDING EXTERNAL LINKS

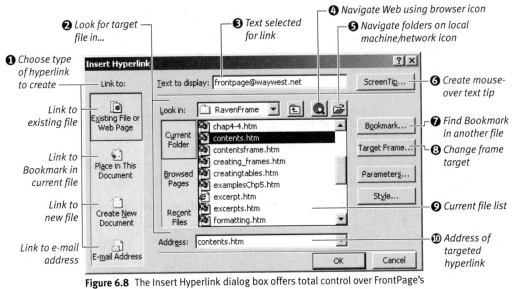

Figure 6.8 The Insert Hyperlink dialog box offers total control over FrontPage's hyperlinks.

Insert Hyperlink options

The Insert Hyperlink dialog box offers total control over FrontPage's hyperlinks (**Figure 6.8**). To reach the dialog box, choose Insert > Hyperlink ((Ctrl)(K)). By default, the dialog box initially displays the Web site you're working on.

❶ **Choose type of hyperlink to create:**
Click one of the four buttons in *Link to* column, based on the type of link you need to create.

◆ **Link to existing file:** Click the *Existing File or Web Page* button to link to a file on your local computer, local network, or the Web. Use in tandem with the dialog box's *Look in* buttons and icons to navigate to the file. (For details, see *Look for target file in* on the next page).

◆ **Link to Bookmark in current file:**
Click the *Place in This Document* button to link to a bookmark (FrontPage's term for anchor links) that already exists in the page you're working on. To create a bookmark from scratch, see page 145.

◆ **Link to new file:** Click the *Create New Document* button if you want to create a link to a page on your Web site that you've not yet created (see page 142). The New dialog box will open, allowing you to create a normal page or one based on FrontPage's templates.

◆ **Link to e-mail address:** Click the *E-mail Address* button to link your selected text or image to an email address. For details, see *To create an email link* on page 141.

❷ **Look for target file in:** Use the three buttons (*Current Folder, Browsed Pages,* and *Recent Files*) and the two navigation icons (*Navigate Web using browser* and *Navigate folders on local machine/network*) to select a target file for the hyperlink. By default, the *Current Folder* button is selected and its contents will be displayed in the Current file list. Clicking *Browsed Pages* will display the URLs for Web pages you've browsed in Microsoft Internet Explorer. The number of pages listed reflects the content of Internet Explorer's History folder (cache). Clicking *Recent Files* will list all the files recently opened within FrontPage—no matter which Web site they are stored in.

❸ **Text selected for link:** By default, the *Text to display* window contains the text you initially selected for the hyperlink. In most cases, you won't want to change this, but you can type new text into the window and it will replace the original linked text after you click *OK*.

❹ **Navigate Web using browser icon:** Click to launch your Web browser and hunt down an external page out on the Web. Once you reach the page, switch back to FrontPage and the address is pasted automatically into the *Address* window.

❺ **Navigate folders on local machine/network icon:** Click to navigate to any file on your hard drive or your local network. The file location will be pasted automatically into the *Address* window.

❻ **Create mouseover text tip:** Based on Windows' own screen tip feature, the ScreenTip button lets you create a small text message that appears when a browser's cursor moves over the link. The text will appear only if the Web visitor is using the Windows version of Internet Explorer 4 or later.

❼ **Find Bookmark in another file:** By selecting a file in the Current file list, you can use the *Bookmark* button to link to a bookmark (anchor) in a file other than the current page. (To use a bookmark in the current page, click the *Place in This Document* button instead.) For more information, see *Using Bookmarks* on page 145.

❽ **Change frame target:** Click *Target Frame* only if your Web site contains frames (see *Creating and Formatting Frames* on page 273).

❾ **Current file list:** By default, the list shows the current Web site's files but it will change if you click the *Browsed Pages* or *Recent Files* buttons. Use the far-right scroll bar to see all the files and folders in your site.

❿ **Address of targeted hyperlink:** FrontPage automatically fills in the address for your targeted hyperlink based on your choices in the *Link to* and *Look in* columns. You also can type directly in the window if you already know a file's URL (Uniform Resource Locator). FrontPage automatically begins the URL with an http:// but just type ftp:// to replace it if you're creating a File Transfer Protocol link for visitors to download a file.

To link to a page in your Web site

1. Make sure you're in page view by clicking the Page icon in the Views Bar (**Figure 6.1**).

2. Select the text you want to link, right-click, and choose *Hyperlink* from the shortcut menu ([Ctrl][K]) (**Figure 6.3**).

3. When the Insert Hyperlink dialog box appears, the *Link to* column's *Existing File or Web Page* button will be selected by default. Use the *Look in* buttons and folder icons to find the desired file in your Web site. If the file is in the *Current Folder*, use the dialog box's scroll bar to find the file, click it, and the name will be pasted into the *Address* text box (**Figure 6.9**). If the file's elsewhere on your computer, click the Navigate folders on local machine/network icon and use the Link to File dialog box to reach the desired file (**Figures 6.10** and **6.11**).

4. Click *OK* in either the Insert Hyperlink or Link to File dialog box, depending on your choice in step 3. The dialog box will close and your selected text will be linked to the file—as indicated by an underline in the Web page.

Figure 6.9 If a file's already part of your Web site, select it in the scrolling list and its name will be pasted into the *Address* text box.

Figure 6.10 To link to a file on your computer, click the Navigate folders on local machine/network icon in the Insert Hyperlink dialog box.

Figure 6.11 Once you track down a local file, click *OK* in the Link to File dialog box.

Figure 6.12 To add an email link, click the *Link to* column's *E-mail Address* button.

Figure 6.13 Type in the *E-mail address*, add a *Subject*, and click *OK*.

To create an email link

1. Select the text you want linked to an email address, right-click, and choose *Hyperlink* from the shortcut menu (Ctrl K) (**Figure 6.3**).

2. When the Insert Hyperlink dialog box appears, click the *Link to* column's *E-mail Address* button (**Figure 6.12**). The right side of the Insert Hyperlink dialog box will change and display email-related fields (**Figure 6.13**). The text selected in step 1 will appear in the *Text to display* window, which you can change if you need to.

3. Fill in the *E-mail address* window, but don't type the *mailto:* portion of the address since it will be inserted automatically. You also may want to fill in the *Subject* window, although not all email programs will display it when receiving the message. Click *OK* and the address will be applied to the selected text in the Web page.

✔ Tip

■ By clicking any item in the *Recently used e-mail addresses* list, you can quickly fill out the fields—including the *Subject*. Over time, the list will grow longer, which can save you lots of time addressing frequent contacts.

LINKING TO EMAIL

Linking to pages not yet created

On the face of it, this sounds weird: Why would you link to a non-existent page? In truth, it's common as you're creating links to realize you've forgotten to create a necessary page. This option lets you quickly make the new page and link to it from the page you're already working on.

To create a new page and link to it

1. Select the text you want linked to a not-yet-created page, right-click, and choose *Hyperlink* from the shortcut menu (Ctrl K) (**Figure 6.3**).

2. When the Insert Hyperlink dialog box appears, click the *Create New Document* button and the right side of the Insert Hyperlink dialog box will change to reflect your choice (**Figure 6.14**). The text selected in step 1 will appear in the *Text to display* window, which you can change if you need to. Also by default, the *Edit the new document now* button will be selected.

3. Unless you want to drop everything and immediately build the page, however, select the *Edit the new document later* button (**Figure 6.15**). (See *Tip* if you want to create the page right now.) Use the *Name of new document* window to create a name for the page that will jog your memory when you do return later to edit it later.

4. Click *OK* and the link will be applied to the selected text in the Web page. If you open the Folder List, you'll see that the selected text now links to the newly created (blank) page (**Figure 6.16**).

✔ Tip

- If you want to create the new page immediately, click the *Change* button in the Insert Hyperlink dialog box (**Figure 6.14**). FrontPage will open the Create New Document dialog box.

Figure 6.14 To link to a not-yet-created page, click the *Create New Document* button and the right side of the Insert Hyperlink dialog box will change to reflect your choice.

Figure 6.15 To avoid having to immediately build the page, select the *Edit the new document later* button and then fill in the *Name of new document* window.

Figure 6.16 After the link is created, the new, but blank, page appears in the Folder List.

Figure 6.17 To change a link, right-click it and choose *Hyperlink Properties* from the shortcut menu.

Figure 6.18 Use the Edit Hyperlink dialog box to change a link's *Address*.

Changing links

FrontPage automatically updates links as you move pages around on your Web site. But if you want to completely change a link address, or delete a link, it's easy. If you've deleted entire pages—especially without using FrontPage in the first place—running an update will guard against broken links (see *To update links* on the next page).

To edit a link

1. Right-click on any link you want to change and choose *Hyperlink Properties* from the shortcut menu (**Figure 6.17**). Or type Alt Enter.

2. When the Edit Hyperlink dialog box opens, the link's present *Address* will be highlighted (**Figure 6.18**). You can:
   ❶ Type a *new* URL directly into the text window.
   ❷ Click the *Address* text window's right-side arrow to choose from a drop-down menu of recent URLs.
   ❸ Click any of the *Look in* buttons or icons to navigate to a new file.
   ❹ Click one of the three other *Link to* buttons to change the type of hyperlink entirely.

3. When you've changed the *Address*, click *OK* and the link will be updated to reflect the new address.

To delete a link

1. Right-click on any link you want to change and choose *Hyperlink Properties* from the shortcut menu (**Figure 6.17**). Or type [Alt][Enter].

2. When the Edit Hyperlink dialog box opens, click the *Remove Link* button (**Figure 6.19**). The dialog box will close and the Web page text will no longer be linked.

To update links

1. Choose Tools > Recalculate Hyperlinks (**Figure 6.20**).

2. FrontPage will warn you that this might take a few minutes, depending on the size of your Web site. It rarely takes that long, so click *Yes*. FrontPage will repair any links broken when site pages were rearranged, but it can't fix a link if you entered the wrong URL in the first place.

Figure 6.19 To delete a link, click the *Remove Link* button in the Edit Hyperlink dialog box.

Figure 6.20
If you delete pages without using FrontPage, update their links by choosing Tools > Recalculate Hyperlinks.

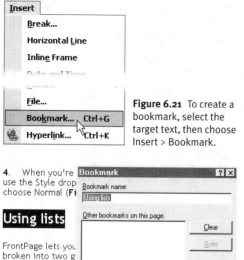

Figure 6.21 To create a bookmark, select the target text, then choose Insert > Bookmark.

4. When you're use the Style drop choose Normal (**Fi**

Using lists

FrontPage lets you broken into two g lists. Unordered, o series of items tha supplies. Use orde

Figure 6.22 By default, the bookmark (right) assumes the name of the selected text (left). Type in another name if you prefer.

Using lists|

FrontPage lets you creat broken into two general lists. Unordered, or bull

Figure 6.23 FrontPage places a dashed line beneath bookmarked text.

Using Bookmarks

Bookmarks, often called anchor links, let visitors jump to specific spots, such as section headings, within a long Web page. Creating anchors is a two-step process: first you create the bookmark itself (the anchor), then you create hyperlinks (the anchor links) that point to the bookmark. The bookmark can be in the current page or FrontPage lets you browse to another page containing bookmarks.

Insert anchor links into your Web pages to let readers jump ahead or back without scrolling through the whole document. Anchors aren't limited to headings. Feel free to link to a citation, word or image, or single character.

If you ever want to update or remove some bookmarks in a lengthy Web page and don't want to search for them one by one, FrontPage makes it easy to find them.

To create a bookmark

1. Select the text you want the reader to jump to, that is, the target or destination.

2. Choose Insert > Bookmark ([Ctrl][G]) (**Figure 6.21**).

3. When the Bookmark dialog box opens, it automatically uses the selected text as the name of the bookmark (**Figure 6.22**). However, you can type in another name if that suits your purposes.

4. When you're done naming the bookmark, click *OK* and the selected text will be bookmarked, as indicated by a dashed underline (**Figure 6.23**). See the next page to complete the process.

To link to a bookmark in the current page

1. Select the text you want linked to a bookmark, right-click, and choose *Hyperlink* from the shortcut menu (Ctrl K) (**Figure 6.3**). The Insert Hyperlink dialog box will open.

2. Click the *Link to* column's *Place in This Document* button and the right side of the Insert Hyperlink dialog box will change to reflect your choice (**Figure 6.24**).

3. Pick a bookmark in the *Select a place in this document* list, click *OK*, and your selected text will be linked to the bookmark.

Figure 6.24 To link to a bookmark in the current page, click the *Link to* column's *Place in This Document* button, choose a bookmark, and click *OK*.

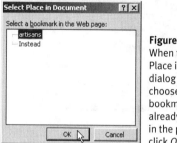

Figure 6.25 To link to a bookmark in another page, navigate to the file, select it in the folder list, and click the *Bookmark* button.

Figure 6.26
When the Select Place in Document dialog box appears, choose one of the bookmarks you've already created in the page, and click *OK*.

Figure 6.27 When the Insert Hyperlink dialog box reappears, the location of the bookmark will appear in the *Address* window. Click *OK*.

To link to a bookmark in another page

1. Select the text you want linked to a bookmark, right-click, and choose *Hyperlink* from the shortcut menu (Ctrl K) (**Figure 6.3**). The Insert Hyperlink dialog box will open.

2. Navigate to the other page containing the bookmark you want using the *Current Folder*, *Browsed Pages*, or *Recent Files* buttons, the Web browser, or the open folder icons. Select the page in the scrolling list of files and click the *Bookmark* button (**Figure 6.25**).

3. When the Select Place in Document dialog box appears, choose one of the bookmarks you've already created in the page, and click *OK* (**Figure 6.26**).

4. When the Insert Hyperlink dialog box reappears, the location of the bookmark will appear in the *Address* window (**Figure 6.27**). Click *OK* and your selected text will be linked to the bookmark.

✔ Tips

■ The Select Place in Document dialog box will display the bookmarks for only one page at a time, not the entire site. To reach bookmarks in another page, you must first select the file in the Insert Hyperlink dialog box.

■ Revising the link to a bookmark follows the same steps, except that in step 2, the Edit Hyperlink dialog box will appear. For details, see *To edit a link* on page 143.

USING BOOKMARKS

To find bookmarks

1. Start by finding any bookmark in a page (marked by a dashed underline). Right-click it and choose *Bookmark Properties* from the shortcut menu (⟨Alt⟩⟨Enter⟩) (**Figure 6.28**).

2. The Bookmark dialog box will appear with the selected bookmark highlighted in the top text window. Highlight any other bookmark by clicking it within the list, then click *Goto* (**Figure 6.29**).

3. The Bookmark dialog box will remain open, but your Web page will jump to the chosen bookmark (**Figure 6.30**). Once you find the bookmark, click *OK,* and you'll be returned to the Web page. To clear the bookmark, see the next page.

Figure 6.28 To find any bookmarks in a page, right-click any bookmark and choose *Bookmark Properties* from the shortcut menu.

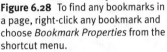

Figure 6.29 Choose the bookmark you're looking for in the *Other bookmarks* list, then click *Goto*.

Figure 6.30 After clicking *Goto*, the Bookmark dialog box remains open but your Web page jumps to the chosen bookmark.

USING BOOKMARKS

Figure 6.31 To clear a bookmark after you've found it, click *Clear*.

Figure 6.32 Once you've cleared a bookmark, the text remains highlighted but without a dashed underline.

To clear a bookmark

1. To find a bookmark you want to clear, first follow the steps in *To find bookmarks* on the previous page.

2. Once you find the bookmark, click *Clear* in the Bookmark dialog box (**Figure 6.31**). The Bookmark dialog box will close, returning you to the Web page, where the text remains highlighted but without the dashed underline of a bookmark (**Figure 6.32**).

Setting Link Colors

By default, FrontPage follows the Web convention of showing unvisited links as blue and visited ones as dark purple. However, you can assign any Web-safe color you want to your hyperlinks. FrontPage also lets you set colors for active links (the instant you click them) and rollover links (when your cursor moves over them).

To change a link's color

1. Make sure you're in page view by clicking the Page icon in the Views Bar.

2. Right-click anywhere in the page and choose *Page Properties* from the shortcut menu (**Figure 6.33**).

3. When the Page Properties dialog box opens, click the *Background* tab (**Figure 6.34**).

4. To change the color for any of a link's three states, in the *Colors* section click the far-right arrows and pick a new color from the pop-up box (**Figure 6.35**). If you want to create a custom color, choose *More Colors* in the pop-up box. When the More Colors dialog box appears, click the *Select* button, then pick a color and click *OK* (**Figure 6.36**).

5. When the Page Properties dialog box reappears, if you've already changed the link colors on another page, check *Get background information from another page*, then click the *Browse* button to find that page and automatically apply its colors to the current page's links (**Figure 6.37**).

6. When you've finished making your color choices for the hyperlinks, click *OK,* and the links *for that page only* will be changed.

Figure 6.33 To change a link's color, right-click in the page and choose *Page Properties* from the shortcut menu.

Figure 6.34 To reach the color section, click the *Background* tab in the Page Properties dialog box.

Figure 6.35 Use the pop-up box to change the color of your hyperlinks. To pick a custom color, click *More Colors*.

Figure 6.36 The More Colors dialog box lets you use any Web-safe color for your links.

Figure 6.37 To apply link colors from another page, click the *Background* tab's *Get background information from another page* checkbox. Click the *Browse* button to locate the other page.

Figure 6.38 To trigger a color change when a cursor moves over a link, choose the *Background* tab's *Enable hyperlink rollover effects* checkbox and click *Rollover style*.

Figure 6.39 The *Background* tab also lets you change the page's background color and the text color.

Figure 6.40 Check *Background picture*, then click *Browse* to add a tiled background graphic to a page.

✔ Tips

- Make sure your custom color stands out against the background and that unvisited and visited link colors are not so similar that it's unclear which is which.

- If you ever change your mind and want to use the default link colors, just choose *Automatic* within each link's pop-up box in step 4.

- The *Background* tab includes an option to have your links change color whenever a visitor's cursor moves over the link. Just check *Enable hyperlink rollover effects*, then click the *Rollover style* button (**Figure 6.38**). When the Font dialog box opens, use the *Color* pop-up menu to make your choice.

- The *Background* tab also lets you change the page's background color and the text color (**Figure 6.39**). Click the arrows to make your choices, then click *OK* to apply them to the current page.

- If you absolutely must add a background (tiled) picture to the page, the *Background* tab includes a checkbox to do just that (**Figure 6.40**). Check the *Background picture* box, click *Browse* to find your image, then click *OK* to apply the picture to the current page. Tile images plagued the Web early on—with headache inducing results. It's best to use a simple, light-toned image that doesn't obliterate your text.

- To change the link colors in a *theme*, see *To modify a theme* on page 82.

Creating Image Links

Obviously the Web isn't limited to text-only links and FrontPage makes it easy to insert links into any image. You can link an entire image to a file or you can create what's called a hotspot, which links a defined area of the image to another file. By putting multiple hotspots in an image, you can create links to multiple files.

To link an entire image to a file

1. Make sure the Pictures toolbar is visible by choosing View > Toolbars > Pictures (**Figures 6.41** and **6.42**).

2. Open the page containing the image you want linked and click the image to select it (**Figure 6.43**). Square black handles will appear on the image's corners, indicating it's selected.

3. With the image still selected, right-click, and choose *Hyperlink* from the shortcut menu (Ctrl K) (**Figure 6.44**).

4. When the Insert Hyperlink dialog box opens, you have all the choices already explained in *Insert Hyperlink options* on page 138. To link the image to another page in your current Web site, choose a file in the center window and click *OK*. The image will be linked to the selected page—as indicated by the status bar and the cursor pop-up (**Figure 6.45**).

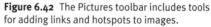

Figure 6.41 Before working with images, choose View > Toolbars > Pictures.

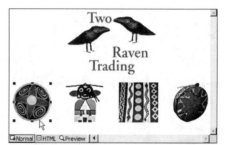

Figure 6.42 The Pictures toolbar includes tools for adding links and hotspots to images.

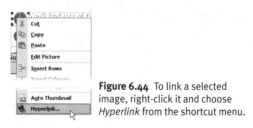

Figure 6.43 Once an image is selected, square black handles will appear on the image's corners.

Figure 6.44 To link a selected image, right-click it and choose *Hyperlink* from the shortcut menu.

Two Raven Trading

Use Ctrl+Click to follow a hyperlink

Native American Crafts on the Web

Figure 6.45 Once linked, an image displays pop-up instructions whenever FrontPage's cursor moves over it. The link address appears in the bottom status bar.

CREATING IMAGE LINKS, HOTSPOTS

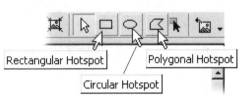

Figure 6.46 To create a hotspot, first select the entire image.

Rectangular Hotspot | Polygonal Hotspot

Circular Hotspot

Figure 6.47 Click a shape for your hotspot—rectangle, circle, or polygon—in the Pictures toolbar.

Figure 6.48 Once you choose a shape tool, the cursor becomes a pencil, allowing you to draw a hotspot boundary around the image. Don't worry if it's not exact—you can adjust it later.

To create an image hotspot

1. Make sure the Pictures toolbar is visible by choosing View > Toolbars > Pictures (**Figure 6.41**).

2. Open the page containing the image you want linked and click the image to select it (**Figure 6.46**).

3. Decide what shape your hotspot will be (rectangle, circle, or freeform polygon) and click the appropriate symbol in the Pictures toolbar (**Figure 6.47**).

4. Once you choose a shape tool, the cursor will turn into a pencil, allowing you to draw the hotspot's boundary in the image (**Figure 6.48**). Don't worry about getting the boundary exactly right—you can fix it in a moment.

5. The Insert Hyperlink dialog box will open, allowing you to choose which file to link to the hotspot. Choose the file, click *OK,* and you'll be returned to the image.

(continued)

CREATING IMAGE LINKS, HOTSPOTS

6. Now you can click *inside* the hotspot and move it exactly where you want it (left, **Figure 6.49**).

7. If you need to resize the hotspot—and you'll want it big enough for visitors to click on it easily—use your cursor to grab the hotspot's black rectangular "handles" to enlarge or shrink the hotspot (right, **Figure 6.49**). If you need to reposition the hotspot, repeat step 6.

8. Repeat steps 3–7 if you want to add more hotspots to the image and link them to separate files. When you're done, the image will contain multiple hotspots, each with its own link (**Figure 6.50**).

✔ Tips

■ Your hotspots cannot overlap, nor extend beyond the edge of the selected image. For both reasons, you may realize the image itself needs to be enlarged. Just grab one of the *image's* handles and drag it to give your hotspots more room, then reposition and resize the hotspots as needed. If you wind up enlarging the image more than about 10 percent, however, go back and create a larger original. Otherwise the image will wind up looking fuzzy.

■ Hotspots don't have to link to *another* file. You also can use them with anchors to link to text somewhere else in the *same* file.

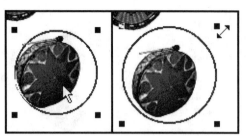

Figure 6.49 Once you've linked the image, click *inside* the hotspot and move it exactly where you want (left). To resize the hotspot, drag any image handle (right).

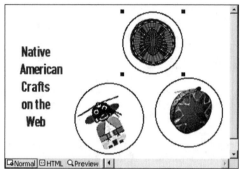

Figure 6.50 By adding several hotspots, a single image can link to multiple files.

Figure 6.51 If an image obscures your view of its hotspots, click the Pictures toolbar's Highlight Hotspots button.

Native American Crafts on the Web

Figure 6.52 With highlighting applied, an image's hotspots are clearly outlined with the active hotspot in black.

Figure 6.53 To edit a hotspot link, right-click it and choose *Picture Hotspot Properties* from the shortcut menu.

Finding image hotspots

Sometimes your image can keep you from easily seeing your hotspot boundaries. FrontPage includes a feature that lets you see the hotspots—without the images.

To find image hotspots

1. While in page view, select the image you want to inspect by clicking on it.

2. Click the Highlight Hotspots button in the Pictures toolbar (**Figure 6.51**). The image's hotspots will be outlined against a clean background. When a hotspot is selected, it will turn black (**Figure 6.52**).

3. To see the image again, click anywhere outside the image.

To delete a hotspot

◆ Click on the hotspot you want removed and press [←Backspace] or [Delete].

To change a hotspot link

1. Right-click on the hotspot you want to edit and choose *Picture Hotspot Properties* ([Alt][Enter]) from the shortcut menu (**Figure 6.53**).

2. When the Edit Hyperlink dialog box appears, use the buttons and arrows to navigate to the new link. For details, see *To edit a link* on page 143.

CREATING IMAGE LINKS, HOTSPOTS

Using Hover Buttons

Through the use of what FrontPage calls hover buttons, it's incredibly easy to add cool effects activated by your visitors' mouse actions. You can have a button change appearance or even trigger sounds when the mouse hovers over the button. Essentially hover buttons trigger different kinds of links, which is why they're discussed in this chapter.

To add a hover button

1. Make sure you're in page view by clicking the Page icon in the Views Bar. Also be sure the Normal tab is clicked at the bottom of the page window.

2. Click where you want to add a hover button and choose Insert > Web Component (**Figure 6.54**).

3. When the Insert Web Component dialog box appears, click *Hover Button* in the list labeled *Choose an effect* (*Dynamic Effects* will already be selected in the *Component type* list), and click *Finish* (**Figure 6.55**).

4. When the Hover Button Properties dialog box appears, set your button's text and font, its link, color, hover effect, and size (**Figure 6.56**). For details see *Hover Button options* on the next page.

5. Once you've made your choices, click *OK*.

6. Click the *Preview* tab at the bottom of the page window to see how the effect will appear whenever a browser's cursor rolls over the button (**Figure 6.57**).

✔ Tips

■ Be sure you've saved all your pages and images, otherwise the hover buttons may not appear in Preview.

■ Be careful using the color pop-up menus: Unless you keep a short leash on your cursor, it's all too easy to change a hover color without even realizing it.

Figure 6.54 To add a hover button, choose Insert > Web Component.

Figure 6.55 Click *Hover Button* in the *Choose an effect* list. *Dynamic Effects* will already be selected in the *Component type* list.

Figure 6.56 The Hover Button Properties dialog box controls the button's appearance and action.

Figure 6.57 After you've applied a button effect, switch to Preview to see the result. "The Land" button glows when the cursor moves over it.

Hover button options

The Hover Button Properties dialog box lets you apply all kinds of mouse-over special effects (**Figure 6.56**). To reach the dialog box, choose Insert > Component > Hover Button or double-click an existing hover button.

❶ **Button text:** Type the button's name or label into the text box, and use the *Font* button to change the font face, style, size, and most importantly, the color. Make sure the color contrasts with the Button color and Effect color, explained below.

❷ **Link to:** Either type a URL/file path directly into the text box or click *Browse* to open the Select Hover Button Hyperlink dialog box, which works exactly like the Insert Hyperlink dialog box (**Figure 6.8**).

❸ **Button color:** Use the pop-up menu to reach the standard color dialog box, explained earlier in *Setting Link Colors* on page 150.

❹ **Effect:** Use the drop-down menu to pick one of seven effects, which will be triggered when the visitor's cursor passes over the button. For the best look, try different combinations using the *Effect color* pop-up menu and the text's color, reached with the *Font* button.

❺ **Width:** Enter numbers in the text box to set the button's width. You also can adjust the button's size in Normal view by clicking and dragging its corner handles.

❻ **Custom:** Click to reach the Custom dialog box, where you can select sounds or custom graphics that are triggered when a visitor's cursor hovers over or clicks the button.

❼ **Background color:** Use the pop-up menu to reach the standard color dialog box.

❽ **Effect color:** Click the arrow to reach the color pop-up menu. Use with the *Effect* pop-up menu and the *Font* button to give your effect maximum graphic snap.

❾ **Height:** Works just like the *Width* box.

To edit a hover button

1. Make sure the Normal tab is clicked at the bottom of the page window.

2. Right-click the button and choose *Hover Button Properties* from the shortcut menu ((Alt)(Enter)) (**Figure 6.58**). Or just double-click the button.

3. When the Hover Button Properties dialog box appears, use it to change your button's characteristics (**Figure 6.56**). Click *OK* when you're done and the changes will be applied.

4. Switch to Preview and move your cursor over the button to see the change in the hover effect.

To customize hover buttons

1. To add a sound or custom graphic to a button, double-click any hover button to reach the Hover Button Properties dialog box (**Figure 6.56**).

2. Click the *Custom* button in the box's lower-left corner.

3. When the Custom dialog box opens, use the *Browse* buttons to navigate to the appropriate file (**Figure 6.59**). Once you've found the file, click *OK* in the Custom dialog box.

4. Switch to Preview and move your cursor over the button to check its custom sound or graphic.

✔ Tip

- When adding custom art for a hover button, click the drop-down menu next to the Select Picture dialog box's *Open* button to reach FrontPage's collection of clip art (**Figure 6.60**). For more information, see *Clip Art options* on page 166.

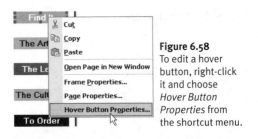

Figure 6.58
To edit a hover button, right-click it and choose *Hover Button Properties* from the shortcut menu.

Figure 6.59 When linking a sound or special graphic to a hover button, click *Browse* in the Custom dialog box to reach the appropriate file.

Figure 6.60 To use FrontPage's clip art for your hover buttons, click the drop-down menu next to the Select Picture dialog box's *Open* button.

Figure 6.61 The hyperlinks view shows links *into* your page on the left and links *out from* the page on the right. The ⊞ marks indicate pages with links of their own.

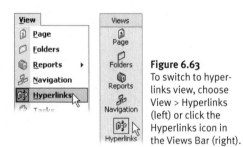

Figure 6.62 In hyperlinks view, external links are marked by a globe icon (top), internal Web site links by a plain page (middle), and email links by an envelope (bottom).

Figure 6.63
To switch to hyperlinks view, choose View > Hyperlinks (left) or click the Hyperlinks icon in the Views Bar (right).

Figure 6.64 In hyperlinks view, a peripheral page (top) can be inspected by right-clicking it and choosing *Move to Center*. The peripheral page will jump to the center with its links showing (bottom).

Using the Hyperlinks View

Sometimes the easiest way to spot a missing link, or to analyze the links you already have is to use FrontPage's hyperlinks view (**Figure 6.61**). Each page's link type is marked by a distinct icon, which makes for easy reviewing (**Figure 6.62**). Want to quickly look at links for one of the peripheral pages appearing in the hyperlink view? For details, see *To inspect links on another page* below.

To switch to hyperlinks view

◆ Choose View > Hyperlinks or click the Hyperlinks icon in the Views Bar (**Figure 6.63**). The hyperlinks view will appear in the right pane with the current page in the center (**Figure 6.61**).

To inspect links on another page

◆ If you want to see the links for a page sitting on the periphery of a hyperlinks view, right-click it and choose *Move to Center* from the shortcut menu. The peripheral page will jump to the center of the view, showing all its links (**Figure 6.64**).

ADDING AND
EDITING IMAGES

Putting pictures on the Web requires using images in the right formats, as discussed in *Web Image Formats*, this chapter's first section. The second section, *Adding Images*, covers adding images to a Web page and setting such basic aspects of the image as its size, alignment, and whether it should have borders. *Editing Images* covers tricks built right into FrontPage's Pictures toolbar (**Figure 7.1**). The final section, *Positioning Images Absolutely*, explains how images can escape the confines of grid-like layouts. To add images, links, or hotspots, see *Creating Image Links* on page 152. To use built-in graphic themes, see *Using Templates and Themes* on page 77. To add videos to Web pages, see *Adding Multimedia and Web Components* on page 229.

Create thumbnail · Position absolutely · Rotate left · Rotate right · More contrast · Less contrast · Crop · Format picture · Set transparent color · Add/remove buttons · Create hotspots · Add text · Select

Insert picture · Bring forward · Send back · Flip vertical · Flip horizontal · Dimmer · Brighter · Set color · Line style · Resample picture · Bevel border · Restore picture

Figure 7.1 The Pictures toolbar contains a variety of image-editing tools.

Web Image Formats

The world's awash with a virtual alphabet soup of image formats: BMPs, TIFFs, TGAs, EPSs, RASs—the list goes on and on. Fortunately when it comes to the World Wide Web, it really boils down to just two formats—GIFs and JPEGs. GIFs (CompuServe's Graphical Interchange Format) are used for everything but medium to large photographs, which are best formatted as JPEGs (developed by the Joint Photographic Experts Group).

Another file format, PNG (Portable Network Graphics) has been touted for several years now because it compresses images nicely without losing as much information as a JPEG and sidesteps an ongoing dispute over GIF rights. While version 4 and later browsers support PNG, the inability of earlier browsers to display the format has hampered its growth and acceptance. GIFs and JPEGs remain your best bets. For details, see *Converting image formats* on page 168.

Let's get small

Before you start adding images to a Web page, make sure the files are as small—no, make that as *tiny*—as possible. Bloated images can slow the downloading of your pages so much that visitors simply click on rather than wait. Take the time on your end to shave those files to save the viewer's time.

With the exception of cropping, most of this graphical liposuction should be done in a Web-savvy graphics program, such as Photoshop, DeBabelizer, or Fireworks. Start by cropping the image's width and height to remove everything but the visual gist of the picture. Who needs that blurry background or that parking lot foreground?

The real key to small files, however, is how well you compress the images. For GIFs, that means reducing the number of colors in the

Table 7.1

GIF vs JPEG: What's best?	
WEB PAGE ITEM	BEST FORMAT
buttons, arrows	GIF
illustrations	GIF
animations	GIF
blocks of solid color	GIF
button-size photographs	GIF
all but tiny photographs	JPEG

Table 7.2

Bit depth, number of colors, & file size		
NON-INDEXED ORIGINAL IMAGE		
24 bits	17 million colors	1.1 MB (original size)
15 bits	32,768 colors	816K
INDEXED AS A GIF		
8 bits	256 colors	417K
7 bits	128 colors	111K
6 bits	64 colors	94K
5 bits	32 colors	77K
4 bits	16 colors	60K
3 bits	8 colors	43K
2 bits	4 colors	17K
1 bit	2 colors	9K

image. For JPEGs, it's a matter of how much compression you can apply to the photograph while keeping it from looking artificial.

The number of colors in an image, commonly called the bit depth, has a big influence on the file's size (**Table 7.2**). Many Web surfers still use 8-bit monitors, which can only render 256 colors anyway. And since up to 40 of those colors wind up being reserved for the computer's operating system, most GIFs use just 216 colors in what's called a Web- or browser-safe palette. Converting a high-resolution image to one with a Web-safe palette is sometimes called *indexing* or *mapping* the image. That's because the color information for every pixel in the image is stored as a grid-like index.

While taking a graphic containing millions of colors and indexing it down to a few hundred may seem crazy, the whole point of the Web is that it works no matter which operating system and monitor are used. To find that balance point between a minimum bit depth and decent image quality, experiment in your graphics program with saving images at various bit depths to see just how low you can go.

Photographs don't lend themselves to bit depth reduction—skin tones especially end up looking just terrible in GIFs. That's where JPEGs come in, which use an entirely different compression method. With JPEGs, you can use FrontPage to control the file size by experimenting with the level of compression. For details, see *To convert image formats* on page 168. One limitation to JPEGs is that they don't work well for one-color transparency (they wind up looking termite damaged).

Finally, if you've trimmed and slimmed an image down to a willowy minimum and it's still big, consider using FrontPage's auto thumbnail feature. For details, see *Creating auto thumbnails and photo galleries* on page 183.

WEB IMAGE FORMATS

Adding Images

Once you've done the sometimes tedious work within a graphics program of slimming your image files down to the smallest possible size, adding them to a FrontPage Web page is a breeze.

To insert an image

1. Switch to page view by clicking the Page icon in the Views Bar, then click where you want the image placed within a page.

2. Choose Insert > Picture, then choose *Clip Art* or *From File* from the submenu (**Figure 7.2**).

3. If you choose *Clip Art*, the Insert Clip Art task pane will appear on the main window's right side. Use the *Search text* window and *Search* button to find an image (**Figure 7.3**). Click the image in the task pane and it will be added to the Web page. For details on using clip art, see *Clip Art options* on page 166.

   or

   If you choose *From File*, the Picture dialog box will appear (**Figure 7.4**). Use the *Look in* buttons or navigation icons to find a picture and click *Insert* to add the image to the Web page.

4. Save the page and its new image (Ctrl S). If the image didn't come from your current Web site, the Save Embedded Files dialog box will appear (**Figure 7.5**).

5. Click *Rename* if you want to change the file name and *Change Folder* if you want to save the file in another location. When you're done, click *OK* and the image will be saved.

6. Once the image is inserted and saved, you can edit it, if necessary. See *Editing Images* on page 178.

Figure 7.2 To insert an image, choose Insert > Picture, then choose *Clip Art* or *From File* from the submenu.

Figure 7.3 The Insert Clip Art task pane provides a central access point for royalty free art.

Figure 7.4 The Picture dialog box lets you choose images from your computer or the Web itself.

Figure 7.5 The Save Embedded Files dialog box lets you rename images added to your Web site and choose where they're stored.

ADDING IMAGES

Figure 7.6 If the Picture dialog box does not show a preview of the picture, click the Views drop-down menu and choose Preview.

Figure 7.7 If the Pictures toolbar is active, you can insert an image from your computer's hard drive.

Insert Picture From File

Figure 7.8 If the Folder List is visible, you can click and drag an image into a page from your Web site.

Figure 7.9 To change the picture's format, click *Picture Options* and choose *JPEG* or *GIF* in the Picture Options dialog box.

✔ Tips

- Three of the four choices at the bottom of the submenu in step 2 (**Figure 7.2**) (*New Drawing*, *AutoShapes*, and *WordArt*) are covered in *Adding and Editing Drawings* on page 197. For more information on the last choice (*Video*), see *Adding Videos or Animations* on page 230. For more information on the *New Photo Gallery* choice, see *To create a thumbnail photo gallery* on page 185.

- If the Picture dialog box does not show a preview of the picture, click the drop-down menu for the Views icon and choose Preview (**Figure 7.6**).

- If the Pictures toolbar is active, you also can insert a picture by clicking the first icon (**Figure 7.7**).

- If the Folder List is visible and you're inserting an image already in your Web site folder, just click and drag the file into the page pane (**Figure 7.8**).

- Every FrontPage Web site automatically includes an Images folder, but imported images don't always get saved to it. To keep your images together, use the *Change Folder* button to select the folder as you add images to your site (**Figure 7.5**).

- In step 6, if you want to change the picture's format, say from a GIF to a JPEG, click *Picture Options* and make your choice in the dialog box that appears (**Figure 7.9**). (For more information, see *Converting image formats* on page 168.)

ADDING IMAGES

165

Clip Art options

FrontPage 2002 comes with a bunch of clip art. If you've installed Office 2000 or Office XP, FrontPage can use the ample clip art that comes with those programs as well. The Insert Clip Art task pane provides a central access point for clips, whether they're on your hard drive or online (**Figure 7.10**). To reach the Insert Clip Art task pane, choose Insert > Picture > Clip Art.

❶ **Search text:** Type in the text window one or more keywords that describe the clip's subject. Use with the *Other Search Options* menus to expand or narrow which files are searched. The trick is to not define your search so narrowly that you find nothing nor so broadly that you get hundreds of results.

❷ **Search:** Click to start the clip search after entering your search terms.

❸ **Restore:** Click to return to the search criteria used in your previous search. This makes it easy to toggle between a narrow and a broad search.

❹ **Search in:** By default, the drop-down menu is set to search *All collections*, which comprises all the clip collections that come with FrontPage or Office, plus your own clips. Use the drop-down menu to expand or narrow the search by checking or unchecking individual item boxes. Click the ⊞ or ⊟ symbols to expand or collapse a category's listings (left, **Figure 7.11**).

❺ **Results should be:** By default, the drop-down menu is set to search *All media file types*. Use the drop-down menus to expand/narrow the search by checking or unchecking the item boxes (right, **Figure 7.11**).

Figure 7.10 The Insert Clip Art task pane provides a central access point for clips, whether they're on your hard drive or online.

Figure 7.11 Use the drop-down menus and check-boxes to expand or narrow your clip art search.

Figure 7.12 The Clip Organizer covers the same clips as the Search button but lets you browse by category.

Figure 7.13 The first time you use the Clip Organizer, you'll be asked if you want to build an index of all your existing clips.

Figure 7.14 Microsoft's Design Gallery Live offers an online trove of searchable clip art.

❻ **Clip Organizer:** The organizer covers the same clips as the Search button but lets you browse by category instead of zeroing in on particular keyword-based clips (**Figure 7.12**). When you first launch the organizer, it will ask if you want to create a catalog of your existing images (**Figure 7.13**). This can take some time, so you may want to use the *Later* option. Items found in the Clip Organizer can be dragged directly into your Web page.

❼ **Clips Online:** Click to search Microsoft's online collection of clips. Be sure to connect to the Internet before clicking this button. After accepting Microsoft's end user agreement, you'll be linked to Design Gallery Live, where you can search for still more clips (**Figure 7.14**).

❽ **Tips for Finding Clips:** Click to launch FrontPage's Help system for more details on using clip art.

CLIP ART OPTIONS

Converting image formats

By default, FrontPage saves images created in any other format as GIFs or JPEGs. If the image's color depth is 8 bits or less, it's saved as a GIF; anything over 8 bits is saved as a JPEG. FrontPage also makes it easy to convert a GIF to a JPEG, a JPEG to a GIF, or either to a PNG.

To convert image formats

1. Right-click the image you want to convert and choose *Picture Properties* from the shortcut menu ((Alt)(Enter)) (**Figure 7.15**).

2. When the Picture Properties dialog box appears, click the *General* tab. Within the *Type* section, an option button will indicate the image's current format. To change it, select the button for the other format: *JPEG* or *GIF* (**Figure 7.16**).

3. Once you've made your choice, click *OK* and the Picture Properties dialog box will close. Save your change ((Ctrl)(S)), and the image format change will trigger the appearance of the Save Embedded Files dialog box. Click *Picture Options* (**Figure 7.17**).

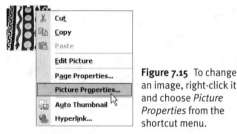

Figure 7.15 To change an image, right-click it and choose *Picture Properties* from the shortcut menu.

Figure 7.16 To convert an image's format, click the *General* tab in the Picture Properties dialog box.

Figure 7.17 Click the *Picture Options* button to set details for your image's format.

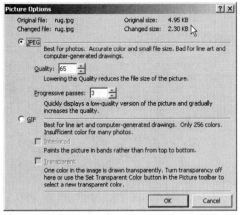

Figure 7.18 If you want an image saved as a *JPEG*, set the compression *Quality* and how many *Progressive passes* a browser will make to download it.

4. When the Picture Options dialog box appears, set the *JPEG Quality* and *Progressive passes* levels using the right-side arrows (**Figure 7.18**). Once you've made your choices, click *OK* and the image changes will be applied. For details, see *Tips* below.

✔ Tips

- In setting the quality of a JPEG, the higher the *Quality* number, the more accurate—but less compressed—the image will be. The default is 75 for moderate compression; 100 is the maximum, which would leave the image uncompressed. The *Progressive passes* number controls how many passes it takes a Web browser to completely download the picture. As you change the settings, you can compare the image's *Changed size* with its *Original size* (upper right, **Figure 7.18**).

- If you choose *GIF* as the file type, you can make the image *Interlaced*, which will cause the image to download in several increasingly detailed passes. The full image downloads no faster this way, but interlacing gives the viewer a quick sense of its content.

- The GIF *Transparent* option will be dimmed unless you've previously made one color transparent. The checkbox can only be used to turn *off* GIF transparency. For details on turning transparency *on*, see *To make a GIF color transparent* on page 191.

Creating alternates for images

It's common for folks using a slow dial-up Web connection to set their browsers to not download images. By creating alternate text for each image on your site, you can give those visitors at least some sense of a page's images before they finish downloading. The text will download almost immediately—enabling visitors to judge whether they even want to wait for the download (top, **Figure 7.19**). If viewers use Internet Explorer, their cursor will even display the alternate text as a pop-up label, giving you an easy way to add a caption (bottom, **Figure 7.19**). Finally, visually impaired Web users depend on special programs that read aloud what's on the page. With alternate text, those users get dealt in—not left out.

FrontPage also offers another tool for dealing with slow-to-download images: low-resolution images that act as quick-to-appear placeholders. See *To create low-resolution alternate images* on page 172.

To create alternate text

1. Right-click the image and choose *Picture Properties* from the shortcut menu (Alt Enter) (**Figure 7.15**).

2. When the Picture Properties dialog box appears, click the *General* tab (**Figure 7.16**).

3. Within the *Alternative representations* section type a label or brief description in the *Text* window (**Figure 7.20**).

4. When you're done, click *OK* and the alternate text will become part of the image's HTML coding.

Figure 7.19 By creating alternate text for images (top), visitors can get a sense of an image's content before it completely downloads (bottom). In Internet Explorer, alternate text appears as pop-up text.

Figure 7.20 Use the *General* tab's *Alternative representations* section to enter a brief description of an image—or instructions for users who have images turned off.

Figure 7.21 To see how alternate text looks in Web browsers without images on, use Internet Explorer's Tools menu to reach the *Multimedia* settings.

Figure 7.22 Web browsers with images turned off will display the alternate text instead.

✔ Tip

■ To check that the ordinarily invisible alternate text will appear in Web browsers where images have been turned off, launch Internet Explorer. Choose Tools > Internet Options, click the dialog box's *Advanced* tab and uncheck *Show pictures* under *Multimedia* (**Figure 7.21**). Click *OK* to close the dialog box, switch back to FrontPage, and click the Standard toolbar's Preview in browser icon (**Figure 7.22**).

To create low-resolution alternate images

1. Right-click the regular resolution image within its Web page and choose *Picture Properties* from the shortcut menu (Alt Enter) (**Figure 7.15**).

2. When the Picture Properties dialog box appears, click the *Appearance* tab. Within the *Size* section, note the image's *Width* and *Height* (**Figure 7.23**). Click *Cancel* to close the dialog box.

3. Now switch to whatever graphics program you use to create images and make a duplicate of your original image. When you save the duplicate, however, save it at 18 dpi instead of the usual 96 dpi. Be sure to give the duplicate the same physical dimensions as the original (75 by 75 pixels in our example)—otherwise at 18 dpi it's going to be a tiny, tiny picture.

4. Switch back to FrontPage, right-click your *regular resolution* image and once more choose *Picture Properties* from the shortcut menu (Alt Enter) (**Figure 7.15**).

5. When the Picture Properties dialog box appears, click the *General* tab.

6. Within the dialog box's *Alternative representations* section, click *Browse* to navigate to your low-resolution version of the image.

Figure 7.23 Before creating a low-resolution alternate image, note the original image's *Width* and *Height* in the Picture Properties dialog box.

Figure 7.24 Use the *Alternative representations* section of the Picture Properties dialog box to pair low-resolution and regular-resolution versions of an image.

7. When you return to the Picture Properties dialog box the name of the low-resolution image will appear in the text window (**Figure 7.24**). Click *OK*, and the low-resolution version will be paired with the regular resolution image. That way, when Web browsers download the page, the low-resolution version will download almost immediately to hold the page space until the regular-resolution image takes its place.

Aligning images

Sometimes the trickiest thing about creating a Web page is getting the text to align and wrap correctly around your images.

To align images

1. Right-click the image within its Web page and choose *Picture Properties* from the shortcut menu ([Alt][Enter]) (**Figure 7.15**).

2. When the Picture Properties dialog box appears, click the *Appearance* tab (**Figure 7.23**).

3. To quickly set how text flows around the picture, click *None*, *Left*, or *Right* in the *Wrapping style* section. To fine-tune how the picture aligns with adjacent text or pictures, use the *Layout* section's *Alignment* drop-down menu (**Figure 7.25**). (The *Alignment* drop-down menu's *Left* and *Right* choices do the same thing as *Left* and *Right* in *Wrapping style*.)

4. Click *OK* and the alignment will be applied to the image (**Figure 7.26**). To see the effect, however, you'll have to click the *Preview* tab. **Figure 7.27** shows each alignment choice affects the image.

Figure 7.25 Use the *Appearance* tab's *Layout* section to set how an image aligns with adjacent text. It also controls borders and spacing around the image.

Figure 7.26 The top image is aligned right, the bottom image aligned left.

Figure 7.27 FrontPage's alignment choices control how the image lines up with same-line text and graphics.

Figure 7.28 A 6-pixel border has been applied to the top image, a 2-pixel border to the bottom image.

Figure 7.29 A horizontal spacing of 30 has been applied to the top image; a vertical spacing of 15 to the bottom one.

To add an image border

1. Right-click the image within its Web page and choose *Picture Properties* from the shortcut menu (Alt Enter) (**Figure 7.15**).

2. When the Picture Properties dialog box appears, click the *Appearance* tab (**Figure 7.23**).

3. Within the *Layout* section, you can type a number directly into the *Border thickness* text window or use the arrows just to the right to choose a number. (The numbers represent pixels.) Click *OK* and the border will be applied to the image (**Figure 7.28**).

To add space around an image

1. Right-click the image within its Web page and choose *Picture Properties* from the shortcut menu (Alt Enter) (**Figure 7.15**).

2. When the Picture Properties dialog box appears, click the *Appearance* tab (**Figure 7.23**).

3. Within the *Layout* section, you can type a number directly into the *Horizontal spacing* and *Vertical spacing* text windows or use the arrows to set how many pixels of blank space should be placed around the image (**Figure 7.25**). Click *OK* and the space will be added to the page (**Figure 7.29**).

ADDING BORDERS/SPACE TO IMAGES

Adding horizontal lines

OK, OK, it's not exactly an image. But a horizontal line is a basic *graphic* element for Web pages. A couple of other graphic-based approaches for dressing up pages—changing the page color and adding a background image—are covered in the tips for *To change a link's color* on page 150.

To insert a horizontal line

1. Make sure you're in page view by clicking the Page icon in the Views Bar, then click where you want the rule placed within a page (**Figure 7.30**).

2. Choose Insert > Horizontal Line (**Figure 7.31**). The line will be inserted into the page (**Figure 7.32**).

To edit a horizontal line

1. Right-click on the line and choose *Horizontal Line Properties* from the shortcut menu ((Alt)(Enter)) (**Figure 7.33**).

2. When the Horizontal Line Properties dialog box appears, you can adjust the line's size, alignment, and color (**Figure 7.34**). For details see *Horizontal line options* on the next page.

3. When you're done editing the line, click *OK* and the changes will be applied.

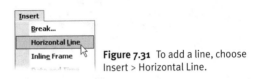

Figure 7.30 Click where you want to insert a horizontal line.

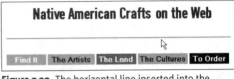

Figure 7.31 To add a line, choose Insert > Horizontal Line.

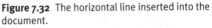

Figure 7.32 The horizontal line inserted into the document.

Figure 7.33 To edit a horizontal line, right-click it and choose *Horizontal Line Properties* from the shortcut menu.

Figure 7.34 Use the Horizontal Line Properties dialog box to adjust a line's size, alignment, and color.

Horizontal line options

Use the Horizontal Line Properties dialog box to adjust a line's size, alignment, and color (**Figure 7.34**).

❶ **Size:** By default, FrontPage sets the line width as a percentage of the browser window's width. Choose *Pixels* if you want to set an absolute width. The *Height* is always set in pixels. Use the arrows to adjust the numbers or enter numbers directly in the text windows.

❷ **Alignment:** By default, FrontPage centers the line. Choose *Left* or *Right* to have the line start from either side.

❸ **Color:** Click the arrow just to the right of *Automatic* (the default color) and a pop-up menu lets you pick from *Standard colors* (HTML's 16 predefined colors), the *Document's colors* (very handy for maintaining the color scheme of a page or site), or *More Colors*, which displays FrontPage's standard color wheel of all 216 Web-safe colors. By default, FrontPage adds a shadowed effect to the line. Check *Solid line (no shading)* to cancel the effect.

❹ **Style:** This button can only be used if you've created style sheets for your Web site. See *Building Style Sheets and Dynamic Effects* on page 335.

ADDING HORIZONTAL LINES

Editing Images

For major image editing, it's best to use a dedicated graphics program, but FrontPage's Pictures toolbar can easily handle a lot of basic editing (**Figure 7.1**). Remember that when using FrontPage to edit images all changes are applied to the actual image. To be safe, always keep a duplicate of the original stored outside your Web site. The Restore button, explained below, also will become one of your best friends.

To undo image editing

◆ Select the image, then click the Restore button in the Pictures toolbar (**Figure 7.35**). The image will revert to the last saved version.

Figure 7.35 To undo an image change, click the Restore button.

Figure 7.36 Use the *Appearance* tab's *Size* section to set an image's width and height.

Resizing images

The simplest way to resize an image is to grab one of its square black handles with the cursor and drag it. If you're looking for more precision with *minor* resizing, the following method will do it. Also see *Resampling images* on the next page.

To resize images

1. Right-click the image within its Web page and choose *Picture Properties* from the shortcut menu ((Alt)(Enter)) (**Figure 7.15**).

2. When the Picture Properties dialog box appears, click the *Appearance* tab (**Figure 7.23**).

3. Within the *Size* section, check *Specify size* and either type numbers into the *Width* and *Height* text windows or use the arrows just to the right (**Figure 7.36**). By default, the numbers represent pixels, unless you choose *in percent*.

4. Check *Keep aspect ratio* if you want to preserve the image's overall proportions even as you shrink or enlarge it.

5. Click *OK* and the image will be resized.

✔ Tip

- If you're making anything other than minor size adjustments (10 percent or less), you should go back to your image editing program, create a new image, and insert it into your Web page.

RESIZING IMAGES

Resampling images

If you want to significantly enlarge or shrink an image, you'll get better looking results resizing it with a separate graphics program. But resampling, which involves FrontPage making its best guess at adding or deleting image pixels, is OK for minor size changes. In general, using resampling to shrink an image creates less distortion than enlarging it.

To resample an image

1. Be sure to click the Normal tab and the Page icon, then select your image by clicking on it.

2. Drag any of the image's square black handles to shrink or enlarge it (**Figure 7.37**). Use a corner handle if you want to maintain the image's original proportions.

3. Once you've shrunk or enlarged the image, click the Resample button in the Pictures toolbar to apply the resampling (**Figure 7.38**).

Figure 7.37 To resample an image, first drag any of the image's square black handles to shrink or enlarge it.

Figure 7.38 Once you've shrunk or enlarged the image, click the Resample button to apply the change.

Figure 7.39 To add text to images, first click the Text button and a text box will appear centered within the image.

Figure 7.40 Type into the box, resizing if necessary by clicking and dragging its handles.

Figure 7.41 Once you've adjusted the text's position, font and color, the changes are applied.

To add text to images

1. Be sure to click the *Normal* tab and the Page icon, then select your image by clicking on it.

2. Click the Text button (**Figure 7.39**) and a text box will appear centered within the image. Type in your text (**Figure 7.40**). You may need to enlarge the text box by clicking and dragging its handles for all your text to show, though the box cannot extend beyond the image's edges.

3. To move the text box, select it and drag any of its square black handles. To set the text size or color, right-click the text box, choose *Font* from the shortcut menu, make your choices in the dialog box and click *OK*. The changes will be applied to the text (**Figure 7.41**).

✔ Tips

- Make sure the text is readable against the image. Change the text's color or size by right-clicking it and choosing *Font* from the shortcut menu. Or use the Pictures toolbar's Wash Out button. See the next page.

- To delete an image's text, select the text box and press (←Backspace) or (Delete).

- A great thing about the Text button is that you can go back and change the text or move the box even after you've saved it.

ADDING TEXT TO IMAGES

To wash out an image

1. Be sure to click the *Normal* tab and the Page icon, then select your image by clicking on it (**Figure 7.42**).

2. Click the Pictures toolbar's Color button and choose Wash Out from the drop-down menu (**Figure 7.43**). The image will be brightened in a single step, making it easier to use the image as a backdrop for text or another image (**Figure 7.44**).

Figure 7.42 Click to select the image you want to wash out.

Figure 7.43 Use the Color button's Wash Out choice to reduce the image's contrast.

Figure 7.44 Once an image has been washed out, it will be easier to see objects placed atop it.

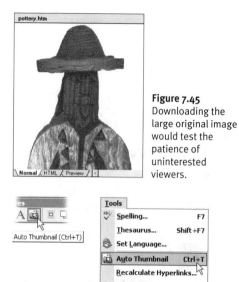

pottery.htm

Figure 7.45
Downloading the large original image would test the patience of uninterested viewers.

Figure 7.46 To create a thumbnail of a large image, click the Auto Thumbnail button or choose Tools > Auto Thumbnail ([Ctrl][T]).

Figure 7.47 The thumbnail image includes a hyperlink to the larger image for viewers wanting a detailed look.

Creating auto thumbnails and photo galleries

Thumbnails let visitors get the gist of an image without waiting for the detailed, slow-to-download original. If they want to see the larger file version, clicking the thumbnail automatically takes them to it. Thumbnails are particularly useful for quickly presenting a catalog-style page of products. FrontPage also gives you control over thumbnail properties, so you can set default size, border, and beveling.

What FrontPage calls auto thumbnails in fact involve manually creating thumbnails one at a time. Photo galleries, new in FrontPage 2002, overcome this drawback by letting you convert an entire folder of images into a hyperlinked set of thumbnails.

To create auto thumbnail images

1. Be sure to click the *Normal* tab and the Page icon, then select your image by clicking on it (**Figure 7.45**).

2. Click the Pictures toolbar's Auto Thumbnail button or choose Tools > Auto Thumbnail ([Ctrl][T]) (**Figure 7.46**). (If the image is already fairly small, the button will be dimmed.) A smaller version of the image will be created and automatically linked to the large original image (**Figure 7.47**).

CREATING AUTO THUMBNAILS

To set auto thumbnail properties

1. Choose Tools > Page Options (**Figure 7.48**).

2. When the Page Options dialog box appears, the *Auto Thumbnail* tab will be selected by default (**Figure 7.49**). Use the *Set* drop-down menu to pick any of the four settings, then use the *Pixels* text window to change the default. If you want, check *Border thickness* and use the *Pixels* text window to set its width. You also can add a *Beveled edge*.

3. Click *OK* and the settings will be applied to all new thumbnails created.

Figure 7.48 To set thumbnail properties, choose Tools > Page Options.

Figure 7.49 The Auto Thumbnail tab lets you set the size, border, and bevels applied to thumbnails.

Figure 7.50 To create a thumbnail photo gallery, choose Insert > Web Component.

Figure 7.51 Choose *Photo Gallery* in the *Component type* list, then choose a layout in the right-hand pane.

Figure 7.52 To compile the gallery, click the *Add* button and choose either *Pictures from Files* or *Pictures from Scanner or Cameras*.

To create a thumbnail photo gallery

1. Click on the Web page where you want the photo gallery to appear and choose Insert > Web Component (**Figure 7.50**).

2. When the Insert Web Component dialog box appears, choose *Photo Gallery* in the *Component type* list, then choose a layout in the right-hand pane, and click *Finish* (**Figure 7.51**).

3. When the Photo Gallery Properties dialog box appears, the *Pictures* tab will be chosen by default. Click the *Add* button and choose *Pictures from Files* from the drop-down menu (**Figure 7.52**).

(continued)

4. When the File Open dialog box appears, navigate to the images you want to use, select one or more (⌃Ctrl–click to select multiple images), and click *Open* (**Figure 7.53**). The selected images will be added to the list in the Photo Gallery Properties dialog box (**Figure 7.54**).

5. The list of files reflects the order images will be displayed in the gallery, so if necessary, select a listing and use the *Move Up* or *Move Down* buttons to change the order. Use *Remove* to drop a file from the gallery only; the file itself will not be deleted from your hard drive.

6. If you prefer, select an image in the list and use the *Width* and *Height* windows to change the *Thumbnail size*. By default, each image's horizontal-to-vertical ratio is preserved, unless you uncheck *Maintain aspect ratio*. (If you check *Set as default size*, the currently selected image's *Width* and *Height* will be applied to all the images in the list—overriding each image's original aspect ratio.)

Figure 7.53 Use the File Open dialog box to navigate to the images you want to use in the photo gallery.

Figure 7.54 The selected images are added to the Photo Gallery Properties dialog box's list. Use the *Move Up* or *Move Down* buttons to change the order.

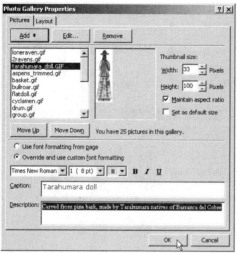

Figure 7.55 Use the *Caption* or *Description* text window to add information about a selected image.

Figure 7.56 The photo gallery as it appears in the Web page.

7. To add information about a particular image, select it in the list and type in the *Caption* or *Description* text windows (**Figure 7.55**). By default, the text will *Use font formatting from page*. To apply particular fonts or styles, choose *Override and use custom font formatting* and use the formatting drop-down menus and icons to set the *Caption* or *Description*. Repeat for each image needing text description.

8. Click *OK* and the gallery will be generated and added to your Web page (**Figure 7.56**). Each thumbnail image can be clicked to reach the original image.

✔ Tip

- If you choose *Pictures from Scanner or Cameras* when you click *Add* in step 3, FrontPage will import images directly from either connected device without having to first copy them to your hard drive (**Figure 7.52**).

CREATING A THUMBNAIL PHOTO GALLERY

To change a photo gallery

1. Open the Web page containing the gallery, right-click the gallery, and choose *Photo Gallery Properties* from the shortcut menu (**Figure 7.57**).

2. When the Photo Gallery Properties dialog box appears, the *Pictures* tab is selected by default, enabling you to reorder the list, change the size of the thumbnails, or edit the text information as described in *To create a thumbnail photo gallery*.

3. To change the gallery's basic arrangement, click the dialog box's *Layout* tab and select a new setting in the *Choose a layout* list (**Figure 7.58**). Set the *Number of pictures per row* if that choice is available.

4. You also can make some basic changes to any photo in the gallery by clicking the Photo Gallery Properties dialog box's *Pictures* tab and then clicking the *Edit* button (top, **Figure 7.59**). The Edit Picture dialog box will open, where you can change the size of the original picture itself, instead of just its thumbnail (bottom, **Figure 7.59**). You also can rotate or crop the picture and even use the *Previous* and *Next* buttons to move through the rest of the gallery list. Click *OK* to apply the changes and return to the Photo Gallery Properties dialog box.

5. Once you have finished making all your changes, click *OK* in the Photo Gallery Properties dialog box and the changes will be applied to the photo gallery.

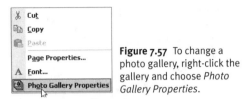

Figure 7.57 To change a photo gallery, right-click the gallery and choose *Photo Gallery Properties*.

Figure 7.58 To change the gallery's basic arrangement, click the *Layout* tab and select a new setting in the *Choose a layout* list.

Figure 7.59 By clicking the *Edit* button (top), you can make basic changes to any photo in the gallery (bottom).

Figure 7.60 The original image before being flipped or rotated.

Rotate Left | Flip Vertical

Rotate Right | Flip Horizontal

Figure 7.61 The Pictures toolbar includes four rotate/flip buttons.

Figure 7.62 Left: The image after being rotated to the left. Right: The image after being flipped vertically.

To rotate or flip images

1. Be sure to click the *Normal* tab and the Page icon, then select your image by clicking on it (**Figure 7.60**).

2. Click one of the four rotate/flip buttons in the Pictures toolbar (**Figure 7.61**). The image will be rotated or flipped, depending on your choice (**Figure 7.62**).

✔ Tip

■ To undo any rotate or flip action, click the same button again and the image will be restored to its original position.

To change image contrast

1. Be sure to click the *Normal* tab and the Page icon, then select your image by clicking on it (**Figure 7.63**).

2. Click the More Contrast or Less Contrast buttons as many times as you need to boost or reduce the image's contrast (**Figures 7.64** and **7.65**). If the image gets too contrasty or too flat, use the other button of the pair to rebalance its appearance. You also can undo each incremental change by pressing Ctrl Z.

To change image brightness

1. Be sure to click the *Normal* tab and the Page icon, then select your image by clicking on it (**Figure 7.66**).

2. Click either the More Brightness or Less Brightness buttons as many times as you need to lighten or darken the image (**Figures 7.67** and **7.68**).

Figure 7.63 The original image before changing its contrast.

Figure 7.64 Click the More Contrast or Less Contrast buttons to boost or reduce the image's contrast.

Figure 7.65 Left: Image contrast boosted to maximum. Right: Image contrast reduced to a minimum.

Figure 7.66 The original image before adjusting the brightness.

Figure 7.67 Click either the More Brightness or Less Brightness buttons to lighten or darken the image.

Figure 7.68 Left: Image brightened. Right: Image darkened.

Figure 7.69 To trim an image, select it and click the Crop button.

Figure 7.70 Click and drag any of the black handles to shape the cropping boundary.

Figure 7.71 After you press (Enter) or click the Crop button again, the image is trimmed.

Figure 7.72 To make a color transparent in a GIF image, click the Set Transparent Color button.

Figure 7.73 Move your cursor back over the selected image and click the eraser-like icon on the color you want made transparent.

Figure 7.74 After making the image's white background transparent, the underlying image shows through.

To crop images

1. Be sure to click the *Normal* tab and the Page icon, then select your image by clicking on it.

2. Click the Crop button (**Figure 7.69**).

3. When a dashed line surrounds the image, click and drag any of the black handles to shape the cropping boundary (**Figure 7.70**).

4. Press (Enter) or click the Crop button again and the image will be trimmed (**Figure 7.71**).

To make a GIF color transparent

1. Be sure to click the *Normal* tab and the Page icon, then select your image by clicking on it.

2. Click the Set Transparent Color button in the Pictures toolbar (**Figure 7.72**). Move your cursor back over the selected image and it will turn into an eraser-like icon (**Figure 7.73**).

3. Click the tip of the icon on the color in the image that you want to be transparent. The change will be applied, though you may not detect the change until you drag the image over another image (**Figure 7.74**).

To remove image color

1. Be sure to click the *Normal* tab and the Page icon, then select your image by clicking on it.

2. Click the Color button in the Pictures toolbar, choose Grayscale from the drop-down menu (**Figure 7.75**), and the previously full-color image will turn to a grayscale image.

✔ Tip

■ The drop-down menu's Black & White choice is only available when working with vector-based images. For more information, see *Adding and Editing Drawings* on page 197.

To add a bevel to an image

1. Be sure to click the *Normal* tab and the Page icon, then select your image by clicking on it.

2. Click the Bevel button in the Pictures toolbar and a button-like beveled edge will be added to the image (**Figure 7.76**).

Figure 7.75 To remove color from an image, click the Color button and choose *Grayscale* from the drop-down menu.

Figure 7.76 To add a bevel to an image, click the Bevel button (left) and the effect is applied (right).

REMOVING COLOR, ADDING BEVELS

Positioning Images Absolutely

FrontPage supports Cascading Style Sheets (CSS) for version 4 or later browsers, which means you can position images in ways not possible before. Without CSS, images and other objects can only be positioned in sequence, that is, one after another across and down the Web page. With CSS 2.0 you can position images absolutely, for example, stacking them in front of or behind other images and objects. Two wrinkles to consider: First, visitors without version 4 or later browsers will see the absolutely positioned images aligned to the left, which might not look so good; second, absolute positioning can't be used with Dynamic HTML. Because Web browser support for CSS 2.0 remains spotty, use absolute positioning only if you are sure the bulk of your audience is using version 4 or later browsers. In general, it's best to stick with CSS 1.0, which only affects formatting. For more information, see *Using Cascading Style Sheets* on page 337.

To position images absolutely

1. Be sure to click the *Normal* tab and the Page icon, then select your image by clicking on it (**Figure 7.77**).

2. Click the Position Absolutely button in the Pictures toolbar (**Figure 7.78**).

3. A four-arrowed icon will appear as you grab the image and begin moving it into position (**Figure 7.79**). Once you've positioned the image, click anywhere outside the image to deselect it.

✔ Tip

■ The click and drag method may not be precise enough if you're working with a design requiring that images be positioned at predetermined x, y coordinates. For pixel-based precision, choose View > Toolbars > Positioning to activate the Positioning toolbar (**Figure 7.80**). Use the number-entry windows to set the image's pixel coordinates.

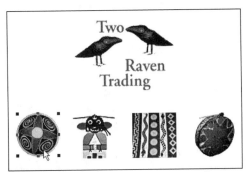

Figure 7.77 To position an image absolutely, first select it.

Figure 7.78 After selecting the image, click the Position Absolutely button.

Figure 7.79 A four-arrowed icon will appear as you grab the image and begin moving it into position.

▼ Positioning			✕
⊞ Left: 121	Top: 119	Width: 75	
Height: 75	Z-Index:	🗗 🗗	

Figure 7.80 For greater precision, use the Positioning toolbar's number-entry windows to set the image's pixel coordinates.

Figure 7.81 Use the Bring Forward or Send Backward buttons to place the selected image in front of or behind other page items.

Figure 7.82 The Mimbres pot has been sent behind the raven.

Figure 7.83 Left: Clicking the pot winds up selecting the raven image because it's in front and larger. Right: After sending the ravens to the back, the pot can be selected.

Figure 7.84 By making the white areas transparent in all three images, the stacking arrangement is more flexible.

To move absolutely positioned images forward and backward

1. Select your image by clicking on it (**Figure 7.77**).

2. Depending on whether you want to place the selected image in front of or behind the other page items, click the Bring Forward or Send Backward buttons in the Pictures toolbar (**Figure 7.81**). The stack order of the selected image will change (**Figure 7.82**).

✔ Tips

■ If you have multiple overlapping images, you may need to click the Bring Forward or Send Backward buttons several times to get the stack order right.

■ If you position an image completely behind a much larger one, you won't be able to select it by clicking it. To reach the smaller image, first select the larger image, then click the Send Backward button until the smaller image moves forward to where you can click it (**Figure 7.83**).

■ For more flexibility when stacking images, remember the option of making the background color transparent. In the GIFs used in these examples, the white background color was made transparent (**Figure 7.84**).

■ Bear in mind that many of the layered effects created by absolute positioning also can be simulated using a graphics program—without the browser compatibility problems.

POSITIONING IMAGES ABSOLUTELY

ADDING AND EDITING DRAWINGS

If you have ever used Microsoft PowerPoint to create an organization chart, you have created vector-based drawings. As bit-mapped images, GIFs and JPEGs are made of differently colored pixels. Drawings, however, are vector-based images. As mathematically generated objects, vector-based images create much smaller files than their GIF or JPEG equivalents. That means they download more quickly over the Web. But there's a catch: only version 5 or later Web browsers can read the Vector Markup Language coding used to generate vector-based drawings.

Microsoft FrontPage includes a partial solution to this problem by also creating a GIF version of any drawing. Web browsers that cannot handle the VML code will, instead, display the substitute GIF. The problem is that the GIF file will be larger (and slower to download) than the original vector-based image. As with so many things Web, using drawings involves a trade off. Unless you're publishing Web pages for an audience where *everyone* uses Internet Explorer 5, for example, you may want to think twice before packing your pages with drawings.

Virtually all of FrontPage's drawings can be created using the Drawing toolbar (**Figure 8.1**) or the WordArt toolbar (**Figure 8.2**). FrontPage's drawings fall into three broad categories: simple shapes such as lines, arrows, squares and circles; AutoShapes; and WordArt. The AutoShapes feature offers a variety of pre-drawn shapes at the click of your cursor. You'll also find the tools for drawing freeform shapes tucked away in the AutoShapes menu. For more information, see *To draw a freeform shape* on page 202. WordArt makes it easy to create fancy text and banner effects. For more information, see *Using WordArt* on page 206.

FrontPage's drawing tools also allow you to create a drawing canvas, which has advantages when creating more complicated drawings containing multiple shapes. For more information, see *Using the Drawing Canvas* on page 216. For creating complex layouts, you may want to use the Drawing toolbar's text box feature. For more information, see *Using Vector-based Text Boxes* on page 224.

To turn on the Drawing toolbar

◆ To view the Drawing toolbar, choose View > Toolbars > Drawing.

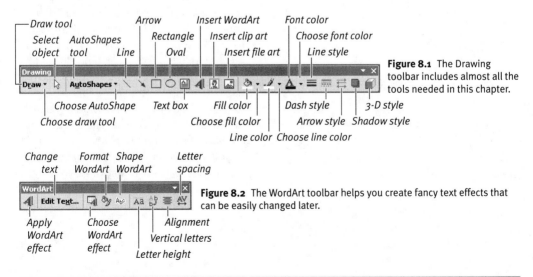

Figure 8.1 The Drawing toolbar includes almost all the tools needed in this chapter.

Figure 8.2 The WordArt toolbar helps you create fancy text effects that can be easily changed later.

Figure 8.3 To draw a simple shape, click the toolbar's line, arrow, rectangle, or oval icon.

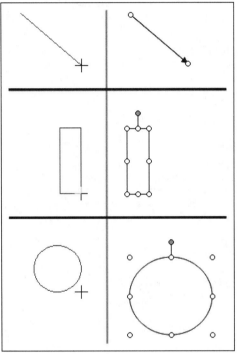

Figure 8.4 Whether you add an arrow, rectangle, or circle, the click-and-drag basics of drawing the shape remain the same.

To draw a simple shape

1. Turn on the Drawing toolbar, then click one of the toolbar's four simple shapes (line, arrow, rectangle, or oval) (**Figure 8.3**).

2. Click and drag in the page where you want the shape to appear (left, **Figure 8.4**). Release the cursor when the shape reaches the desired size (you can adjust its location and size later). The shape will appear on the page, with small circles marking its boundary (right, **Figure 8.4**). For more information on moving or adjusting a shape, see *Changing Drawn Objects* on page 209.

To add an AutoShape

1. Turn on the Drawing toolbar, click AutoShapes in the toolbar, choose a shape category, then choose a specific shape from the drop-down menu (**Figure 8.5**).

2. Click and drag in the page where you want the shape to appear (left, **Figure 8.6**). Release the cursor when the shape reaches the desired size (you can adjust its location and size later). The shape will appear on the page, with a series of small circles marking its boundary (right, **Figure 8.6**). For more information on moving or adjusting AutoShapes, see *Changing Drawn Objects* on page 209.

✔ Tips

- You also can add AutoShapes to a page by choosing Insert > Picture > AutoShapes and then choosing a shape from the AutoShapes toolbar (**Figure 8.7**).

- If you plan on creating a bunch of AutoShapes all at once, you may find it easier to have a separate AutoShapes toolbar on your desktop. Just click the Drawing toolbar's AutoShapes icon and move your cursor over the top of the drop-down menu until it becomes a four-headed arrow. You can then drag the AutoShapes toolbar to the desktop (**Figure 8.8**).

Figure 8.5 To add an AutoShape, choose a shape category, and a specific shape from the drop-down menu.

Figure 8.6 Click and drag in the page where you want the shape to appear (left), and release the cursor when the shape reaches the desired size (right).

Figure 8.7 You also can add AutoShapes to a page by choosing Insert > Picture > AutoShapes (left), and then choosing a shape from the AutoShapes toolbar (right).

Figure 8.8 To put a separate AutoShapes toolbar on your desktop, click the AutoShapes icon and drag the drop-down menu to the desktop.

Figure 8.9 To reach the Curve tool, choose AutoShapes > Lines and click the icon in the drop-down menu.

Figure 8.10 Left: To draw a curve, click where the line should begin, draw to the curve's midpoint, and click again. Middle: Continue drawing to the end of the line and the first click point becomes the curve's middle flex point. Right: When you're done drawing, double-click to select your new curved line.

Figure 8.11 To adjust a curve's arc, move your cursor over the mid-point and drag the hollow-circle handle.

Figure 8.12 Create a separate Lines toolbar by clicking and dragging the top of the Lines drop-down menu onto your desktop.

To draw a curved line

1. Turn on the Drawing toolbar, then choose AutoShapes > Lines and click the Curve tool (**Figure 8.9**).

2. Click in your page where the line should begin, draw a line to the approximate midpoint of your curve, and click again (left, **Figure 8.10**). Continue drawing the line until you reach where you want the line to end and you'll notice that the previous cursor click created a flex point for the curve (middle, **Figure 8.10**). Double-click and the curved line will appear as a selected object on the page, denoted by its hollow-circle handles (right, **Figure 8.10**).

3. To adjust the curve's arc, move your cursor over any handle until the cursor becomes a double-headed arrow, at which point you can click and drag the handle (**Figure 8.11**).

4. Deselect the curved line by clicking elsewhere on your Web page and the line's handles will disappear.

✔ Tip

■ Because curves, freeform, and scribble shapes often require a bit of adjustment, put the Lines toolbar on your desktop where you can reach its tools in a single click. Choose AutoShapes > Lines and then click and drag the top of the Lines drop-down menu onto your desktop (top, **Figure 8.12**). Release the cursor and the tiny Lines toolbar will detach itself from the main Drawing toolbar (bottom, **Figure 8.12**).

DRAWING A CURVED LINE

To draw a freeform shape

1. Turn on the Drawing toolbar, then choose AutoShapes > Lines and click the Freeform tool (**Figure 8.13**).

2. Click in your page where the line should start and begin drawing, clicking at each spot where you want the line to change direction (left, **Figure 8.14**).

3. Double-click when you are done drawing the shape and it will appear as a selected object on the page, denoted by its hollow-circle handles (right, **Figure 8.14**).

4. To adjust the shape, right-click it and choose Edit Points from the drop-down menu (**Figure 8.15**).

5. When the shape's handles change to solid-black squares, click and drag any handle to adjust its position (**Figure 8.16**).

6. Repeat with any other handles you want to adjust. When you are done, deselect the freeform shape by clicking elsewhere on your Web page and the handles will disappear.

Figure 8.13 To reach the Freeform tool, choose AutoShapes > Lines and click the icon in the drop-down menu.

Figure 8.14 Left: Click where the freeform line should start, and begin drawing, clicking when you want to change direction. Right: Double-click when you are done to select the freeform shape.

Figure 8.15 To adjust the freeform shape, right-click it and choose Edit Points from the drop-down menu.

Figure 8.16 Once the black handles appear, click and drag any handle to a new position.

Figure 8.17 To reach the scribble tool, choose AutoShapes > Lines and click the icon in the drop-down menu.

Figure 8.18 To draw a scribble shape, click where the line should begin and draw in a continuous motion. Double-click when you're done to select the shape (right).

Figure 8.19 To adjust the shape, right-click it and choose Edit Points from the drop-down menu.

Using the scribble tool

Despite its unassuming name, the scribble tool is a powerful—and tricky—tool to use. More commonly known as a Bezier tool in such programs as Adobe Illustrator or Macromedia FreeHand, this tool lets you create shapes with a combination of straight and curved lines. You can then adjust the curves by clicking-and-dragging their handles. Be prepared to practice getting the hang of it.

To draw a scribble shape

1. Turn on the Drawing toolbar, then choose AutoShapes > Lines and click the Scribble tool icon (**Figure 8.17**).

2. Click in your page where the line should begin, then draw your shape without clicking (left, middle, **Figure 8.18**).

3. Double-click and the shape will appear as a selected object on the page, denoted by its hollow-circle handles (right, **Figure 8.18**).

4. To adjust the shape, right-click it and choose Edit Points from the drop-down menu (**Figure 8.19**).

(continued)

USING THE SCRIBBLE TOOL

5. When the shape's handles change to solid-black squares, click and drag any handle to adjust its position (**Figure 8.20**). You can change how a particular handle responds to adjustments by right-clicking that handle and choosing one of the four point types listed in the shortcut menu (*Auto, Smooth, Straight,* or *Corner*) (**Figure 8.21**). While the handle will not change its appearance, the line segments on each side of the point (shown as dashed lines) will respond quite differently based on the point type chosen (**Figure 8.22**).

6. Once you are finished adjusting the shape, deselect the freeform shape by clicking elsewhere on your Web page and the handles will disappear.

Figure 8.20 Once the black handles appear, click and drag any handle to a new position.

Figure 8.21 To change how a handle responds to adjustments, right-click it and choose one of the four point types listed in the shortcut menu.

Figure 8.22 Adjustments vary based on the point type. From left, the same handle as: an auto point, a smooth point, and a corner point.

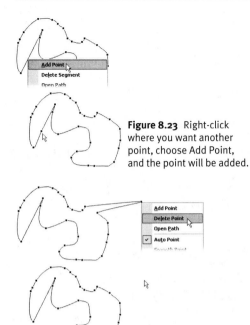

Figure 8.23 Right-click where you want another point, choose Add Point, and the point will be added.

Figure 8.24 Right-click a point, choose Delete Point, and the point will be removed—along with the line segment on each side of it.

Figure 8.25 To delete a single line segment, right-click it and choose Delete Segment.

Figure 8.26 A straight line segment (left) adjusts differently than a curved segment (right). To change one type to the other, right-click it and choose the other type in the drop-down menu (middle).

✔ Tips

- Adding handles (points) gives you finer control over a shape's outline. Right-click where you want another point, choose Add Point from the shortcut menu, and the point will be added (**Figure 8.23**).

- Deleting handles (points) simplifies a shape's outline. Right-click a point, choose Delete Point from the shortcut menu, and the point will be removed— along with the line segment on each side of it (**Figure 8.24**).

- You can delete a single line segment— without affecting any point—by right-clicking the segment and choosing Delete Segment from the shortcut menu (**Figure 8.25**).

- A shape's line segments are either straight or curved, but FrontPage lets you change one type to the other. This affects how the segment responds when adjusted (left, right, **Figure 8.26**). To change a segment's type, right-click it and choose Straight Segment or Curved Segment from the shortcut menu (middle, **Figure 8.26**).

- To enclose an open-ended shape, right-click it and choose Close Path from the shortcut menu (**Figure 8.27**).

Figure 8.27 To enclose an open-ended shape, right-click it and choose Close Path from the shortcut menu.

Using WordArt

A new feature in FrontPage 2002, WordArt gives you lots of flexibility. Because it is vector based, WordArt can be changed at any time. That's especially handy for creating, and then changing, text for buttons and other navigation-related labels. For example, if you restructure your Web site, it's much quicker to change a button that uses a WordArt label than redoing a GIF-based button. While the WordArt gallery is full of wild type effects, don't overlook the usefulness of the relatively plain, but easier to read, gallery choices.

To turn on the WordArt toolbar

◆ To view the WordArt toolbar, choose View > Toolbars > WordArt or click the WordArt icon in the Drawing toolbar.

To add WordArt

1. Choose Insert > Picture > WordArt or click the Insert WordArt icon in the Drawing toolbar (**Figure 8.28**).

2. When the WordArt Gallery dialog box appears, choose one of the 30 styles and click *OK* (**Figure 8.29**).

3. When the Edit WordArt Text dialog box appears, choose your *Font*, *Size* and whether you want to use bold or italic, then type in the *Text* window (**Figure 8.30**). When you are done, click *OK* and the text will appear in the Web page (**Figure 8.31**).

Figure 8.28 To add WordArt, choose Insert > Picture > WordArt (left), or click the WordArt icon in the Drawing toolbar (right).

Figure 8.29 The WordArt Gallery dialog box offers you the choice of 30 type styles.

Figure 8.30 Use the Edit WordArt Text dialog box to enter your text and set its *Font*, *Size*, and whether you want to use bold or italic.

Figure 8.31 After you enter your text, it appears on the page in the chosen WordArt style.

Figure 8.32 To change the WordArt text at any time, click the WordArt toolbar's Edit Text icon.

Figure 8.33 The WordArt toolbar's shape icon offers dozens of choices.

Figure 8.34 The WordArt toolbar's horizontal/vertical icon lets you reorient your text.

To change WordArt

1. Click to select the WordArt, denoted by the appearance of small hollow circles (handles) around its boundary.

2. To change the text, click the WordArt toolbar's Edit Text icon (**Figure 8.32**), which will reopen the Edit Text dialog box.

3. As long as the WordArt object remains selected, you can click any of the other WordArt toolbar icons and apply a second effect (**Figures 8.33–8.36**).

Figure 8.35 The WordArt toolbar's alignment icon offers five choices for adjusting your text.

Figure 8.36 The WordArt toolbar's letter spacing icon offers five pre-set choices and a custom spacing option.

✔ Tips

■ The first and third icons in the WordArt toolbar both open the WordArt Gallery.

■ To quickly apply or change several WordArt effects, right-click the WordArt and choose Format WordArt or click the bucket icon in the WordArt toolbar (**Figure 8.37**). When the Format WordArt dialog box appears, use the tabs and menus to change the shape's properties (**Figure 8.38**). Click *OK* and all your changes will be applied to the selected WordArt. If you check the *Default for new objects* box, those settings will be used for any new WordArt.

■ WordArt properties that can be set within the Format WordArt dialog box include: fill color and transparency: line color, style, and size; size and rotation; alignment and positioning, and alternate text.

■ Some WordArt effects can only be applied using the WordArt toolbar: editing the text, making all characters the same height, reopening the WordArt Gallery, and changing the letter spacing (kerning).

Figure 8.37 To change several WordArt effects at once, right-click the WordArt and choose Format WordArt (left) or click the WordArt toolbar's bucket icon (right).

Figure 8.38 Use the tabs and menus in the Format WordArt dialog box to simultaneously change multiple WordArt properties.

CHANGING WORDART

Figure 8.39 To resize an object, move the cursor over the handle you want to move, then click and drag it to a new location.

Figure 8.40 To resize lines and arrows, click and drag either point to a new location.

Figure 8.41 Some AutoShapes include a diamond-shaped handle, which you can use to adjust the shape's internal proportions.

Changing Drawn Objects

All three types of FrontPage drawings—simple shapes, AutoShapes, and WordArt—are generated as mathematical objects. That means you can easily resize, move, or even rotate drawings at any time. You also can change such properties as the color or style using the Drawing toolbar's icons. FrontPage also lets you group and arrange multiple objects. For more information, see *Aligning, Arranging, and Grouping Drawn Objects* on page 213.

To resize a drawn object

1. Click to select the drawn object, denoted by the appearance of small hollow circles (handles) around its boundary.

2. Move the cursor to the handle on the side that you want to expand or reduce. The cursor will become a two-headed arrow (left, **Figure 8.39**).

3. Click on the handle and drag it in the direction you want to expand or shrink. A dashed line will mark your progress (middle, **Figure 8.39**).

4. When the object reaches the desired size, release your cursor and the object will be resized (right, **Figure 8.39**).

✔ Tips

■ You also can resize lines or arrows by clicking either point, dragging the point to a new spot, and releasing the cursor (**Figure 8.40**).

■ Some of the more complex AutoShapes may include a diamond-shaped handle, which you can use to further adjust the shape's internal proportions (**Figure 8.41**).

CHANGING DRAWN OBJECTS

To move a drawn object

1. Click to select the drawn object and drag the object to its new destination (left, **Figure 8.42**). A dashed line will mark your progress (middle, **Figure 8.42**).

2. Release your cursor and the object will move to the new location (right, **Figure 8.42**).

To rotate a drawn object

1. Move your cursor over the object's protruding green handle until the cursor becomes a spiraling arrow (left, **Figure 8.43**).

2. Click and drag the cursor either clockwise or counter-clockwise. A dashed line will mark your progress (middle, **Figure 8.43**).

3. Release your cursor and the object will rotate to the new location (right, **Figure 8.43**).

To flip a drawn object

1. Click to select the drawn object or objects (**Figure 8.44**).

2. In the Drawing toolbar, choose Draw > Rotate or Flip and then make a choice in the drop-down menu (**Figure 8.45**). The selected object will be flipped based on your choice (**Figure 8.46**).

✔ Tip

- If you choose Rotate Left or Rotate Right, the object will be rotated exactly 90 degrees.

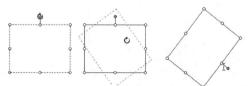

Figure 8.42 To move an object, click to select it, then drag it to a new location and release your cursor.

Figure 8.43 To rotate an object, move your cursor over the protruding green handle until the cursor becomes a spiraling arrow (left). Click and drag to rotate the object in either direction (right).

Figure 8.44 To flip an object, click to select it and its handles will become visible.

Figure 8.45 In the Drawing toolbar, choose Draw > Rotate or Flip and then make a choice in the drop-down menu.

Figure 8.46 After flipping the object, it remains selected, making it easy to apply another action if necessary.

Figure 8.47 Once you select an object, you can apply any of the effects included in the Drawing toolbar's last eight icons.

Figure 8.48 The Drawing toolbar's 3-D settings can turn a square (top) into a shaded cube (bottom).

To change other drawn object properties

1. Click to select the drawn object, click any of the last eight icons in the Drawing toolbar, and select an effect from the icon's drop-down menu (**Figure 8.47**).

2. Release the cursor and the effect will be applied to the object.

3. As long as the object remains selected, you can click one of the other seven icons (top, **Figure 8.48**) and apply a second effect (bottom, **Figure 8.48**).

✔ Tips

■ The Drawing toolbar's icons offer a tremendous number of effects, including line shapes, shadows, and 3D shadings (**Figure 8.49**). It's worth your time to explore what's available.

■ To quickly apply multiple effects, right-click an object and choose Format AutoShape (**Figure 8.50**). (This works even if the object is a simple shape and not an AutoShape.) When the Format AutoShape dialog box appears, use the tabs and menus to change the shape's properties (left, **Figure 8.51**). Click *OK* and all your changes will be applied to the selected shape (right, **Figure 8.51**). If you check the *Default for new objects* box, the settings will be used for any new shapes— a great time saver if you need to create a series of similar, custom shapes.

Figure 8.49 The Drawing toolbar's icons offer a tremendous number of effects.

Figure 8.50 To quickly apply multiple effects, right-click an object and choose Format AutoShape.

Figure 8.51 Use the tabs and menus in the Format AutoShape dialog box (left) to change multiple aspects of a shape (right).

Figure 8.52 Select several objects that you want to align by Ctrl-clicking each object.

Figure 8.53 To align or distribute the selected objects, choose Draw > Align or Distribute and then make a choice in the drop-down menu.

Figure 8.54 In this example, the two WordArt objects have been centrally aligned.

Aligning, Arranging, and Grouping Drawn Objects

FrontPage includes several options for moving and positioning drawn objects, which can be particularly helpful when working with multiple objects. Aligning lets you rearrange objects along a common axis; distributing lets you evenly space three or more objects. By default, FrontPage displays drawn objects in the order they were created with the most recent atop, that is, in front of, the earlier objects. By arranging, or ordering, the objects, you can change their so-called stack order. Finally, grouping lets you turn multiple objects into a single object, or group. This enables you to move the objects as a unit or apply property changes to all of them simultaneously. By creating groups of groups, known as subgroups, you can build fairly complex drawings and yet easily change selected sections.

To align or distribute drawn objects

1. Select several objects that you want to align by Ctrl-clicking each object (**Figure 8.52**).

2. In the Drawing toolbar, choose Draw > Align or Distribute and then make a choice in the drop-down menu (**Figure 8.53**). The previously selected objects will be aligned or distributed based on your choice (**Figure 8.54**).

✔ Tip

■ If you're not sure how a particular setting will affect the objects, take a look at the icons in the *Align or Distribute* drop-down menu.

To arrange drawn objects

1. Select the object you want to move forward or backward in the stack order (**Figure 8.55**).

2. In the Drawing toolbar, choose Draw > Order and then make a choice in the drop-down menu (**Figure 8.56**). The object will change its position in the stack order.

3. Depending on the stack order, you may need to select another object and choose Draw > Order and apply a second choice in the drop-down menu (or right-click the object and use the *Order* shortcut menu) (**Figure 8.57**).

4. Keep applying the various Draw > Order choices until the stack order is arranged how you want it (**Figure 8.58**).

✔ Tip

■ If you select multiple objects by Ctrl-clicking, you can move them forward or backward simultaneously. However, you can do this only if you use the Drawing toolbar's Draw icon (right-clicking overrides the multiple selection).

Figure 8.55
Begin by selecting the object you want to rearrange.

Figure 8.56 To rearrange the object, choose Draw > Order and then make a choice in the drop-down menu.

Figure 8.57 You also can right-click an object and change its order using the shortcut menu.

Figure 8.58
It may take several changes to rearrange the objects in the desired order.

Figure 8.59
Select several objects that you want to group by Ctrl -clicking each object.

Figure 8.60 To group objects, choose Draw > Group in the Drawing toolbar.

Figure 8.61
The previously separate objects are now grouped, as denoted by the single set of handles.

Figure 8.62 If you try to select an individual object in a group, its handles will be darkened to indicate that it cannot be selected.

Figure 8.63 To select a single object in a group, you must first choose Draw > Ungroup to cancel the grouping.

To group drawn objects

1. Select the objects you want to group by Ctrl -clicking each object (**Figure 8.59**).

2. In the Drawing toolbar, choose Draw > Group (**Figure 8.60**). The objects will become a single group, denoted by the appearance of a single set of handles (**Figure 8.61**).

✔ Tip

■ If you try to select an individual object in a group, its handles will be darkened and marked with Xs to indicate that it cannot be selected (**Figure 8.62**). To select the individual item, first choose Draw > Ungroup to cancel the grouping (**Figure 8.63**).

Using the Drawing Canvas

When adding drawings to a Web page, you can draw them directly on the page or create what FrontPage calls a drawing canvas. The canvas has several advantages over drawing individual figures directly on a Web page: you can move a canvas in a single step, instead of having to individually select all the drawings before moving them. You can easily resize the canvas and even rescale it—right along with all the drawn objects it contains. The Drawing Canvas toolbar, naturally enough, contains all the commands you need for working with the canvas (**Figure 8.64**).

To turn on the Drawing Canvas toolbar

◆ Choose View > Toolbars > Drawing Canvas or right-click an existing drawing canvas and choose Show Drawing Canvas Toolbar from the shortcut menu (**Figure 8.65**).

Enlarge canvas

Fit canvas to drawings　*Scale canvas up or down*

Figure 8.64 The Drawing Canvas toolbar lets you resize the canvas, which can contain more complex drawings.

Figure 8.65 To turn on the Drawing Canvas toolbar, choose View > Toolbars > Drawing Canvas (left), or right-click an existing canvas and choose Show Drawing Canvas Toolbar from the shortcut menu (right).

Figure 8.66
To create a
drawing canvas,
choose Insert >
Picture > New
Drawing.

Figure 8.67 To resize a drawing canvas, click and drag the solid-black corner or side handles.

Figure 8.68 When the canvas is resized, the rest of the Web page contents will reflow to accommodate the change.

Figure 8.69 It's easy to add multiple shapes to the Drawing canvas.

To create a drawing canvas

1. Click in the Web page where you want to add the drawing canvas and choose Insert > Picture > New Drawing (**Figure 8.66**).

2. When the drawing canvas appears on the page, click and drag the solid-black corner or side handles to resize it as needed (**Figure 8.67**). A dashed line will mark your progress. Release the cursor and the canvas will assume its new size (**Figure 8.68**).

3. To begin drawing, choose a shape icon in the Drawing toolbar and begin drawing inside the canvas area. If necessary switch to other icons to add other shapes until you are done (**Figure 8.69**).

CREATING A DRAWING CANVAS

To select a drawing canvas

1. Move your cursor over the drawing until it becomes a four-headed arrow.

2. Click once and the hashed border will appear (**Figure 8.70**). At that point, you can then move, resize, or rescale the drawing canvas

To move a drawing canvas

1. Select the drawing canvas (top, **Figure 8.71**).

2. Click and drag the cursor to where you want the drawing canvas moved (middle, **Figure 8.71**).

3. Release your cursor and the drawing canvas—along with all its contents—will move to the new destination (bottom, **Figure 8.71**).

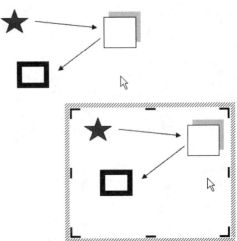

Figure 8.70 To see the sometimes hidden edges of a canvas, click your cursor on the drawing and its hashed border will appear.

Figure 8.71 To move a drawing canvas, select it and then drag your cursor to the new location. Release the cursor and the canvas will appear in the new spot (bottom).

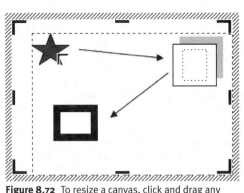

Figure 8.72 To resize a canvas, click and drag any handle.

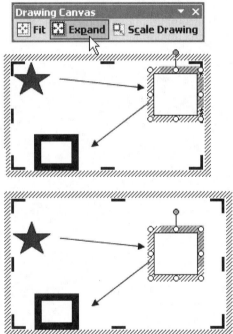

Figure 8.73 To incrementally enlarge a canvas, select it and click the Expand icon repeatedly until the canvas reaches the desired size.

Resizing a drawing canvas

Maybe you need space for more shapes, or now that you're done drawing you want to make the canvas a bit smaller. FrontPage offers several ways to resize the canvas while leaving the shapes within it unchanged.

To resize a drawing canvas by hand

1. Click on the hashed boundary of the drawing canvas to select it.

2. Click and drag one of the black handles on the corners or side of the drawing canvas. Whether you enlarge or reduce the canvas, a dashed line will mark your progress (**Figure 8.72**).

3. Release the cursor and the canvas will assume its new size, without affecting the shapes within.

To expand a drawing canvas with the toolbar

1. Make sure the Drawing Canvas toolbar is visible, then select the canvas by clicking on its hashed boundary.

2. Click the Expand icon in the Drawing Canvas toolbar and the canvas will expand to the right and downward (**Figure 8.73**).

3. Continuing clicking the Expand icon until the canvas reaches the desired size.

To fit a canvas to its contents

1. Make sure the Drawing Canvas toolbar is visible, then select the canvas by clicking on its hashed boundary (left, **Figure 8.74**).

2. Click the Fit icon in the Drawing Canvas toolbar and the canvas will shrink to just fit around its contents (right, **Figure 8.74**).

✔ Tip

■ The Fit icon is available only when the canvas contains more than one shape. For a canvas containing a single shape, resize the canvas by clicking and dragging.

Figure 8.74 To fit a canvas to its contents, select the canvas (left), click the Fit icon, and the canvas will shrink to just fit around its contents (right).

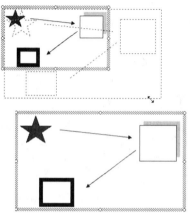

Figure 8.75 Select the canvas (left), then click the *Scale Drawing* icon in the toolbar and the previously solid-black handles will become hollow circles (right).

Figure 8.76 To preserve the proportions of its contents while scaling the canvas, click and drag a corner handle.

Rescaling a drawing canvas

Rescaling a canvas affects everything inside the canvas—unlike resizing a canvas, which does not change the size of its contents. When rescaling a canvas, you can choose to keep the height and width of its contents in proportion to each other or affect only one of the dimensions.

To preserve proportion while scaling a canvas

1. Select the canvas by clicking on its hashed boundary, then click the *Scale Drawing* icon in the toolbar and the previously solid-black handles will become hollow circles (**Figure 8.75**).

2. Click and drag any corner handle of the canvas. You can enlarge or shrink the canvas and a dashed line will mark your progress (top, **Figure 8.76**).

3. Release your cursor and the canvas will be rescaled proportionately, along with its contents (bottom, **Figure 8.76**).

4. Once you're done scaling the canvas, click the toolbar's *Scale Drawing* icon again to turn off the scaling feature.

To change proportion while scaling a canvas

1. Select the canvas by clicking on its hashed boundary, then click the *Scale Drawing* icon in the toolbar and the previously solid-black handles will become hollow circles (**Figure 8.75**).

2. Click and drag the handles on the sides, top, or bottom of the canvas. Clicking a side handle will change the content's width but not its height; clicking a top or bottom handle will change the height but not its width. You can enlarge or shrink the canvas and a dashed line will mark your progress (top, **Figure 8.77**).

3. Release your cursor and the canvas will be rescaled in only one dimension and change the proportions of its contents (bottom, **Figure 8.77**).

4. Once you're done scaling the canvas, click the toolbar's *Scale Drawing* icon again to turn off the scaling feature.

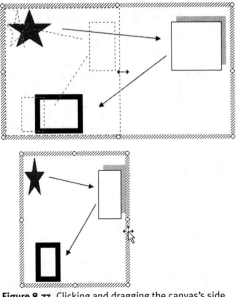

Figure 8.77 Clicking and dragging the canvas's side handle (top) will change the content's width but not the height (bottom).

Figure 8.78 To change the drawing canvas format, right-click the canvas and choose Format Drawing Canvas from the shortcut menu.

Figure 8.79 Use the tabs in the Format Drawing Canvas dialog box to change several canvas settings simultaneously.

Figure 8.80 By default, a drawing canvas's *Positioning style* is set to *None*, which lets the page content flow around the canvas.

Formatting a drawing canvas

By default, the drawing canvas automatically flows the page contents around its boundary. That makes it possible to quickly drop a drawing into your Web page without having to readjust the surrounding content.

To change the drawing canvas format

1. Select the drawing canvas you want to reformat, then right-click and choose Format Drawing Canvas from the shortcut menu (**Figure 8.78**).

2. When the Format Drawing Canvas dialog box appears, use the *Colors and Lines* tab to set the canvas's background color or border (**Figure 8.79**). Use the *Size* tab to resize or rescale the canvas using pixels. Use the *Layout* tab's *Wrapping style* and *Positioning style* to control the placement of the canvas amid the page's content (**Figure 8.80**). The *Picture* and *Text Box* tabs, used in formatting text boxes, are not available and, so will be dimmed. But you can use the *Web* tab to create alternate text.

3. Once you are done changing the formatting for the drawing canvas, click *OK* to close the dialog box and apply the changes to the canvas.

Using Vector-based Text Boxes

FrontPage's Drawing toolbar includes a handy, if confusingly named, feature called text boxes. Based on the same VML code that generates other FrontPage drawings, text boxes make it easy to create what are called sidebars. Common in print publishing but often a pain to create on a Web page, sidebars let you run a separate box of type next to—or even floating over—your page's main text. The great thing about vector-based text boxes is that you can add them after you've already created a page. That makes them extremely helpful when creating complex page layouts.

Despite their name, text boxes can also contain graphics. And, if that wasn't confusing enough, these vector-based text boxes have nothing to do with the short text boxes long used in HTML form pages. Finally, as with all other FrontPage drawings, remember that only version 5 or later browsers can display vector-based text boxes.

To add a vector-based text box

1. Turn on the Drawing toolbar and click the Text Box icon (**Figure 8.81**).

2. Click and drag your cursor in the page until you have created roughly the size text box you need (**Figure 8.82**). Release the cursor and a solid box will appear, blocking out the underlying page.

3. Right-click the edge of the text box and choose Format Text Box from the shortcut menu (**Figure 8.83**).

Figure 8.81 To add a vector-based text box, click the Drawing toolbar's Text Box icon.

Figure 8.82 Click and drag your cursor in the page to create the size text box needed.

Figure 8.83 To set its properties, right-click the text box and choose Format Text Box from the shortcut menu.

Figure 8.84 By default, the Format Text Box dialog box's *Layout* tab is set to *Absolute* positioning so the box floats atop the rest of your Web page.

Figure 8.85 To flow your Web page content around the text box, set the *Positioning style* to *None* and then choose an appropriate *Wrapping style*.

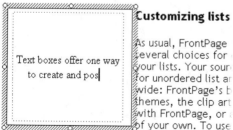

Customizing lists

As usual, FrontPage
several choices for
your lists. Your sour
for unordered list a
wide: FrontPage's t
themes, the clip art
with FrontPage, or
of your own. To use
built into FrontPage's theme, see *To apply a th*
page or Web site on page 000.

Figure 8.86 With the rest of the page wrapping around the text box, it's easier to see how the box relates to the page.

Text boxes offer one way
to create and pos

4. When the Format Text Box dialog box appears, click the *Layout* tab (**Figure 8.84**). By default, the *Positioning style* is set to *Absolute*, which is why text boxes initially float on top of your page's content. In a few cases, *Absolute* positioning may be what you want. More likely, you will want to change the *Positioning style* to *None* to let the rest of the page's content flow around the text box (**Figure 8.85**).

5. To give the text box a background color or border, use the dialog box's *Colors and Lines* tab. Use the *Size* tab to set the text box to precise x-y coordinates, the *Text Box* tab to set the margin surrounding the text, and the *Web* tab to create alternate text. Once you are done, click *OK* to close the dialog box and apply the changes to the text box.

6. With the rest of the page now wrapping around the text box, enter the text you want in the box (**Figure 8.86**).

(continued)

USING VECTOR-BASED TEXT BOXES

7. Once you have entered the text, select it, right-click, and choose Font from the shortcut menu (**Figure 8.87**).

8. Use the Font dialog box to style the text as you need and click *OK* to apply it. At that point, you may need to resize the text box to accommodate the restyled text by clicking and dragging any of its circular handles (**Figure 8.88**). If you add a picture, you may need to further adjust the text box's size or scale the picture before getting a decent overall layout (**Figure 8.89**).

9. To add a picture, click in the text box where you want the picture placed, choose Insert > Picture, and choose a submenu item.

✔ Tips

■ You can double-click the box's border to quickly open the Format Text Box dialog box and change any of its settings.

■ To move a text box to another place on the page, move the cursor to the edge of the box, where it will become a four-headed arrow. Then click and drag the box to its new destination.

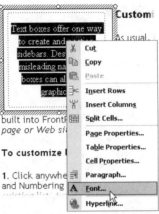

Figure 8.87 To change the text style in the box, select it, right-click and choose Font from the shortcut menu.

Figure 8.88 After restyling your text in the Font dialog box, you may need to resize the text box to accommodate your text.

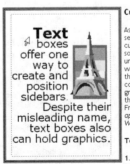

Figure 8.89 Text boxes also can contain graphics. You may need to resize and realign the box once the graphic's inserted.

USING VECTOR-BASED TEXT BOXES

PART 3

CREATING ADVANCED PAGES

ADDING MULTIMEDIA AND WEB COMPONENTS

9

Used judiciously, a bit of multimedia can juice up your Web pages and grab visitor attention. As always, bear in mind that visitors won't wait around for downloads, so use FrontPage's download progress indicator to gauge how long pages with multimedia elements will take to appear on screen (see page 16).

FrontPage gives you three basic categories for turning your Web pages into a multimedia extravaganza: videos or animations; background page sounds; and Web Components, which include such things as banner ads, ticker-tape marquees, and visitor-driven hit counters. FrontPage now includes more than 25 of these components. A few, such as Hover Buttons, you've already used. See *Adding Web Components* on page 236 to learn how to put them to work on your pages. One other multimedia-style element—moving type in layers—is covered in *Building Style Sheets and Dynamic Effects* on page 335.

Adding Videos or Animations

Although you technically could add an hour-long training video to your Web site, there are precious few network connections fast enough to handle such a huge file. In practice, Web videos/animations are best kept small—things like logos with moving type or animated arrows. Just remember: a little motion goes a long way.

To insert a video or animation

1. Switch to page view and click where you want the video or animation placed within a page.

2. Choose Insert > Picture > Video (**Figure 9.1**).

3. When the Video dialog box appears, it will show all the files already in your Web site (**Figure 9.2**). If the video/animation you want isn't listed, use the drop-down menus, folder icons, or buttons to navigate to the desired file.

4. Once you find the file and return to the Video dialog box, click *Open* to insert the video/animation into the Web page (**Figure 9.3**).

Figure 9.1 To insert a video or animation, choose Insert > Picture > Video.

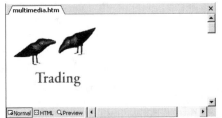

Figure 9.2 The Video dialog box, which lists all of your current Web site's files, also can be used to find a file on your hard drive or the Web itself.

Figure 9.3 Once the video/animation is inserted, FrontPage will display its first frame.

Figure 9.4 If the video/animation didn't come from your current Web site, the Save Embedded Files dialog box will give you a chance to save it.

Figure 9.5 Use the Clip Organizer to search for royalty-free movie clips.

5. Save the page with its new video/animation ([Ctrl][S]). If the file didn't come from your current Web site, the Save Embedded Files dialog box will appear (**Figure 9.4**).

6. Click *Rename* if you want to change the file name and *Change Folder* if you want to save the file in another location. When you're done, click *OK* and the video/animation will be saved.

7. Once the video/animation is inserted and saved, you can set how often it repeats and other aspects. See *To set loops for videos/animations* on page 232.

✔ Tip

- To use a clip art video/animation in step 3, click *Open* and choose *Open From Clip Organizer* in the shortcut menu (top, **Figure 9.5**). When the Select Movie dialog box appears, search for the movie clip you need (bottom, **Figure 9.5**). For more information, see *Clip Art options* on page 166.

To set loops for videos/animations

1. Switch to page view, right-click the video/animation and choose *Picture Properties* from the shortcut menu ((Alt)(Enter)) (**Figure 9.6**).

2. When the Picture Properties dialog box appears, click the *Video* tab (**Figure 9.7**).

3. If you want to substitute another video/animation for the current one, click *Browse* to find it.

4. Use the arrows and text windows in the *Repeat* section to set how many times the video/animation will play (or check the *Forever* box) and how long the delay should be between the loop finishing and starting again.

5. By default, the video/animation is set to start as soon as the file opens, but you can give more control to the user by selecting *On mouse over* in the *Start* section.

6. Once you've made your choices, click *OK* and the changes will be applied to the video/animation.

Figure 9.6 To set looping for a video or animation, right-click it and choose *Picture Properties*.

Figure 9.7 The *Video* tab in the Picture Properties dialog box lets you set how the video/animation repeats.

Figure 9.8 Playback controls let users pause, rewind, stop, or repeat the video.

Figure 9.9 To add video playback controls, choose Insert > Web Component.

Adding video playback controls

By adding playback controls to your video, the Web page user can pause, rewind, stop, or repeat the video (**Figure 9.8**). Many times, of course, this isn't necessary, but it's a nice option. Before taking these steps, first insert the video file as explained on page 230.

To add video playback controls

1. Choose Insert > Web Component (**Figure 9.9**).

2. When the Insert Web Component dialog box appears, click *Advanced Controls* in the left-hand *Component type* list, *Plug-In* in the right-hand list, and then click *Finish* (**Figure 9.10**).

3. When the Plug-In Properties dialog box appears, click *Browse* (**Figure 9.11**).

(continued)

Figure 9.10 When the Insert Web Component dialog box appears, click *Advanced Controls* in the left-hand *Component type* list, *Plug-In* in the right-hand list, and then click *Finish*.

Figure 9.11 Click *Browse* in the Plug-In Properties dialog box to reach the video file.

4. When the Select Plug-In Data Source dialog box appears, navigate to the video file to which you want playback controls added and click *Open* (**Figure 9.12**).

5. When the Plug-In Properties dialog box reappears, the path to the file will appear in the *Data source* text window (**Figure 9.13**). Add an alternate text *Message for browsers without plug-in support* (though most support them), set the video's *Size* and *Layout* properties, and click *OK*. A plug-in placeholder icon will appear on the page in FrontPage's *Normal* view (left, **Figure 9.14**).

6. Switch to FrontPage's *Preview* view to see the video with the playback controls added (right, **Figure 9.14**).

✔ Tip

- FrontPage also will let you configure the video's playback controls using ActiveX (**Figure 9.15**). The major drawback to using Microsoft's proprietary format is that it only works with Microsoft's Internet Explorer browser. About 79 percent of all Web surfers use Internet Explorer, but using ActiveX potentially shuts out one in five users, so think twice before going this route.

Figure 9.12 Once you find the video file, click *Open*.

Figure 9.13 When the Plug-In Properties dialog box reappears, the path to the file will appear in the *Data source* text window. Set alternate text, the size and layout, then click *OK*.

Figure 9.14 Left: A placeholder icon appears on the page in *Normal* view. Right: In *Preview* view, the video's playback controls appear.

Figure 9.15 By inserting an ActiveX Control component (top), you gain precise control over many elements (bottom). But non-Microsoft browsers won't work properly.

Figure 9.16 To add a page background sound, right-click anywhere in the page and choose *Page Properties*.

Figure 9.17 Click the *General* tab of the Page Properties dialog box to reach the *Background sound* section.

Figure 9.18 Click *Browse* to find a sound file. By default, playing the sound *Forever* is checked. Or use the *Loop* number window to limit the repetitions.

Adding Sounds

Short sound loops can be effective mood setters on the appropriate pages—and maddening on strictly business pages. Pick and choose your sound pages carefully.

To add a page background sound

1. Switch to page view, right-click anywhere in the page and choose *Page Properties* from the shortcut menu (**Figure 9.16**).

2. When the Page Properties dialog box opens, click the *General* tab (**Figure 9.17**).

3. Within the *Background sound* section, click *Browse* to locate a sound file (**Figure 9.18**). By default, *Forever* is checked. If you want the sound to play a short time, uncheck the box and use the text window or arrows to set the number of loops.

4. Click *OK* and the sound will become part of your Web page. Click the *Preview* tab at the bottom of FrontPage's main window to hear the sound or test it with your Web browser.

✔ Tips

- Since background sounds are linked to specific pages, you can give different pages different sounds.

- To remove a sound from a page, right-click in the page, choose *Page Properties* from the shortcut menu, and delete the file from the *Location* window.

Adding Web Components

FrontPage includes more than two dozen other multimedia components that can make your pages more interactive. These Web Components, one of which you used in creating video playback controls, have been greatly expanded in FrontPage 2002. Besides the components included in FrontPage 2000 (rotating banners, page hit counters, and scrolling marquees), the 2002 version adds the ability to create tables of content, lists of a site's most used pages, dynamically updated content, and time-sensitive pages.

Some of these Web Components, however, require that FrontPage 2002 extensions be installed on the hosting Web server. While these components do cool things, they tend to exclude Web users not using Microsoft products. That makes their use a tough call—and one only you can make.

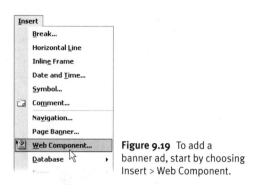

Figure 9.19 To add a banner ad, start by choosing Insert > Web Component.

Figure 9.20 To add a banner ad, choose *Dynamic Effects* in the left-hand *Component type* list and *Banner Ad Manager* in the right-hand list.

Using banner ads

With a constantly rotating selection of images, banner ads are powerful attention getters. No wonder they've become a staple of commercial Web sites. Banner ads, however, need not be confined to product advertising. Corporate intranets, for example, can use them to alert users to items of company wide interest, whether it's a new pension policy or the Friday beer bash.

To add a banner ad

1. Switch to page view, click in the page where you want the banner ad, and choose Insert > Web Component (**Figure 9.19**).

2. When the Insert Web Component dialog box appears, click *Dynamic Effects* in the left-hand *Component type* list, *Banner Ad Manager* in the right-hand list, and then click *Finish* (**Figure 9.20**).

(continued)

3. When the Banner Ad Manager Properties dialog box appears (**Figure 9.21**), set the dimensions for the banner images ❶.

4. Using the drop-down menu, select a *Transition effect* for moving from one image to another ❷.

5. Decide how long you want to *Show each picture for* and enter the number of seconds in the text window ❸.

6. Use the *Browse* button to select which Web page users will be linked to if they click the banner ad ❹.

7. Use the *Add* button ❻ to locate each of the images you want displayed by the banner ad ❺. Use the *Move Up* and *Move Down* buttons to rearrange the display order of the images.

8. Once you've made your choices, click *OK*, then save the page ([Ctrl][S]). The banner ad will be inserted into the Web page.

9. FrontPage can only show the banner ad's first image, so launch your Web browser to see the images actually change (**Figure 9.22**).

✔ Tips

■ By default, the Banner Ad Manager is set to show each image for 5 seconds but that's often a tad slow—3 seconds sets a better pace. Experiment to find what's best for your particular images.

■ You can freely mix JPEGs and GIFs in your banner ad's rotation of images.

■ You cannot link each image to a separate Web page. Every image in a banner ad must link to the same page.

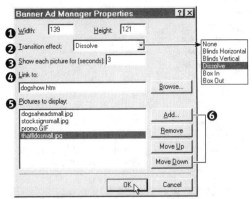

Figure 9.21 Use the Banner Ad Manager Properties dialog box to set the ad's size, transition from one image to another, and images used.

Figure 9.22 FrontPage can only display a banner ad's first image (top); switch to your Web browser to see the full image rotation (bottom).

Figure 9.23
To change a banner ad, right-click it and choose *Banner Ad Manager Properties*.

To change a banner ad

1. Right-click the banner and choose *Banner Ad Manager Properties* from the shortcut menu (**Figure 9.23**).

2. When the Banner Ad Manager Properties dialog box appears, choose another transition effect, add or remove images, and rearrange the image order (**Figure 9.21**).

3. When you're satisfied with the changes, click *OK*, and save the page (Ctrl S).

4. To see the banner changes, switch to your Web browser and open the Web page.

To delete a banner ad

◆ Right-click the banner, and choose *Cut* from the shortcut menu. The banner will be deleted.

USING BANNER ADS

To add a page hit counter

1. Switch to page view, and click in the page where you want the counter to appear.

2. Choose Insert > Web Component.

3. When the Insert Web Component dialog box appears, click *Hit Counter* in the left-hand *Component type* list, choose a counter style in the right-hand list, and then click *Finish* (**Figure 9.24**).

4. When the Hit Counter Properties dialog box appears (**Figure 9.25**), check *Reset counter to* and enter a number in the text window if you want the counter to start with a particular number.

5. Check *Fixed number of digits* if you want the counter to roll back to zero when it reaches 10, 100, 1,000, or whatever.

6. Once you've made your choices, click *OK*. A hit counter placeholder will appear on your page, but you will not see the actual counter until you publish the site (**Figure 9.26**).

✔ Tip

■ The hit counter only works if FrontPage's extensions have been installed on your Web server. Check with the server administrator to be sure. Most Internet Service Providers, such as EarthLink, will install the extensions if asked.

Figure 9.24 To add a page hit counter, choose *Hit Counter* in the left-hand *Component type* list and choose a counter style in the right-hand list.

Figure 9.25 Use the Hit Counter Properties dialog box to pick a *Counter Style* or *Custom Picture*.

Figure 9.26 After you add a hit counter, a placeholder will appear on the page. The actual counter won't show until you publish the site.

Figure 9.27
To change a hit counter, right-click it and choose *FrontPage Component Properties*.

To change a hit counter

1. Right-click the counter and choose *FrontPage Component Properties* from the shortcut menu (**Figure 9.27**).

2. When the Hit Counter Properties dialog box appears, change the *Counter Style*, reset the counter, or limit the number of digits (**Figure 9.25**).

3. When you're satisfied with the changes, click *OK*, and save the page ((Ctrl)(S)).

To delete a hit counter

◆ Make sure you're in page view, right-click the counter, and choose *Cut* from the shortcut menu. The counter will be deleted.

USING HIT COUNTERS

To add a marquee

1. Switch to page view and click in the page where you want the marquee to appear.

2. Choose Insert > Web Component.

3. When the Insert Web Component dialog box appears, click *Dynamic Effects* in the left-hand *Component type* list, choose *Marquee* in the right-hand list, and then click *Finish* (**Figure 9.28**).

4. When the Marquee Properties dialog box appears, enter the text you want displayed in the marquee; set its direction, speed, behavior, and alignment; its size; how often it should repeat; and the background color (**Figure 9.29**). For details, see *Marquee options* on the next page.

5. Once you've made your choices, click *OK*, then save the page (⌈Ctrl⌉⌈S⌉). The marquee will be inserted into the Web page.

6. To see how the marquee looks and decide if it needs adjustment, click FrontPage's *Preview* tab (**Figure 9.30**). To edit the marquee, see *To change a marquee* on page 244.

Figure 9.28 To add a marquee, choose *Dynamic Effects* in the left-hand *Component type* list and *Marquee* in the right-hand list.

Figure 9.29 Use the Marquee Properties dialog box to enter the display text and control its motion and appearance.

Figure 9.30 Click the *Preview* tab to see if the marquee needs adjusting.

Marquee options

To reach the Marquee Properties dialog box (**Figure 9.29**), see *To add a marquee* or right-click an existing marquee and choose *Marquee Properties* from the shortcut menu.

❶ **Text:** Type in the message you want the marquee to display.

❷ **Direction:** By default, *Left* will be selected since Western languages are read left to right. Choose *Right* for languages that read right to left.

❸ **Speed:** The marquee's speed is controlled by two factors. *Delay* sets how *often* (in milliseconds) the marquee moves. *Amount* controls the *distance* (in pixels) the marquee moves each time. Experiment with both settings to find the best speed.

❹ **Behavior:** The difference between *Scroll* and *Slide* is subtle and only appears at the end of your text message (**Figure 9.31**). With *Scroll*, the message keeps moving until the marquee is *blank*, then the message repeats. With *Slide*, the marquee is never blank. *Alternate* switches from *Scroll* to *Slide* after each sequence.

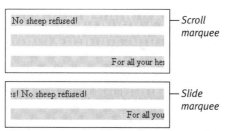

Figure 9.31 A subtle difference: marquee *scroll* (top sequence) leaves the marquee blank before the text begins again; marquee *slide* does not.

❺ **Size:** Set the *Width* and *Height* of the marquee in pixels or as a percent of the browser window.

❻ **Repeat:** Set the marquee to run *Continuously* or use the text window or arrows to set a limited number of repetitions.

❼ **Background color:** Use the drop-down menu to choose a marquee color. Since the text is always black, choose a lighter color for good contrast.

❽ **Style:** This button can only be used if you've created style sheets for your Web site. See *Building Style Sheets and Dynamic Effects* on page 335.

To change a marquee

1. Right-click the marquee and choose *Marquee Properties* from the shortcut menu ((Alt)(Enter)) (**Figure 9.32**).

2. When the Marquee Properties dialog box appears (**Figure 9.29**), make your changes to the marquee, and click *OK*.

3. Save the page ((Ctrl)(S)) and the changes will be applied to the marquee.

4. To see the changes, click the *Preview* tab.

✔ Tip

■ If you just need to resize the marquee, don't bother with the Marquee Properties dialog box. Instead, click on the marquee while in page view and drag any of its handles to resize the marquee's text area (**Figure 9.33**).

To delete a marquee

◆ Make sure you're in page view, right-click the marquee, and choose *Cut* from the shortcut menu. The marquee will be deleted.

Figure 9.32 To change a marquee, right-click it and choose *Marquee Properties*.

For all your herding needs

Figure 9.33 To resize a marquee, click and drag any of its handles.

Figure 9.34 To add a table of contents, choose *Table of Contents* in the left-hand *Component type* list and *For This Web Site* in the right-hand list.

Figure 9.35 If you want another page to be the starting point for a table of contents, click *Browse* and navigate to that page.

Adding a Web site table of contents

FrontPage includes a component that makes it relatively easy to build a dynamically updated table of contents for your Web site. This acts like a map of your Web site, offering a helpful way for visitors to find what they need.

To add a table of contents

1. Create a new Web page on which to display the table of contents, then choose Insert > Web Component.

2. When the Insert Web Component dialog box appears, click *Table of Contents* in the left-hand *Component type* list, choose *For This Web Site* in the right-hand list, and then click *Finish* (**Figure 9.34**).

3. When the Table of Contents Properties dialog box appears, it will list the index page for the site by default as the *Page URL for starting point of table* (**Figure 9.35**). If you want another page to be the starting point for the table, click *Browse* and navigate to that page.

(continued)

4. Adjust the *Heading font size* if desired, then check which *Options* you want used. By default, *Show each page only once* and *Show pages with no incoming hyperlinks* are checked. If you want the table of contents automatically updated as you change the site, also check *Recompute table of contents when any other page is edited.*

5. Click *OK* and a placeholder table of contents will appear on your Web page (**Figure 9.36**). Choose File > Preview in Browser and the actual table of contents will appear (**Figure 9.37**).

✔ Tips

■ You also can build a table of contents using page categories by choosing *Based on Page Category* from the right-hand list in step 2. For more information on using categories, see *Organizing Files* on page 364.

■ To change the particular properties of a table of contents, right-click the table and choose *Table of Contents Properties* from the shortcut menu (**Figure 9.38**). Make your changes when the Table of Contents Properties dialog box appears.

Figure 9.36 A placeholder table of contents appears on the Web page.

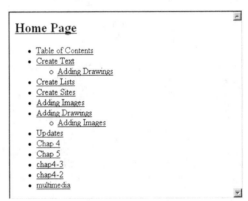

Figure 9.37 To see the actual table of contents, choose File > Preview in Browser.

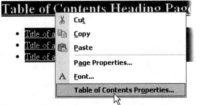

Figure 9.38 To change a table of contents, right-click the table and choose *Table of Contents Properties* from the shortcut menu.

Figure 9.39 To add a Top Ten list, choose *Top 10 List* in the left-hand *Component type* list and one of the seven choices in the right-hand list.

Figure 9.40 Use the Top 10 List Properties dialog box to choose the *List settings* and *List Style*.

Top 10 Visited Pages (August 2001)	
Name of Page	XX
Name of Page	XX
Name of Page	XX
Name of Page	XX
Name of Page	XX
Name of Page	XX
Name of Page	XX
Name of Page	XX
Name of Page	XX
Name of Page	XX

Figure 9.41 Until you actually publish a Web site, a place-holder table appears on the Web page.

Adding a Top Ten list

New in FrontPage 2002, the Top Ten list feature lets you share information about your Web site with your visitors. You can, for example, create a continuously updated list of the ten most visited pages on your site. In contrast, FrontPage's reporting features (see page 359) are available only to members of your publishing team.

To create a Top Ten list

1. Create a new Web page on which to display the list, then choose Insert > Web Component.

2. When the Insert Web Component dialog box appears, click *Top 10 List* in the left-hand *Component type* list, choose one of the seven choices in the right-hand list, and then click *Finish* (**Figure 9.39**).

3. When the Top 10 List Properties dialog box appears, type in the *Title Text* (**Figure 9.40**). Check *Include date usage processing was last run* if you want users to see just how current the list is, then choose a *List Style*.

4. Click *OK* and a placeholder list will appear on your Web page (**Figure 9.41**). To see the actual table of contents, you will have to actually publish your Web site (see page 394).

CREATING AND FORMATTING TABLES

Tables make it easy to present related text or images in a quick-to-scan form. With their rows and columns composed of individual cells, tables also lend themselves to clean-looking border and color treatments. A major plus of using tables is their consistent appearance no matter which browser Web visitors use. That's why so many commercial Web sites are designed around page-sized tables, similar to the layout grids favored by traditional paper-based designers. Rather than use a single table to build a page, how-ever, remember to use several tables. That way the top of the page will appear more quickly as the tables farther down the page are still downloading. By the way, you'll find it much quicker building tables using the Tables toolbar (**Figure 10.1**). Activate it by choosing View > Toolbars > Tables.

Figure 10.1 Using the Tables toolbar lets you bypass many of FrontPage's menu commands for building tables.

Creating Tables

FrontPage offers two main ways to create tables: one based on freehand drawing and one driven by dialog boxes. With the free-handed approach, you use a pencil-shaped cursor to draw directly in your Web page. It's straightforward and will quickly become your favorite way to handle tables. If you ever need absolute precision, however, the dialog box approach lets you create a table of pre-determined dimensions.

To draw a table

1. Switch to page view and click where you want a table placed in the page.

2. Choose Table > Draw Table or, if the Tables toolbar is active, click the Draw Table button in the Tables toolbar (**Figure 10.2**).

3. A pencil icon will appear on the page. Click and drag the pencil until the dashed box is roughly the size of the table you want, release the mouse, and a simple table will appear on the page (**Figure 10.3**).

4. To further divide the table into columns and rows, click and drag the pencil to draw in their boundaries (**Figure 10.4**).

5. To resize any part of the table, move your cursor over the cell border until the cursor becomes a two-headed arrow. Then click and drag the border until you're satisfied, release the cursor, and the table is resized (**Figure 10.5**). Double-click to switch the pencil back to an I-beam cursor.

✔ Tip

■ Unfortunately, FrontPage won't let you proportionately resize the table by grabbing one of its corners.

Figure 10.2 To draw a table directly, choose Table > Draw Table from the menu (left) or click the Draw Table button in the Tables toolbar (right).

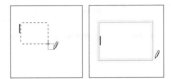

Figure 10.3 Draw a table by dragging the pencil icon across the page (left), then release the cursor (right).

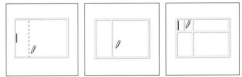

Figure 10.4 To further divide a table into columns and rows, click, drag, and release the pencil cursor.

Figure 10.5 To resize any part of a table, move the cursor until it becomes a two-headed arrow. Then click, drag, and release the cursor.

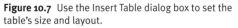

Figure 10.6 To insert a table, choose Table > Insert > Table from the menu.

Figure 10.7 Use the Insert Table dialog box to set the table's size and layout.

Figure 10.8 Black areas show changes in cell *padding*, which is the area *inside* the cells (top), versus changes in cell *spacing*, which is the area *between* cells (bottom).

Figure 10.9 For quick tables, click the Insert Table button in the Standard toolbar and drag your cursor to choose how many rows and columns you want.

To insert a table

1. Switch to page view and click where you want a table placed in the page.

2. Choose Table > Insert > Table (**Figure 10.6**).

3. When the Insert Table dialog box appears (**Figure 10.7**), use the *Size* section to set how many *Rows* and *Columns* the table should have.

4. Use the dialog box's *Layout* section to set the table's *Alignment* (left, center, or right), the *Border size* (the area around the outside of the entire table), and the *Cell padding* and *Cell spacing* (**Figure 10.8**).

5. Check *Specify width* to set the width of the entire table, and use the option buttons to choose whether the width should be absolute (*In pixels*) or relative to the width of the visitor's Web page (*In percent*).

6. Once you're done, click *OK* and the table will be inserted into your Web page.

✔ Tips

■ Whatever changes you make in the Insert Table dialog box become the *default* settings for the next time you insert a table. That's great if you're churning out copies of that same customized table but a pain if you just want a plain vanilla table. To avoid constantly monkeying with the default settings, insert a plain table. Then customize it as explained in *To format tables* on page 266.

■ For quick tables using the default settings, click the Insert Table button in the Standard toolbar and drag your cursor into the pop-up table to choose how many rows and columns you want (**Figure 10.9**). Release the cursor and a table of that size will be inserted into the page.

■ If you want a borderless table, set *Border size* to 0 in the Insert Table dialog box.

To add table text

1. If your cursor doesn't have the familiar I-beam shape, first click outside the table. Then click inside any table cell (**Figure 10.10**).

2. Start typing and the cell will grow to accommodate your text (**Figure 10.11**).

To add table images

1. If your cursor doesn't have the familiar I-beam shape, first click outside the table. Then click inside any table cell (**Figure 10.10**).

2. Click the Insert Picture From File button in either the Standard or Pictures toolbar (**Figure 10.12**).

3. When the Picture dialog box appears, navigate to the image you want inserted (**Figure 10.13**). For details, see *Adding Images* on page 164.

4. Click *Insert* and the image will be inserted into the table cell, which will expand to accommodate its size (**Figure 10.14**).

✔ Tip

■ FrontPage includes what it calls AutoFit to automatically fit any material inserted into a cell. First, make sure the Tables toolbar is active, then after you've inserted an item, click the AutoFit to Contents button (**Figure 10.15**).

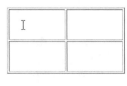

Figure 10.10 To add table text, just click inside a table cell.

Figure 10.11 As you type, the cell grows to accommodate your text.

Figure 10.12 To add images to a table, click the Insert Picture From File button.

Figure 10.13 Use the Picture dialog box to navigate to the image you want inserted in the table.

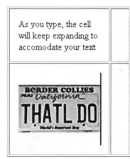

Figure 10.14 When a picture is inserted, the table cell expands to hold it.

Figure 10.15 If material inserted into a cell doesn't fit, click the AutoFit to Contents button in the Tables toolbar.

Figure 10.16 To add a caption, click inside the table and choose Table > Insert > Caption from the menu.

Figure 10.17 By default, captions are centered at the top of tables.

Figure 10.18 Use the Caption Properties dialog box to reposition captions beneath tables.

To add table captions

1. Click anywhere inside the table and choose Table > Insert > Caption (**Figure 10.16**).

2. When the cursor appears, it will be centered at the top of the table. Type in your caption (**Figure 10.17**).

3. Once you've entered the caption, you can change the font or size just like any other FrontPage text.

✔ Tip

■ You can move the caption beneath the table, by right-clicking it and choosing *Caption Properties* from the shortcut menu. When the Caption Properties dialog box appears, choose *Bottom of table* and click *OK* (**Figure 10.18**). The caption will move to the bottom.

Adding Excel spreadsheets

FrontPage offers several ways to add Excel spreadsheets to your Web pages. The first simply creates a table based on the Excel data *at the time you import it*. In other words, it's static data—not a "live" spreadsheet that's dynamically updated.

The second method actually lets you use Excel inside Web pages for entering dynamic numbers and formulas. There's a catch of course: The page's visitors must have Microsoft Office 2000 or Office XP installed on their computers, along with Microsoft's Office Web Components. Obviously, that's not much help if you're a solo worker or don't have a network administrator to handle the component installation But if you're working in a networked office across a corporate intranet, those requirements are easily met. And the payoff is being able to share—and dynamically update—Excel spreadsheets over the Web.

To add static Excel data

1. Make sure you're in page view, then click where you want the Excel data inserted into the Web page.

2. Choose Insert > File (**Figure 10.19**).

3. When the Select File dialog box appears, use the *Files of type* drop-down menu to select *Microsoft Excel Worksheet (*.xls, *.xlw)* (**Figure 10.20**).

4. Navigate to the spreadsheet you need, click *Open*, and the data will be inserted into the Web page as a borderless table (denoted by the dashed outlines) (**Figure 10.21**).

✔ Tip

■ You can easily reformat the borderless Excel-based table into something more "Webby" (**Figure 10.22**). For details, see *To format tables* on page 266.

Figure 10.19 To add static Excel data to a table, choose Insert > File.

Figure 10.20 To find Excel files, use the Select File dialog box's drop-down menu to select *Microsoft Excel Worksheets*.

creatingtables.htm			×
585	66	12	8898
62	58	44	6254
841	36	94	2187
1488	160	150	17339

Figure 10.21 Excel files inserted into FrontPage initially appear as borderless tables, denoted by the dashed outlines.

creatingtables.htm			×
585	66	12	8898
62	58	44	6254
841	36	94	2187
1488	160	150	17339

Figure 10.22 It's easy to reformat an Excel-based table into a more traditional Web-styled table.

Figure 10.23 To add dynamic Excel data, use the Insert Web Component dialog box.

Figure 10.24 A blank Excel spreadsheet inserted into the Web page can be filled in with Excel-based formulas.

Figure 10.25 To import an *existing* Excel spreadsheet into a Web page, click the blank spreadsheet's *Commands and Options* button.

Figure 10.26 Use the *Import* tab in the Commands and Options dialog box to bring existing Excel data into your FrontPage table.

To add dynamic Excel data

1. Make sure you're in page view, click where you want the Excel spreadsheet inserted into the Web page, and choose Insert > Web Component.

2. When the Insert Web Component dialog box appears, click *Spreadsheets and charts* in the left-hand *Component type* list, *Office Spreadsheet* in the right-hand list, and then click *Finish* (**Figure 10.23**). A blank Excel spreadsheet will appear inside the Web page, which can then be filled in with numbers and formulas (**Figure 10.24**).

✔ Tip

■ To import an *existing* Excel spreadsheet into the Web page you just created, click the blank spreadsheet's *Commands and Options* button (**Figure 10.25**). When the Commands and Options dialog box appears, click the *Import* tab (**Figure 10.26**). Leave the *Data type* set to *XML*, enter the spreadsheet's *URL* (or click the folder icon to browse to the file), check *Refresh data from URL at run time*, and click *Import Now*. The latest version of the data will be dumped into your blank spreadsheet.

Selecting Table Elements

Unlike many FrontPage procedures, selecting cells, rows, and columns within tables isn't always a click-and-drag affair.

To select a cell

◆ Press $\boxed{\text{Alt}}$ and click inside any cell. The cell will be selected, denoted by its colors reversing (**Figure 10.27**).

or

◆ Click anywhere in a cell and choose Table > Select > Cell (**Figure 10.28**). The cell will be selected, denoted by its colors reversing (**Figure 10.27**).

To select multiple cells

◆ To select *adjacent* cells, click and hold your cursor in a cell, then drag the cursor to select additional cells (**Figure 10.29**).

or

◆ To select *non-adjacent* cells, press $\boxed{\text{Alt}}$ and click inside any cell, then press $\boxed{\text{Alt}}$ $\boxed{\text{Shift}}$ and click another cell. Repeat until you've selected all the cells you need (**Figure 10.30**).

Figure 10.27 To select a cell, press $\boxed{\text{Alt}}$ and click inside the cell.

Figure 10.28 To select any element of a table, choose Table > Select and make a choice from the submenu.

Figure 10.29 To select *adjacent* cells, click the cursor in a cell, then drag the cursor to select additional cells.

Figure 10.30 To select *non-adjacent* cells, press $\boxed{\text{Alt}}$ and click inside any cell, then press $\boxed{\text{Alt}}$ $\boxed{\text{Shift}}$ as you select other cells.

Figure 10.31 To select a row, move the cursor up to the edge of a row (left). When it becomes a black arrow (middle), click once and the row will be selected (right).

To select a row

◆ Click anywhere in a row and choose Table > Select > Row (**Figure 10.28**). The row will be selected.

or

◆ Click and hold your cursor anywhere in a row, then drag the cursor to select the rest of the cells in the row.

or

◆ Move the cursor slowly up to the left edge of a row until it becomes an arrow, then click once. The row will be selected (**Figure 10.31**).

To select a column

◆ Click anywhere in a column and choose Table > Select > Column (**Figure 10.28**). The column will be selected.

or

◆ Click and hold your cursor anywhere in a column, then drag the cursor to select the rest of the cells in the column.

or

◆ Move the cursor slowly up to the left edge of a column until it becomes an arrow, then click once. The column will be selected.

To select an entire table

◆ Click anywhere in a table and choose Table > Select > Table (**Figure 10.28**). The entire table will be selected.

or

◆ Click your cursor at the table's upper-left or lower-right corner and, while keeping the mouse pressed, drag the cursor to select the entire table.

SELECTING TABLE ELEMENTS

Changing Table Structure

With FrontPage you can go back and expand a table at any time, whether it's by adding a single cell, a row or column, or even inserting another table into the table.

To add cells

1. Click in the cell to the right of where you want to add a cell (**Figure 10.32**).

2. Choose Table > Insert > Cell (**Figure 10.33**).

3. A single cell will be inserted into the table just left of the cell selected in step 1 (**Figure 10.34**).

✔ Tip

■ Adding or deleting single cells in a table can produce a strangely shaped table. So what's the point? Well, if you're using tables to design Web *pages*, this ability might give you just the shape or design you need. The moral: Experiment!

Shiprock	Jemez	Tres Piedras
Lumbre	Rio Grande	Tucumcari
Mogollon	Hatch	Kiowa

Figure 10.32 Click in the cell to the *right* of where you want to add a cell.

Figure 10.33 To add any element of a table, choose Table > Insert and make a choice from the submenu.

Shiprock	Jemez	Tres Piedras	
Lumbre	I	Rio Grande	Tucumcari
Mogollon	Hatch	Kiowa	

Figure 10.34 A single cell is inserted into the table left of the cell selected in Figure 10.32.

Shiprock	Jemez	Tres Piedras
Lumbre	Rio Grande	Tucumcari
Mogollon	Hatch	Kiowa

Figure 10.35 Select the row next to where you want to insert a new row.

Figure 10.36 If the Tables toolbar is active, you also can add rows by clicking the Insert Rows button.

Figure 10.37 Use the Insert Rows or Columns dialog box to set how many rows you want added.

Shiprock	Jemez	Tres Piedras
Lumbre	Rio Grande	Tucumcari
Mogollon	Hatch	Kiowa

Figure 10.38 A new row inserted into the table will be blank.

Figure 10.39 To quickly add rows, right-click and choose *Insert Rows* from the shortcut menu.

To add rows

1. Select a row next to where you want to insert a new row (**Figure 10.35**).

2. Choose Table > Insert, then choose Row or Columns from the submenu (**Figure 10.33**). Or, if the Tables toolbar is active, click the Insert Rows button (**Figure 10.36**).

3. When the Insert Rows or Columns dialog box appears, *Rows* will already be selected (**Figure 10.37**). Use the text window or arrows to choose the *Number of rows* you want to add and decide whether to add the rows above or below the row selected in step 1.

4. Click *OK* and the row(s) will be inserted into the table (**Figure 10.38**).

✔ Tip

■ You also can select a row, right-click, and choose *Insert Rows* from the shortcut menu (**Figure 10.39**). When the Insert Rows or Columns dialog box appears, follow steps 3 and 4.

To add columns

1. Select a column next to where you want to insert a new column (**Figure 10.40**).

2. Choose Table > Insert, then choose Row or Columns from the submenu (**Figure 10.33**). Or, if the Tables toolbar is active, click the Insert Columns button (**Figure 10.41**).

3. When the Insert Rows or Columns dialog box appears, *Columns* will already be selected (**Figure 10.42**). Use the text window or arrows to choose the *Number of columns* you want to add and decide whether to add the columns to the left or right of the column selected in step 1.

4. Click *OK* and the column(s) will be inserted into the table (**Figure 10.43**).

✔ Tip

■ You also can select a column, right-click, and choose *Insert Columns* from the shortcut menu (**Figure 10.44**). When the Insert Rows or Columns dialog box appears, follow steps 3 and 4.

Figure 10.40 Select the column next to where you want to insert a new column.

Figure 10.41 If the Tables toolbar is active, you also can add columns by clicking the Insert Columns button.

Figure 10.42 Use the Insert Rows or Columns dialog box to set how many columns you want added.

Figure 10.43 A new column inserted into the table will be blank.

Figure 10.44 To quickly add columns, right-click and choose *Insert Columns* from the shortcut menu.

Figure 10.45 To delete any part of a table, select it and choose Table > Delete Cells from the menu (left) or click the Delete Cells button (right).

Figure 10.46 To quickly remove any table element, select it, right-click and choose *Cut*.

To delete any part of a table

1. Select the parts of the table you want to delete, whether it's a cell, a single row, or several rows or columns.

2. Choose Table > Delete Cells, or if the Tables toolbar is active, click the Delete Cells button (**Figure 10.45**). All the selected cells will be deleted.

✔ Tip

■ For even faster deletion, select any part of the table, right-click and choose *Cut* from the shortcut menu (**Figure 10.46**).

Splitting and merging cells

While it's easy to add or delete parts of a table, sometimes you'll want to create or delete an individual cell and not affect the overall dimensions of the rest of the table. That's where the ability to split a cell into two cells, or merge several cells into a single cell, becomes especially handy. You can, for example, create a large cell in the center of a table by merging several adjacent cells and avoid messing up anything else in the table.

To split cells

1. Click inside the cell you want to split.

2. Choose Table > Split Cells (**Figure 10.47**) or if the Tables toolbar is active, click the Split Cells button (right, **Figure 10.48**).

3. When the Split Cells dialog box appears, choose whether you want the selected cell divided horizontally into rows or vertically into columns (**Figure 10.49**).

4. Use the arrows or enter numbers directly in the text window to set the *Number of rows* or *Number of columns* you want the cell split into. When you're done, click *OK* and the cell will be split.

✔ Tip

■ The fastest way to split a cell is simply to right-click inside it, choose *Split Cells* from the shortcut menu, and follow steps 3 and 4, above.

Figure 10.47 To split a cell, click inside it and choose Table > Split Cells.

Figure 10.48 If the Tables toolbar is active, you also can combine cells with the Merge Cells button or split them with the Split Cells button.

Figure 10.49 Use the Split Cells dialog box to divide a cell vertically into columns or horizontally into rows.

Figure 10.50 To merge cells, select them and choose Table > Merge Cells.

Figure 10.51 The Eraser button in the Tables toolbar offers a quick way to merge cells.

Figure 10.52 Drag the eraser-shaped cursor across a cell border until it's highlighted, release the mouse, and the border disappears.

To merge cells

1. Select the cells you want merged.

2. Choose Table > Merge Cells (**Figure 10.50**) or if the Tables toolbar is active, click the Merge Cells button (left, **Figure 10.48**). The selected cells will be combined into a single cell.

✔ Tips

■ Akin to the freehand Pencil button, the Tables toolbar's Eraser button offers a quick way to merge cells (**Figure 10.51**). Click the button, press and drag your now eraser-shaped cursor across a cell border until it's highlighted, and then release the mouse. The border will disappear (**Figure 10.52**). To deactivate the eraser, double-click anywhere outside the table.

■ You also can expand a cell by increasing its span, explained in *To format cells* on page 268.

Evening up rows and columns

Inevitably as you work on a table things get messy. Fortunately, FrontPage offers a way to tidy things up by making all your rows the same height or all your columns the same width. The process, by the way, initially seems a bit backward because you select a *column* to even up the *row* height and select a *row* to even up the *column* width.

To make rows the same height

1. Select a *column* containing a cell from each uneven *row* (**Figure 10.53**).

2. Choose Table > Distribute Rows Evenly (left, **Figure 10.54**). If the Tables toolbar is active, you also can click the Distribute Rows Evenly button (left, **Figure 10.55**). The height of the rows will be evened up (**Figure 10.56**).

Figure 10.53 To make rows the same height, select a *column* containing a cell from each uneven row.

Figure 10.54 To even up a table, choose Table > Distribute Rows Evenly (left) or Table > Distribute Columns Evenly.

Figure 10.55 If the Tables toolbar is active, you also can even up a table with the Distribute Rows Evenly button (left) or the Distribute Columns Evenly button (right).

Figure 10.56 Once evened up, the rows will have the same height.

Figure 10.57 To make columns the same width, select a *row* containing a cell from each uneven column.

Figure 10.58 Once evened up, all the columns will have the same width.

To make columns the same width

1. Select a *row* containing a cell from each uneven *column* (**Figure 10.57**).

2. Choose Table > Distribute Columns Evenly (right, **Figure 10.54**). If the Tables toolbar is active, you also can click the Distribute Columns Evenly button (right, **Figure 10.55**). The width of the columns will be evened up (**Figure 10.58**).

✔ Tip

- If the Tables toolbar is active and you want to tidy up a whole table at once, select all of it. That will activate the Distribute Rows Evenly button *and* the Distribute Columns Evenly button, allowing you to click one button right after the other without bothering to make a second selection.

Formatting Tables and Cells

Once you've added a table to your page, put some text and images into it, and perhaps changed its structure, you're ready for the final step: formatting the full table and individual cells.

To format tables

1. Right-click the table and choose *Table Properties* from the shortcut menu (**Figure 10.59**).

2. When the Table Properties dialog box appears (**Figure 10.60**), use the *Layout* section to set the table's *Alignment*, width, and the *Cell padding* and *Cell spacing* (**Figure 10.8**). The *Float* drop-down menu lets you have the table "float" on the left or right side of text that ordinarily would appear below the table (**Figure 10.61**).

3. Use the dialog box's *Borders* section to set the table's border. For details, see *To format table borders* on the next page.

4. If you want to apply the same color to every cell in the table, use the pop-up box in the Background section to choose your color. For details, see *To color cells* on page 270.

5. Once you're done, click *OK* and the changes will be applied to your table.

Figure 10.59
To format a table, right-click it and choose *Table Properties*.

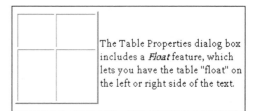

Figure 10.60 Use the Layout section of the Table Properties dialog box to set the table's *Alignment*, width, and the *Cell padding* and *Cell spacing*.

The Table Properties dialog box includes a *Float* feature, which lets you have the table "float" on the left or right side of the text.

Figure 10.61 The Table Properties dialog box *Float* drop-down menu lets you have the table "float" on the left or right side of text.

Borders

| Size: | 10 | Light border: | ■ Automatic |
| Color: | | Dark border: | ■ Automatic |

585	66	12	8898
841	36	94	2187
1488	160	150	17339

Figure 10.62 To create a single-color border, use the *Color* pop-up box and leave the *Light border* and *Dark border* pop-up boxes set to *Automatic*.

Borders

| Size: | 10 | Light border: | |
| Color: | ■ Automatic | Dark border: | |

585	66	12	8898
841	36	94	2187
1488	160	150	17339

Figure 10.63 To create a two-color 3D effect, use the *Light border* and *Dark border* pop-up boxes.

Table AutoFormat

Table AutoFormat

Formats:
None
Simple 1
Simple 2
Simple 3
Classic 1
Classic 2
Classic 3
Classic 4
Colorful 1

Preview

	Jan	Feb	Mar	Total
East	7	7	5	19
West	6	4	7	17
South	8	7	9	24
Total	21	18	21	60

Formats to apply
☑ Borders ☑ Font ☐ AutoFit
☑ Shading ☑ Color

Apply special formats
☑ Heading rows ☐ Last row
☑ First Column ☐ Last Column

OK   Cancel

Figure 10.64 Click the Table AutoFormat icon to preview the preformatted table choices.

None
None
Simple 1
Simple 2
Classic 1
Classic 2
Colorful 1
Colorful 2
Column 1

Figure 10.65
Click the drop-down menu in the Tables toolbar to quickly reach Table AutoFormats.

To format table borders

1. Select the table to which you want borders applied, then right-click and choose *Table Properties* from the shortcut menu (**Figure 10.59**).

2. When the Table Properties dialog box appears (**Figure 10.60**), use the *Borders* section to set the *Size* (width) of your border. The larger the number, the wider the border. For a borderless table, set the number at 0.

3. If you want a single-color border, use the *Color* pop-up box to pick a color and leave the *Light border* and *Dark border* pop-up boxes set to *Automatic* (top, **Figure 10.62**).

   If you want a two-color 3D effect, use the *Light border* and *Dark border* pop-up boxes to pick your colors (top, **Figure 10.63**).

4. Once you've set the width and color, click *OK* and the border will be applied (bottom, **Figures 10.62** and **10.63**).

✔ Tips

- If you use the two-color 3D effect, it will automatically appear instead of whatever single color you set.

- Use the Table AutoFormat icon in the Tables toolbar to preview and modify a variety of preformatted table settings (**Figure 10.64**). Once you learn the names of the preformatted choices, you can reach them directly by clicking the drop-down menu next to the Table AutoFormat button (**Figure 10.65**).

FORMATTING TABLES AND CELLS

267

To format cells

1. Select the cell or cells, then right-click and choose *Cell Properties* from the shortcut menu (**Figure 10.66**).

2. When the Cell Properties dialog box appears (**Figure 10.67**), use the *Layout* section to change the alignment and size of the selected cell.

3. Check *Specify width* and *Specify height* if you want to set the cell's dimensions. Choose *In pixels* to make either dimension absolute or *In percent* to make it relative to the size of the viewer's Web browser window.

4. If you want to have the selected cell span more than one row, enter a number in the *Rows spanned* window. To have the cell span more than one column, enter a number in the *Columns spanned* window.

5. Click *OK* and the changes will be applied to the selected cell(s).

✔ Tips

- While the Cell Properties dialog box offers the option of setting border colors for individual cells, it's more effective visually to adjust borders for an entire table. For details, see *To format table borders* on page 267.

- For details on the dialog box's *Background* section, see *To color cells* on page 270.

Figure 10.66
To format cells, select them, right-click, and choose *Cell Properties*.

Figure 10.67 Use the Cell Properties dialog box to change a cell's alignment, size, and span.

August	Sept.	Oct.	Nov.
585	66	12	8898
62	58	44	6254

Figure 10.68 Select the cell or cells you want to turn into header cells.

August	**Sept.**	**Oct.**	**Nov.**
585	66	12	8898
62	58	44	6254

Figure 10.69 Once you've made cells into headers, the text in the selected cell(s) will be boldfaced.

August 1999	**Sept. 1999**	**Oct. 1999**	**Nov. 1999**
585	66	12	8898
62	58	44	6254

Figure 10.70 To keep cell text on one line, select the text that's wrapping to the next line.

August 1999	Sept. 1999	Oct. 1999	Nov. 1999
585	66	12	8898
62	58	44	6254

Figure 10.71 After No wrap is applied, the text in the selected cell(s) will rewrap to a single line.

Making cells into headers

Header cells typically act as labels for rows or columns within a table. FrontPage makes the text in header cells boldfaced.

To make cells into headers

1. Make sure you're in page view, then select the cell or cells you want as headers (**Figure 10.68**).

2. Right-click and choose *Cell Properties* from the shortcut menu ((Alt)(Enter)) (**Figure 10.66**).

3. When the Cell Properties dialog box appears (**Figure 10.67**), check *Header cell* in the *Layout* section.

4. Click *OK* and the text in the selected cell(s) will become a header, indicated by its boldfaced text (**Figure 10.69**).

To keep cell text on one line

1. Make sure you're in page view, then select the cell or cells with text that's wrapping to the next line (**Figure 10.70**).

2. Right-click and choose *Cell Properties* from the shortcut menu ((Alt)(Enter)) (**Figure 10.66**).

3. When the Cell Properties dialog box appears (**Figure 10.67**), check *No wrap* in the *Layout* section. Line wrapping is the default.

4. Click *OK* and the text in the selected cell(s) will rewrap to a single line (**Figure 10.71**).

FORMATTING TABLES AND CELLS

To color cells

1. Make sure you're in page view and that the Tables toolbar is activated.

2. Select a cell by clicking inside the cell while pressing (Alt).

3. Click and hold the cursor on the arrow next to the paint bucket-shaped Fill Color button. When the pop-up box of colors appears, keep pressing your cursor and move to the color of your choice (left, **Figure 10.72**). Release the cursor and the fill color will be applied to the selected cell.

✔ Tips

- If your fill color is already set to what you want—denoted by the color bar just below the Fill Color button and the pop-up tag (right, **Figure 10.72**), follow steps 1 and 2 above, and then click the button once to fill the cell.

- You also can color a cell by right-clicking it and using the *Background* section of the Cell Properties dialog box (**Figure 10.73**). Click the *Color* arrow to reach a pop-up box of possible colors. Check *Use background picture* and click *Browse* if you want to drop a graphic into the cell. Click *OK* and the changes will be applied to the cell.

Figure 10.72 Left: To add color to a selected cell, click the arrow next to the paint bucket-shaped button and move the cursor to the color of your choice. Right: To fill with the default color—in this case, fuchsia—just click the Fill Color button.

Figure 10.73 You also can color a cell by right-clicking it and using the *Background* section of the Cell Properties dialog box.

Figure 10.74 To align the contents to the top or bottom of the cell, click the respective button in the Tables toolbar.

Figure 10.75 To align the contents equidistant from the cell's top and bottom, click the Center Vertically button.

Figure 10.76 To realign the cell contents *horizontally*, click any of the four alignment buttons in the Formatting toolbar.

To realign cell contents

1. Make sure the Tables and Formatting toolbars are active, then click inside the cell you want realigned.

2. If you want to realign the contents *vertically*, click any of the three alignment buttons in the Tables toolbar (**Figures 10.74** and **10.75**). The changes will be applied to the cell.

3. If you want to realign the contents *horizontally*, click any of the four alignment buttons in the Formatting toolbar (**Figure 10.76**). The changes will be applied to the cell.

✔ Tip

■ You also can realign a cell's contents using the Cell Properties dialog box as explained in *To format cells* on page 268.

CREATING AND FORMATTING FRAMES

Figure 11.1 Left: Each of the four thumbnails contains one darkened *frame*. Right: Collectively, all the frames make up a *frames page*.

One of the big advantages of creating frame-based pages is that you can have site-wide navigation links or buttons that remain visible in one frame even as visitors scroll around in the main frame. That's a great help in keeping visitors oriented while enabling them to easily jump to other parts of your Web site. Version 3 and later browsers support frames, by the way, so you can create frame-based pages without leaving too many folks in the dark.

Frames, however, do have several drawbacks. The page title remains the same even as visitors move from frame to frame, which sometimes creates confusion. It's also not possible for visitors to bookmark a particular frame in their Web browsers. Instead, they'll be sent to the site's home page. One way around these problems, while keeping the site's navigation clear, is to use link bars instead. For more information, see *Using Link Bars and Shared Borders* on page 60.

A couple of terms need explaining: Individual *frames* are collectively displayed in a special page called a *frames page* (**Figure 11.1**). Frames pages used to be called *framesets*, a term you'll still come across. Finally, FrontPage lets you set a hyperlink's *target frame*, which is the frame where the link's content will be displayed.

Creating Frames

Each frame you create can display a separate Web page. Whether you create those content pages before or after you create the frames themselves is up to you. Generally, however, it's less confusing to at least rough out the content pages first, then create the frames that will contain them. At that point, it's common to tweak the content for the frame. In creating frames and frames pages, sometimes it's helpful to see just the content without any frames. For details, see *To show a frame in a new window* on page 274.

A frames page can contain as many frames as you like. Bear in mind, however, that each page and its content must be downloaded, increasing the potential wait for your visitors. Use FrontPage's download progress indicator to gauge how long pages will take to appear on screen (see page 16).

To create a frames page

1. Make sure you're in page view, then choose File > New > Page or Web (Ctrl N) (**Figure 11.2**).

2. When the Task pane appears, click *Page Templates* (**Figure 11.3**).

3. When the Page Templates dialog box appears, click the *Frames Pages* tab (**Figure 11.4**). Use the dialog box's *Preview* area to choose a frames page template and click *OK*. A blank frames page, based on the template, will appear with each frame offering two choices: *Set Initial Page* and *New Page* (**Figure 11.5**).

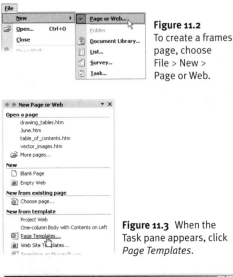

Figure 11.2 To create a frames page, choose File > New > Page or Web.

Figure 11.3 When the Task pane appears, click *Page Templates*.

Figure 11.4 Click the *Frames Pages* tab in the Page Templates dialog box to reach a collection of frames page templates.

Figure 11.5 A new blank frames page offers two choices in each frame: *Set Initial Page* for linking to an existing page and *New Page* for creating a page from scratch.

Figure 11.6 To link a frame to an existing page, use the Insert Hyperlink dialog box to navigate to the page.

Figure 11.7 Once you link an existing page to a frame, the page will appear in the frame.

Figure 11.8 If you choose *New Page* in setting up a frame, a blank page will appear—allowing you to start creating content.

4. To link a frame to an *existing* page on your Web site, click *Set Initial Page*. When the Insert Hyperlink dialog box appears (**Figure 11.6**), navigate to the page you want to use and click *OK*. The existing page will appear in the frame (**Figure 11.7**). For details on using the Insert Hyperlink dialog box, see page 138.

To create a *new* page from scratch for the frame, click *New Page*. A blank page based on the Normal template will appear within the frame (**Figure 11.8**). You then can begin adding content to the frame.

(continued)

5. Press Ctrl S to save any new frame and the *frames page* itself. If you've created a brand new page for any of your frames, that page will be the first to appear in the Save As dialog box (**Figure 11.9**).

6. Give the new page a distinct name and title, then click *Save*. The new page will be saved and a new Save As dialog box will appear for saving the entire frames page, denoted by a heavy blue border surrounding the full page in the preview window (**Figure 11.10**).

7. Give the frames page a distinct name and title, then click *Save*. The frames page will be saved.

Figure 11.9 If you've created a brand new page for any frame, that page's frame will be highlighted in the Save As dialog box's preview area.

Figure 11.10 When you save a frames page, the entire page is highlighted in the Save As dialog box's preview area.

Figure 11.11 To show a frame in a full-sized window, right-click the frame and choose *Open Page in New Window* from the shortcut menu.

To show a frame in a new window

◆ Right-click in the frame and choose *Open Page in New Window* from the shortcut menu (**Figure 11.11**). The content of the frame will expand to a full-size window, replacing your view of the frames page.

✔ Tip

■ If you want to return to the frames page, make sure the Folder List is visible and double-click the frames page file. The frames page will become visible in FrontPage's main window once more.

Setting target frames

In general, FrontPage will automatically set the large, main frame as the target for links clicked in, say, a left-hand table of contents frame. FrontPage, however, gives you a way to directly set any frame as the target of a link.

You won't need to mess with changing the default target frame, because FrontPage usually gets it right based on the context of the rest of the page's frames. But if you need to, see *To change the target frame default* on page 280.

To set a link's target frame

1. Right-click the link for which you want to set a target frame and choose *Hyperlink* from the shortcut menu ((Alt)(Enter)) (**Figure 11.12**).

2. When the Insert Hyperlink dialog box appears, make sure the link's *Address* is correct. If not, change it.

3. If you're happy with the link address, click the *Target Frame* button (**Figure 11.13**). When the Target Frame dialog box appears, you'll see that the *Target setting* text box says *main*, which is the main frame of the current page (**Figure 11.14**).

Figure 11.12 To set a target frame for a link, right-click it and choose *Hyperlink* from the shortcut menu.

Figure 11.13 Click the *Target Frame* button in the Insert Hyperlink dialog box to set or change the target frame.

Figure 11.14 Use the Target Frame dialog box to change your link's targeted frame.

Figure 11.15 Clicking the top frame in the *Current frames page* pastes its name into the *Target setting* text window.

Figure 11.16 When clicked (top), the *Drums* link content replaces the Two Ravens Trading logo in the targeted frame (bottom).

Figure 11.17 You can check what's listed as the *Target Frame* at the bottom of the Insert Hyperlink dialog box.

4. To change the setting, either click a frame in the *Current frames page* thumbnail or click a listing in the *Common targets* window. The frame's name will be pasted into the *Target setting* text window (**Figure 11.15**). For details, see *Target Frame options* on page 281.

5. Click *OK* and when the Insert Hyperlink dialog box reappears, click *OK* again.

6. To check the link target, click the *Preview* tab in FrontPage's main window (top, **Figure 11.16**). When clicked, the link selected in step 1 will now display its linked page in the selected target (bottom, **Figure 11.16**).

✔ Tip

- Much of the time, FrontPage will automatically assign the correct frame as the target. Just check which frame is listed as the *Target Frame* at the bottom of the Insert Hyperlink dialog box (**Figure 11.17**).

SETTING TARGET FRAMES

To change the target frame default

1. Make sure you're in page view, then right-click anywhere in the page and choose *Page Properties* from the shortcut menu (**Figure 11.18**).

2. When the Page Properties dialog box appears, click the *General* tab, then click the Change Target Frame button (**Figure 11.19**).

3. When the Target Frame dialog box appears (**Figure 11.20**), either click a frame in the *Current frames page* thumbnail or click a listing in the *Common targets* window. The frame's name will be pasted into the *Target setting* text window. For details, see *Target Frame options* on the next page.

4. Click *OK*, and when the Page Properties dialog box reappears, the target frame's name will be pasted into the *Default target frame* text box.

5. Click *OK* again and that frame will become the page's default target.

Figure 11.18 To change the target frame default, right-click the page and choose *Page Properties* from the shortcut menu.

Figure 11.19 When the Page Properties dialog box appears, click the *General* tab, then click the Change Target Frame button.

Figure 11.20 Use the Target Frame dialog box to change your link's targeted frame.

Figure 11.21 If you use *Same Frame* as your target frame, clicking the link will replace its frame with the link's content.

Figure 11.22 Left: If you use *Whole Page* as your target, clicking the link replaces the entire frames page. Right: Using *New Window* instead opens another window, leaving the frames page undisturbed.

Target Frame options

To reach the Target Frame dialog box (**Figure 11.20**), right-click a link in a frame, then click the *Target Frame* button in the Insert Hyperlink dialog box.

❶ **Current frames page:** Click any frame in the thumbnail to make it the frame where the link's content will be displayed.

❷ **Common targets:** Click any of these listings, which supplement those in the *Current frames page*.

 Page Default (main): With this option chosen, clicking a link will display its content in the frame designated as the default page—in this example, the main frame of the current frame page.

 Same Frame: With this option, clicking a link in a frame will replace *that same frame* with the linked content (**Figure 11.21**).

 Whole Page: With this option, clicking a link in a frame will replace the entire frames page with a single page showing the linked content (left, **Figure 11.22**).

 New Window: With this option, clicking a link in a frame will open up a new browser window to display the linked content (right, **Figure 11.22**). It's a good choice if you're linking a visitor to a page off your own site because your site will remain visible in the original browser window. That increases the chances the visitor will remain on your site.

 Parent Frame: This advanced option is used in creating discussion groups.

❸ **Target setting:** The text box will be filled automatically based on your choice in either the *Current frames page* or the *Common targets* list.

❹ **Set as page default:** Check this box to make *every* link in the selected page default to the selected target frame.

Setting a frames page as the home page

By default, FrontPage names your home page index.htm. If your site already has a frameless home page that you'd like to replace with a frames-based home page, you simply have to replace the old index.htm with a new one containing your frames page. (On some servers, the home page is named default.htm. The steps are the same.)

To make a frames page your home page

1. Make sure the Folder List is visible, find the index.htm file, and click it so that its name becomes highlighted (left, **Figure 11.23**).

2. Type in a new name, for example framelessindex.htm, being sure to preserve the .htm suffix (right, **Figure 11.23**).

3. Again looking in the Folder List, find the frame-based file you want to use as your home page, and click it so that its name becomes highlighted (left, **Figure 11.24**).

4. Replace its name by typing in index.htm as the file's new name (right, **Figure 11.24**). Now when FrontPage looks for the home page, it will open your frames-based page.

Figure 11.23 To make a frames page your home page, find the original home page in the Folder List (left) and rename it (right).

Figure 11.24 To finish making a frames page your home page, change the frames page's name (left) to index.htm (right).

Figure 11.25 Top: To select a *frame*, click anywhere inside it. Bottom: To select an entire *frames page*, it's easiest to click its border in the lower right.

Figure 11.26 To delete a frame, click inside the frame and choose Frames > Delete Frame.

Formatting Frames

Once you've created some frames and set targets for the links inside them, you may find yourself wanting to reformat or modify some frames. FrontPage includes options for resizing, splitting, and changing basic properties of your frames. It also lets you customize a message to help visitors whose Web browsers don't support frames.

To select a frame

◆ To select a frame, click anywhere *inside* the frame. A dark blue border will highlight the selected frame (top, **Figure 11.25**).

To select a frames page

◆ To select the whole frames page, click the page's outer border. Because the outer border is so narrow, it's easiest to find it by clicking in the bottom-right corner of the status bar. Once you click the right spot, a dark blue border will surround the frames page (bottom, **Figure 11.25**).

To delete a frame

◆ Click inside the frame you want to delete and choose Frames > Delete Frame (**Figure 11.26**). The frame will be removed *from the frames page*, although the page that had been displayed in the frame will remain part of your Web site's files.

To resize a frame

1. Make sure you're in page view, then select the frame you want to resize by clicking anywhere inside the frame.

2. Move your cursor over one of the dark blue frame borders where it will become a double-headed arrow (left, **Figure 11.27**). Click and drag the cursor to make the frame smaller or larger (right, **Figure 11.27**). When it reaches the size you want, release the cursor and the frame will be resized.

✔ Tip

■ If you need more precision in resizing a frame, right-click it, choose *Frame Properties* from the shortcut menu, and use the dialog box's *Frame size* area to enter numerical values.

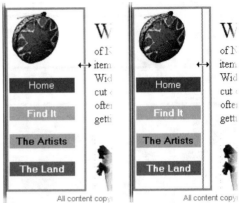

Figure 11.27 To resize a frame, move your cursor over a frame border until it becomes a double-headed arrow (left), then click and drag to make the frame smaller or larger (right).

Figure 11.28 Before a frame is split (left) and afterward (right).

Figure 11.29 To split a frame, choose Frames > Split Frame.

Splitting frames

You can split frames as a quick way to add another frame to an existing frames page.

To split a frame

1. Click inside the frame you want split (left, **Figure 11.28**).

2. Choose Frames > Split Frame (**Figure 11.29**).

3. When the Split Frame dialog box appears, choose whether you want to divide the frame vertically into columns or horizontally into rows (**Figure 11.30**). Click *OK* and the frame will be split into two equal-sized frames (right, **Figure 11.28**).

✔ Tips

- An even faster way to split a frame is to click and drag its border while pressing Ctrl.

- If the frame you split didn't have a scroll-bar initially, you may need to add one to see all its contents. For details, see *Frame Properties options* on page 287.

Figure 11.30 The Split Frame dialog box offers the choice of dividing a frame vertically into columns or horizontally into rows.

To change frames

1. Right-click the frame you want to change and choose *Frame Properties* from the shortcut menu (**Figure 11.31**).

2. When the Frame Properties dialog box appears (**Figure 11.32**), set the frame's name, size, and margins.

3. FrontPage will have assigned the frame a name based on its position (e.g., top, left, center). Type in a new *Name* if you like.

4. Use the dialog box's *Options* section to restrict the user's ability to resize the frame. You also can turn on or off scrollbars for the selected frame.

5. When you're done, click *OK* and the changes will be applied to the selected frame.

To change spacing or borders in frames pages

1. Right-click anywhere in the frames page and choose *Frame Properties* from the shortcut menu (**Figure 11.31**).

2. When the Frame Properties dialog box appears (**Figure 11.32**), click *Frames Page* in the lower right.

3. When the Page Properties dialog box appears, click the *Frames* tab (**Figure 11.33**).

4. Type a number directly into the *Frame Spacing* text window or use the arrows to change the distance *between* the page's frames.

5. To hide the boundaries of the page's frames, uncheck *Show Borders*.

6. Click *OK* to return to the Frame Properties dialog box, then click *OK* again to apply the changes to the frames page.

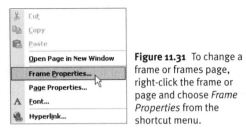

Figure 11.31 To change a frame or frames page, right-click the frame or page and choose *Frame Properties* from the shortcut menu.

Figure 11.32 Use the Frame Properties dialog box to change a frame's name, size, and margins. Or click *Frames Page* in the lower right to change the frames page.

Figure 11.33 Use the Page Properties dialog box's *Frames* tab to set the spacing and borders between a page's frames.

Frame Properties options

To reach the Frame Properties dialog box (**Figure 11.32**), right-click any frame and choose *Frame Properties*.

❶ **Name:** By default, FrontPage assigns a name to the frame based on its position. Type in another name if you prefer.

❷ **Initial page:** Click *Browse* to find a new page to appear in the frame.

❸ **Frame size:** By default, the *Width* is set to *Pixels*. *Row Height* is dimmed unless the current frame is part of a row of frames. Use the drop-down menus of each to change the measures. *Relative* sets the width relative to other frames in the frames page: If you set a value of 1 for one frame and 2 for another, the second frame will be twice as wide. *Percent* sets the frame's width as a percentage of the browser window's width.

❹ **Margins:** The *Width* and *Height* windows set the frame's margin in pixels.

❺ **Resizable in Browser:** By default, this box is checked, allowing the user to resize the frame. Uncheck the box if you want the frame size fixed.

❻ **Show scrollbars:** Use the drop-down menu to choose whether you want the frame to *Always* or *Never* have a scrollbar. *If Needed* will add a scrollbar only if the frame's content extends beyond the visible area.

❼ **Frames Page:** Click the button to change properties for the entire frames page. For details, see *To change spacing or borders in frames pages* on the previous page.

❽ **Style:** This button can only be used if you've created style sheets for your Web site. See *Building Style Sheets and Dynamic Effects* on page 335.

Helping older browsers

No, we're not talking about octogenarian bookstore patrons. We're talking about pre-version 3 Web browsers that can't display frame-based pages. At this point, most folks have switched over to newer browsers. Still, FrontPage offers a way to help out the old-timers by letting you display an explanatory message. More importantly, it makes it easy to link those visitors to a frame-free alternate page.

To set a message for non-frame browsers

1. While displaying your frames page, click the *No Frames* tab at the bottom of FrontPage's main window (**Figure 11.34**).

2. FrontPage's default message somewhat curtly tells visitors using older Web browsers that their browser doesn't support frames (top, **Figure 11.35**). To soften the message—and give visitors an alternate page link—type your own text into the page and create a link to a frame-free page (bottom, **Figure 11.35**).

3. Save the page (Ctrl S) and click the *Normal* tab to return to the frames page.

Figure 11.34 Click the *No Frames* tab at the bottom of the main window to set a message for non-frame browsers.

Figure 11.35 To change the default message that non-frame browsers will display (top), enter your own message and a link to a frame-free page (bottom).

CREATING AND PROCESSING FORMS

Forms enable you to collect information from your users by presenting them with questions, interactive option buttons, check boxes, and multiple-choice menus. The first step in setting up forms is creating the forms and adding the fields you need to collect information. As you add and edit fields within the form, you have the option of setting up data entry rules for the users. FrontPage calls this process validating the data. Once that's done, you can create a confirmation page, which provides crucial feedback to the user and cuts down on incorrect form entries. Finally, you set whether you want the form results saved as a file, email, database entry, or as part of a custom script.

Creating Forms

The fastest way to create a form is use a template and customize it to meet your needs. FrontPage's form templates include a confirmation form and a feedback form, plus a form wizard that walks you through creating a custom form. Of course, you also can build a form from scratch.

To create a form from a template

1. Choose File > New > Page or Web (**Figure 12.1**).

2. When the Task pane appears, click *Page Templates* (**Figure 12.2**).

3. When the Page Templates dialog box appears (**Figure 12.3**), choose *Feedback Form* and click *OK*. When the page appears, save it (Ctrl S).

4. When the Save As dialog box appears, give the form page a distinctive name and title, then click *Save* (**Figure 12.4**). You're now ready to change and add form fields to the template-based form page (**Figure 12.5**). For details, see *Adding Form Fields* on page 292.

Figure 12.1
To create a new form, choose File > New > Page or Web.

Figure 12.2 When the Task pane appears, click *Page Templates*.

Figure 12.3 When the Page Templates dialog box appears, choose *Feedback Form* and click *OK*.

Figure 12.4 Use the Save As dialog box to give the page a distinctive name and title.

sayhey.htm

Tell us what you think about our web site, our products, our organization, or anything else that comes to mind. We welcome all of your comments and suggestions.

What kind of comment would you like to send?

○ Complaint ○ Problem ⦿ Suggestion ○ Praise

What about us do you want to comment on?

[Web Site ▼] Other: [_____]

Enter your comments in the space provided below:

Normal | HTML | Preview

Figure 12.5 By basing your form on a FrontPage template, you can reduce the time needed to add fields.

CREATING FORMS

Figure 12.6
To create a form from scratch, choose Insert > Form > Form.

Figure 12.7 A dashed outline denotes a new form, along with a *Submit* button and a *Reset* button.

Figure 12.8 To give yourself some working space in a new form, press [Enter] several times.

Figure 12.9 To delete a field, right-click it and choose *Cut* from the shortcut menu.

To create a form from scratch

1. Open an existing Web page or create a new page by choosing File > New > Page or Web ([Ctrl][N]) (**Figure 12.1**). If you're creating a new page, go ahead and save it ([Ctrl][S]) and give it a distinctive name in the Save As dialog box (**Figure 12.4**).

2. Click in the page where you want the form inserted and choose Insert > Form > Form (**Figure 12.6**).

3. The form, bounded by a dashed outline, will be inserted into the page, along with a *Submit* button and a *Reset* button (**Figure 12.7**).

4. Give yourself some working space within the form by pressing [Enter] several times (**Figure 12.8**). You're now ready to add whatever form fields you need. For details, see *Adding Form Fields* on page 292.

To delete a field

◆ Make sure the *Normal* tab is active, select the field you want to delete, and press [←Backspace] or [Delete]. The field will be deleted.

or

◆ Right-click the field and choose *Cut* from the shortcut menu (**Figure 12.9**). The field will be deleted.

To change a field's properties

1. Make sure you're in page view, then double-click the field.

2. When the field's properties dialog box opens, make your changes, click *OK,* and they will be applied to the field. For details on the dialog boxes for each field type, see *Adding Form Fields* on page 292.

CREATING, DELETING, AND CHANGING FORMS

Adding Form Fields

Whether you create a form from scratch or start with one of FrontPage's form templates, it's easy to add a variety of form fields to match your needs.

To add a text box

1. Click in the form page where you want to add the field, typically next to text that identifies the field for users (**Figure 12.10**).

2. Choose Insert > Form > Textbox (**Figure 12.11**).

3. When the one-line field appears in the page, right-click it and choose *Form Field Properties* from the shortcut menu ((Alt)(Enter)) (**Figure 12.12**).

4. When the Text Box Properties dialog box appears, FrontPage will have assigned the field an arbitrary name, such as *T1* (**Figure 12.13**). Type in a distinctive name of your own ❶, which won't be visible to site visitors.

5. If you want some text to appear *inside* the one-line box, such as "Enter your name here," type it into the *Initial value* text box ❷.

6. Set how many characters wide you want the line to be ❸ and enter a number for the field's tab order ❹ within the form.

7. If the field will be used for a password ❺, choose *Yes*, otherwise leave it set to the default *No*. By the way, *Style* ❻ is used only if you're building style sheets.

8. If you want to define entry requirements for the field, click *Validate* ❼. For details, see *Text Box Validation options* on page 296.

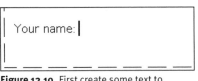

Figure 12.10 First create some text to identify the field for the user, then click in the form page where you want to add the field.

Figure 12.11 To add a single-line text field, choose Insert > Form > Textbox.

Figure 12.12 To modify any form field, right-click it and choose *Form Field Properties* from the shortcut menu.

Figure 12.13 Use the Text Box Properties dialog box to give your field a name, initial value, size, and password.

Figure 12.14 To put a separate Form toolbar on your desktop, choose Insert > Form, move your cursor to the top of the submenu, and drag it to the desktop.

9. When you're done, click *OK* and the properties will be applied to the one-line text field. To see how the field looks and decide if it needs adjustment, click FrontPage's *Preview* tab.

✔ Tips

- If you need to resize a text box, don't bother using the Text Box Properties dialog box. Just click the box and use one of its square black handles to enlarge or shrink it.

- If you're creating a bunch of form fields at once, you may find it easier to have a separate Form toolbar on your desktop. Just choose Insert > Form and move your cursor to the top of the submenu and drag it to the desktop (**Figure 12.14**).

Adding a text area

While a text box contains only a single line of text, a text area can be as large as you need. FrontPage will automatically add a scrollbar if the entire area is not visible on the Web page.

To add a text area

1. Click in the form page where you want to add the text area, typically next to text that identifies the field for users or asks them to enter comments in the field.

2. Choose Insert > Form > Text Area or click the Text Area icon in the Form toolbar (**Figure 12.15**).

3. When the field appears in the page, click it and use the square black handles to enlarge or shrink it (**Figure 12.16**).

4. Right-click the field and choose *Form Field Properties* from the shortcut menu ([Alt][Enter]) (**Figure 12.12**).

Figure 12.15 To add a text area, click the Text Area icon in the Form toolbar.

Figure 12.16 To resize a text area, click and drag the square black handles.

Figure 12.17 Use the TextArea Box Properties dialog box to give the field a name, initial value, and size.

5. When the TextArea Box Properties dialog box appears, FrontPage will have assigned the field an arbitrary name, such as *S1* (**Figure 12.17**). Type in a distinctive name of your own, which won't be visible to site visitors.

6. If you want some text to appear *inside* the box, such as "Enter your name here," type it into the *Initial value* text box.

7. If you aren't happy with your initial resizing, set the *Width in characters* and *Number of lines* using the text boxes. Enter a number for the field's tab order within the form.

8. If you want to define entry requirements for the field, click *Validate*. For details, see *Text Box Validation options* on the next page.

9. When you're done, click *OK* and the properties will be applied to the text area. To see how the field looks and decide if it needs adjustment, click FrontPage's *Preview* tab.

Text Box Validation options

Use the Text Box Validation dialog box to set rules for the kind of data users can enter in text boxes (**Figure 12.18**). To reach the dialog box, click the *Validate* button in the Text Box Properties or TextArea Box Properties dialog boxes (**Figure 12.19**).

❶ **Display name:** Though it sits at the top of the dialog box, this text box won't become available until after you've used the other boxes to set the data entry requirements. Once you've filled out your data requirements, you can then enter a distinctive name.

❷ **Data type:** By default, the drop-down menu is set to *No Constraints*. Use the drop-down menu to narrow the valid options for users. If you choose *Text*, use the *Text format* section to define what text will be allowed. If you choose *Integer* or *Number*, use the *Numeric format* section to define entry requirements.

❸ **Text format:** These options are available only if you choose *Text* as your *Data type*. Check which types of data you will *allow*. Check *Whitespace* to allow spaces, returns, or tabs. Check *Other* to allow such characters as punctuation marks and hyphens. Use the adjacent text box to specify which characters are allowed.

❹ **Numeric format:** These options are available only if you choose *Integer* or *Number* as your *Data type*.

❺ **Data length:** If you don't want the field left blank, check *Required*. Use *Min length* and *Max length* to ensure that users enter a number correctly, for example a 16-digit credit card number.

❻ **Data value:** Use the check boxes, drop-down menus, and text boxes to further define what information users must enter.

Figure 12.18 Use the Text Box Validation dialog box to set data entry rules for one-line text and scrolling text fields.

Figure 12.19 To reach the Text Box Validation dialog box, click the *Validate* button in the Text Box Properties or TextArea Box Properties dialog boxes.

ADDING FORM FIELDS

Figure 12.20 To add a check box, click the Checkbox icon in the Form toolbar.

☐ Please send me more information | Submit | Reset |

Figure 12.21 Once the check box appears in the page, be sure to add some explanatory text.

Submit | Reset |

- Cut
- Copy
- Paste
- Page Properties...
- Form Properties...
- **Form Field Properties...**
- Hyperlink...

Figure 12.22 Right-click the field and choose *Form Field Properties* from the shortcut menu.

Adding check boxes and option buttons

Unlike text boxes in which users can enter a variety of information, check boxes and option buttons have only two states: On (checked) or Off (not checked). The main difference between check boxes and option buttons is that users can choose *several* check boxes, while option buttons force users to make *one* choice among several in a single group.

To add a check box

1. Click in the form page where you want to add the check box.

2. Choose Insert > Form > Check Box or click the Checkbox icon in the Form toolbar (**Figure 12.20**).

3. When the check box appears in the page, add text that explains the field for users (**Figure 12.21**).

4. Right-click the field and choose *Form Field Properties* from the shortcut menu (Alt)(Enter)) (**Figure 12.22**).

(continued)

ADDING FORM FIELDS

5. When the Check Box Properties dialog box appears, FrontPage will have assigned the field an arbitrary name, such as *C1* (**Figure 12.23**). Type in a distinctive name of your own (which, by the way, won't be visible to site visitors).

6. By default, the *Value* will be *ON*. This text is not seen by the user, and you can type in any word that helps you quickly identify the user's response. In **Figure 12.23**, for example, it'd be clearer to use something like *Contact*.

7. By default, the check box's *Initial state* is *Not checked*. Choose *Checked* if you're sure most users will want the box already selected.

8. Enter a number for the field's tab order within the form and click *OK*.

9. If you want to add more check boxes, repeat steps 1–8. Once you're done, you can see how the check boxes look and decide if any need adjustment by clicking FrontPage's *Preview* tab.

Figure 12.23 Use the Check Box Properties dialog box to set the field's name and whether its default is *Checked* or *Not checked*.

CHOOSE A COLOR|

Figure 12.24 Click in the form page where you want to add one or more option buttons. Be sure to add text to prompt users to make a choice.

Option Button

Figure 12.25 To add option buttons, click the Option Button icon in the Form toolbar.

CHOOSE A COLOR ○ Green| | Submit | Reset |

Figure 12.26 Add a label to your first option button when it appears in the form.

Option Button Properties

Group name: R1

Value: V1

Initial state: ⦿ Selected ○ Not selected

Tab order:

| Style... | Validate... | | OK | Cancel |

Figure 12.27 When the Option Button Properties dialog box appears, FrontPage will have assigned the field an arbitrary *Group name*, a *Value*, and set the *Initial state*.

Option Button Properties

Group name: Colors

Value: Green

Initial state: ○ Selected ⦿ Not selected

Tab order:

| Style... | Validate... | | OK | Cancel |

Figure 12.28 Once you've typed in descriptive names for the *Group name* and the *Value*, set the button's *Initial state* and *Tab order*.

To add option buttons

1. Click in the form page where you want to add the option button, typically next to text asking users to choose among what will be several option buttons (**Figure 12.24**).

2. Choose Insert > Form > Option Button or click the Option Button icon in the Form toolbar (**Figure 12.25**).

3. When the option button appears in the form, type in some text identifying that choice (**Figure 12.26**).

4. Click where you want the next option button inserted and repeat steps 2 and 3. Continue until you've added as many option buttons as you need.

5. Right-click the first option button and choose *Form Field Properties* from the shortcut menu ((Alt)(Enter)) (**Figure 12.12**).

6. When the Option Button Properties dialog box appears, FrontPage will have assigned the field an arbitrary *Group name*, such as *R1*, a *Value* of *V1* and set the *Initial state* as *Selected* (**Figure 12.27**).

7. Type in descriptive names of your own for the *Group name* and the *Value*. Since you want the user to pick a color, change the *Initial state* to *Not selected* (**Figure 12.28**). Click *OK* and the changes will be applied to that option button only.

(continued)

8. Select each of the other option buttons you've created and choose *Form Field Properties* from the shortcut menu. In the Option Button Properties dialog box for each, give them the same *Group name*, a different *Value* to match the choice represented by that individual button, and choose *Not selected* as the *Initial state*. Click *OK* to close each dialog box.

9. If you want to make sure that users actually choose one of the option buttons and don't ignore them, double-click any of the option buttons. When the Option Button Properties dialog box appears, click *Validate* to reach the Option Button Validation dialog box (**Figure 12.29**). Check *Data required* and type a message in *Display name* to prompt the user. Click *OK* to close the dialog box.

10. Once you're done, you can see how the option buttons look and decide if any need adjustment by clicking FrontPage's *Preview* tab (**Figure 12.30**).

✔ Tip

- If you create multiple option buttons and expect that most users will choose one choice over the others, set its *Initial state* to *Selected* in step 7.

Figure 12.29 Use the Option Button Validation dialog box to enter a message to prompt users or to require a selection.

Figure 12.30 All three option buttons belong to the same group.

Figure 12.31 To add a drop-down box, click the Drop-Down Box icon in the Form toolbar.

Figure 12.32 When the Drop-Down Box Properties dialog box appears, click *Add* to create menu choices.

Figure 12.33 Use the Add Choice dialog box to create a menu choice, give it a value, and set an initial state.

To add a drop-down box

1. Click in the form page where you want to add the field, typically next to text that identifies the field for users or asks them to pick from the drop-down choices.

2. Choose Insert > Form > Drop-Down Box or click the Drop-Down Box icon in the Form toolbar (**Figure 12.31**).

3. When the drop-down menu appears in the page, right-click the field and choose *Form Field Properties* ([Alt][Enter]) (**Figure 12.12**). Or double-click the field.

4. When the Drop-Down Box Properties dialog box appears, FrontPage will have assigned the field an arbitrary name, such as *D1* (**Figure 12.32**). Type in a distinctive name of your own.

5. To add choices to the drop-down menu, click *Add*. When the Add Choice dialog box appears (**Figure 12.33**), enter your first *Choice*.

6. If you want to create another name for the choice, such as a part number or shorter name, check *Specify Value* and enter it in the text box. Choose whether you want the choice's *Initial state* to be *Selected* or *Not selected*. Click *OK* and the choice will be added to the Drop-Down Box Properties dialog box.

(continued)

ADDING FORM FIELDS

7. Repeat steps 5 and 6 using the *Add* ❷ button until you have added all the choices you want (**Figure 12.34**).

8. To change, delete, or reorder choices, select each in the *Choice* list ❶ and click *Modify* ❸, *Remove* ❹, or *Move Up* or *Move Down* ❺. Set the menu's height ❻, tab order in the form ❼, and whether multiple choices are allowed ❽. For details, see *Drop-Down Box options* on the next page.

9. Once you adjust the drop-down menu, click *OK* and the changes will be applied.

Figure 12.34 Once you've created menu choices, you can rearrange them and allow multiple selections.

Figure 12.35 The Modify Choice dialog box lets you change an item's description, value, and initial state.

Drop-Down Box options

To reach the Drop-Down Box Properties dialog box (**Figure 12.34**), right-click the field and choose *Form Field Properties* from the shortcut menu ([Alt][Enter]) (**Figure 12.12**).

❶ **Choice list:** Click any listing in the window to select it. The window displays all the drop-down menu's choices, whether they will be selected within the menu, and the shorthand value you assigned each choice.

❷ **Add:** Click to add more choices to the drop-down menu.

❸ **Modify:** To change one of your menu choices, select it in the *Choice* list and click *Modify*. The Modify Choice dialog box will appear (**Figure 12.35**), which works identically to the Add Choice dialog box (**Figure 12.33**).

❹ **Remove:** To remove an item, select it in the *Choice* list and click *Remove*. It will be deleted immediately.

❺ **Move Up/Move Down:** To rearrange your choices, select one in the *Choice* list and click *Move Up* or *Move Down*. The item will move up or down by one position.

❻ **Height:** Use the text box to set how many lines of the drop-down menu should appear in the form. If you enter a number and the list has more items than that, a scrollbar will be added to the menu.

(continued)

ADDING FORM FIELDS

❼ Tab order: Enter a number in the text box to set the drop-down menu's tab order within the form.

❽ Allow multiple selections: By default, *No* is chosen. Choose *Yes* if, as in the example, you want users to be able to choose more than one item.

❾ Validate: Click to define entry requirements for the drop-down menu. When the Drop-Down Box Validation dialog box appears (**Figure 12.36**), check *Data Required* if you want users to choose at least one item from the menu. Use the *Minimum Items* and *Maximum Items* text boxes to further refine your requirements. Click *OK* and you'll be returned to the Drop-Down Box Properties dialog box.

Figure 12.36 Use the Drop-Down Box Validation dialog box to set data entry rules for the menu.

ADDING FORM FIELDS

Figure 12.37 Before you create a push button, click in the form where you want it to appear.

Figure 12.38 To add a push button, click the Push Button icon in the Form toolbar.

Push Button Properties

Name: | B1
Value/label: | Button
Button type: | ⦿ Normal ○ Submit ○ Reset
Tab order: |

Style...   OK   Cancel

Figure 12.39 Use the Push Button Properties dialog box to name the button, create a label for it, and choose its type.

Choose a color: ○ GREEN ○ RED ○ BLACK

Choose your features:

Air Conditioning
Power Steering
Moon Roof
Anti-lock Brakes

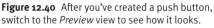
Made your choices? Then click to submit

Figure 12.40 After you've created a push button, switch to the *Preview* view to see how it looks.

Using push buttons

Once you've created a form using text boxes, check boxes, option buttons, or drop-down menus, you'll need to give users some way to submit their information. That's where FrontPage's push buttons, sometimes called command buttons, come in. While you can link push buttons to custom scripts, most of the time you'll be using them to have visitors submit their information or reset the form if they want to start over.

To add a push button

1. Click in the form page where you want to add the push button (**Figure 12.37**).

2. Choose Insert > Form > Push Button or click the Push Button icon in the Form toolbar (**Figure 12.38**).

3. When the button appears in the page, right-click it and choose *Form Field Properties* from the shortcut menu ([Alt][Enter]) (**Figure 12.12**).

4. When the Push Button Properties dialog box appears, FrontPage will have assigned the button an arbitrary name, such as *B1* and labeled it *Button* (**Figure 12.39**). If you like, type in a distinctive name of your own, which won't be seen by site visitors. Type in a button label, such as "Click to Submit," which will help users know what to do.

5. Choose which *Button type* you want to use. By default, the button is set to *Normal*, which is used if you plan on creating your own script that will be triggered by the button. More typically, users will be using the button to *Submit* form information or to *Reset* the form to its original, blank condition.

6. Enter a number for the field's tab order within the form and click *OK*. Your choices will be applied to the button. To see how the button looks, switch to FrontPage's *Preview* view (**Figure 12.40**).

ADDING FORM FIELDS

305

Creating Confirmation Pages

The idea behind a confirmation page is simple: You take some or all of the information your visitors have entered in form fields and present it back to them so they can confirm that it's correct.

While it's relatively easy to create a custom confirmation letter, FrontPage also includes a template to get you started. No matter which route you take, the confirmation pages use the *names* of your form fields to serve back to the user the values they've entered within those fields. If you get the field name wrong, the confirmation page won't work.

To create a confirmation page

1. Make sure you're in page view, choose File > New > Page or Web (Ctrl N), and when the Task pane appears, click *Page Templates*.

2. When the Page Templates dialog box appears, click the *General* tab, select *Confirmation Form,* and click *OK* (**Figure 12.41**).

3. When the new confirmation page appears, save it (Ctrl S).

4. When the Save As dialog box appears, give the confirmation page a distinctive name and title, then click *Save*.

5. You're now ready to modify the page's text and existing confirmation fields, which are set off by [brackets] (**Figure 12.42**). You'll also notice that if you move the cursor over a pair of brackets, it turns into a hand holding a page.

6. To change the field name used in an *existing* confirmation field, right-click it and choose *Confirmation Field Properties* from the shortcut menu (Alt Enter) (**Figure 12.43**).

Figure 12.41 When the Page Templates dialog box appears, click the *General* tab, select *Confirmation Form,* and click *OK*.

Figure 12.42 Confirmation fields are set off by [brackets] and trigger a hand-and-page icon to appear when the cursor moves over them.

Figure 12.43 To rename an *existing* confirmation field, right-click it and choose *Confirmation Field Properties* from the shortcut menu.

Figure 12.44 Use the Confirmation Field Properties dialog box to enter a field name from your form page.

Thank you for sending us your StreetAddress about our [Subject]. If you have asked us to contact you, we will be using the following information:

Figure 12.45 Field names used in confirmation pages must exactly match those used in the form page.

Insert Web Component

Component type:
Table of Contents
Top 10 List
List View
Document Library View
bCentral Web Components
Expedia Components
MSN Components
MSNBC Components
Additional Components
Advanced Controls

Choose an effect:
HTML
Java Applet
Plug-In
Confirmation Field
ActiveX Control
Design-Time Control

Display the information on a confirmation form that a site visitor has entered.

Find components on the web   Cancel   < Back   Next >   Finish

Figure 12.46 When the Insert Web Component dialog box appears, click *Advanced Controls* in the left-hand *Component type* list, *Confirmation Field* in the right-hand list, and then click *Finish*.

Confirmation Field Properties

Name of form field to confirm:
Options

OK   Cancel

Figure 12.47 Give your confirmation field an easy to remember name in the text window and click *OK*.

Thank you for sending us your [St
our [Subject]. If you have asked u
will be using the following informat

[Options]

Figure 12.48 Just like existing confirmation fields, new ones will be marked by brackets in the confirmation page.

---

7. When the Confirmation Field Properties dialog box appears (**Figure 12.44**), type in the name you assigned to a field when creating your form page. Click *OK* and the new name will appear in the brackets (**Figure 12.45**).

8. To add a *new* confirmation field, choose Insert > Web Component.

9. When the Insert Web Component dialog box appears, click *Advanced Controls* in the left-hand *Component type* list, *Confirmation Field* in the right-hand list, and then click *Finish* (**Figure 12.46**).

10. When the Confirmation Field Properties dialog box appears, type an easy to remember name in the text window and click *OK* (**Figure 12.47**).

11. When the empty Confirmation Field Properties dialog box appears (**Figure 12.44**), type the name of the form field you want to use into the text box and click *OK*. The confirmation field will be added to the page (**Figure 12.48**).

12. Continue adding text and confirmation fields, then save the confirmation page (Ctrl S) when you're done.

✔ Tip

■ It's too bad that FrontPage does not present a drop-down menu of your form field names to jog your memory. If you can't remember a field's name, double-click it in the form page and check what's in the *Name* field.

CREATING CONFIRMATION PAGES

307

Saving Form Results

You can save the results collected in a form as a file, email, database record, or data handled by custom scripts. Depending on your choices, FrontPage will configure what are called form handlers to save the results.

If you save the results of a form as a file, FrontPage gives you eight different formats in which to store the data. If you like, by the way, FrontPage lets you save the results as a file *and* as email, rather than forcing you to choose one or the other.

By default, FrontPage uses the Save Results Component to handle your form results. But it also includes a Discussion Form Handler and a Registration Form Handler. FrontPage also recognizes a variety of custom scripts.

To save form results to a file

1. While in page view, right-click the form and choose *Form Properties* from the shortcut menu (**Figure 12.49**).

2. When the Form Properties dialog box appears (**Figure 12.50**), choose *Send to* ❶ in the *Where to store results* section.

3. By default, FrontPage gives the file a name and places it in your Web site's *private* folder, which can't be found by Web search engines. If you want to change the name or folder location, type a new path and name into the text box or click *Browse* if you want the results stored in an existing file.

4. Use the *Form properties* section if you want to give the form another name ❹ or if you want to set a target frame for the form ❺. For details on target frames, see *Setting target frames* on page 278.

5. Click *Options* ❻, and the *File Results* tab of the Options for Saving Results of Form dialog box (**Figure 12.51**) will appear with the file name already entered.

Figure 12.49 To control how form results will be saved, right-click the form and choose *Form Properties* from the shortcut menu.

Figure 12.50 Use the Form Properties dialog box to choose whether form results are saved as a file, email, database record, or customized data.

Figure 12.51 The File Results tab lets you set the file's name, format, and other details of saving the data.

Figure 12.52 The File format drop-down menu offers eight choices for formatting the results data.

Figure 12.53 To test and inspect a form, click the Preview in Browser button in FrontPage's Standard toolbar.

6. Use the *File format* drop-down menu ❶ to choose one of the eight text choices (**Figure 12.52**).

7. Check *Include field names* ❷ if you want to pair the values from each form field with the field's name. Unless you choose *HTML*, the *Latest results at end* ❸ box will be checked, meaning new results will appear at the bottom of the file.

8. If you want to create another file for the results, perhaps in another of the eight formats, use the *Optional second file* section ❹ to enter a new name or *Browse* to an existing file. The section's other choices work identically to those described in steps 6 and 7.

9. Click *OK* to return to the Form Properties dialog box. Click *OK* again and the settings will be applied to the form. To test the form, click the Preview in Browser button in FrontPage's Standard toolbar (**Figure 12.53**).

Form options

To reach the Form Properties dialog box
(**Figure 12.54**), choose Insert > Form >
Form Properties, click the Form Properties
icon in the Form toolbar (**Figure 12.55**), or
right-click the form and choose *Form
Properties* from the shortcut menu.

❶ Send to: Choose this option and use *File
name* to save the form results as a text or
HTML file. Use *E-mail address* and enter
an address in the text box if you want the
results saved in that form.

❷ Send to database: Choose this option to
save the results to a database.

❸ Send to other: Use the drop-down menu
to select a handler other than FrontPage's
default. Use the *Options* button to configure the custom handler you choose.

❹ Form name: By default, FrontPage will
assign a name to the form. If you prefer,
use the text box to type in a distinctive
name for the form.

❺ Target frame: Click the pencil icon to
set a target frame. For details, see *Setting
target frames* on page 278.

❻ Options: Click to configure the details of
how the form results will be saved.

❼ Advanced: Click to set Hidden fields,
which are needed only if you're using CGI
scripts to handle the form results.

Figure 12.54 Use the Form Properties dialog box to
choose whether form results are saved as a file,
email, database record, or customized data.

Figure 12.55 To reach the Form Properties dialog box,
click the Form Properties icon in the Form toolbar.

Figure 12.56 The E-mail Results tab lets you set the message's address, format, subject line, and reply address.

To save form results as email

1. While in page view, right-click the form and choose *Form Properties* from the shortcut menu (**Figure 12.49**).

2. When the Form Properties dialog box appears (**Figure 12.54**), choose *Send to* ❶ in the *Where to store results* section.

3. Type into the *E-mail address* text box the address of where you want the results sent.

4. By default, FrontPage fills in the *File name* text box. If you want your results saved *only* as email, delete the name from the text box. If you want the results saved as email *and* as a file, leave the *File name* as it is.

5. Use the *Form properties* section if you want to give the form another name ❹ or if you want to set a target frame for the form ❺. For details on target frames, see *Setting target frames* on page 278.

6. Click *Options* ❻ and when the Options for Saving Results of Form dialog box appears, click the *E-mail Results* tab (**Figure 12.56**). The address you entered in step 3 will already be entered in the *E-mail address to receive results* text box ❶.

7. Use the *E-mail format* drop-down menu ❷ to choose one of the eight text choices (**Figure 12.52**).

8. Check *Include field names* ❸ if you want to pair the values from each form field with the field's name.

9. By default, the email's subject line ❹ would be *Form Results*. If you want something more descriptive, type it into the text box or check *Form field name* to have it appear in the subject line.

(continued)

10. Type into the *Reply-to line* text box ❺ the address you want used as the *sender* of the email. However, if your form includes a field that collects the user's email address, check *Form field name* and enter that field's name in the text box. That way the reply will go directly to the person who filled out the form in the first place.

11. Click *OK* to return to the Form Properties dialog box. Click *OK* again and the settings will be applied to the form. To test the form, click the Preview in Browser button in FrontPage's Standard toolbar (**Figure 12.53**).

Figure 12.57 The Database Results tab lets you port the form results to an existing or new database.

To save form results to a database

1. While in page view, right-click the form and choose *Form Properties* from the shortcut menu (**Figure 12.49**).

2. When the Form Properties dialog box appears (**Figure 12.54**), choose *Send to database* in the *Where to store results* section.

3. Use the *Form properties* section if you want to give the form another name or if you want to set a target frame for the form. For details on target frames, see *Setting target frames* on page 278.

4. Click *Options* and when the Options for Saving Results to Database dialog box appears, click the *Database Results* tab (**Figure 12.57**).

5. Click *Add Connection* to link to your Web site's database. For details, see *Adding Database Connections* on page 317.

6. Click *OK* to return to the Form Properties dialog box. Click *OK* again and the settings will be applied to the form. To test the form, click the Preview in Browser button in FrontPage's Standard toolbar (**Figure 12.53**).

To save form results with a custom script

1. While in either the folders view or with the Folder List visible, right-click the folder containing your custom script. Choose *Properties* from the shortcut menu (**Figure 12.58**).

2. When the folder's properties dialog box appears, check *Allow scripts or programs to be run* (**Figure 12.59**). Click *OK* to close the dialog box.

3. Switch back to page view, right-click your form, and choose *Form Properties* from the shortcut menu (**Figure 12.49**).

4. When the Form Properties dialog box appears (**Figure 12.54**), choose *Send to other* in the *Where to store results* section and use the drop-down menu to select *Custom ISAPI, NSAPI, CGI, or ASP Script.*

5. Use the *Form properties* section if you want to give the form another name or if you want to set a target frame for the form. For details on target frames, see *Setting target frames* on page 278.

6. Click *Options* and the Options for Custom Form Handler dialog box will appear (**Figure 12.60**).

7. Type the URL for your script into the *Action* text box and use the *Method* drop-down menu to choose which way information will be submitted to the script: *POST* or *GET.*

8. Leave the *Encoding type* text box blank.

9. Click *OK* to return to the Form Properties dialog box. Click *OK* again and the settings will be applied to the form. To test the form, click the Preview in Browser button in FrontPage's Standard toolbar (**Figure 12.53**).

Figure 12.58 Right-click the folder containing your custom script and choose *Properties* from the shortcut menu.

Figure 12.59 When the properties dialog box for the folder containing your custom script appears, check *Allow scripts or programs to be run*.

Figure 12.60 Use the Options for Custom Form Handler dialog box to set the URL for your custom script and the method for submitting the script's data.

✔ Tips

- In step 7, *POST* passes the field name and its value straight to the script; *GET* encodes the same data and presents it as a QUERY_STRING variable. To learn more about custom scripts, get yourself a copy of *Perl and CGI for the World Wide Web, Second Edition: Visual QuickStart Guide* by Elizabeth Castro (Peachpit Press, 2001).

- You also can use the *Send to other* drop-down menu to select handlers for discussion groups and registering users (**Figure 12.54**).

ADDING DATABASE CONNECTIONS

Figuring out how to link databases to Web sites can be a tail-chasing mess of missed deadlines and endless nights. Fortunately, Microsoft FrontPage includes the Database Results Wizard, which walks you step by step through the entire procedure. While a bit lengthy, the process involves five basic steps.

First, you create a connection between FrontPage and the database you want to work with. Once the connection's established, you choose the database records you want to use. The third step involves filtering and sorting out which fields and records will be displayed. At that point, you decide how to format the results. Finally, you have the option of displaying all the results at once or breaking them into smaller groups. Just remember that database connections only work if your Web server includes the FrontPage server extensions and has been configured to handle Active Server Pages.

Importing Databases

Whether the database is part of your Web site or resides on a server somewhere else doesn't really matter. However, if you want to place the database on your Web site, you'll need to import it in a format compatible with FrontPage (**Table 13.1**). If the database uses some other file extension, then use your database application to export it or save it in one of the formats FrontPage supports. Once you've done that, you're ready to import the database using FrontPage.

To import databases into your Web site

1. Use Windows to navigate to the database you want to use, right-click it and choose *Copy* from the shortcut menu (**Figure 13.1**).

2. Switch back to your Web site in FrontPage and make sure the Folder List is visible. Right-click the Web site's folder in the Folder List and choose *Paste* from the shortcut menu (**Figure 13.2**). The database will be added to the Web site.

3. FrontPage will automatically ask if you want to add a database connection to the database (top, **Figure 13.3**). Give the connection an easy to recognize *Name* and click *Yes* (bottom, **Figure 13.3**).

Table 13.1

Compatible Database Formats for FrontPage	
FILE EXTENSION	FORMAT
.MDB	Microsoft Access
.DBF	dBase, Microsoft FoxPro
.XLS	Microsoft Excel
.TXT	Tab-separated text
.CSV	Comma-separated text

Figure 13.1 To import a database to FrontPage, right-click the database and choose *Copy*.

Figure 13.2 Right-click your Web site folder in the Folder List and choose *Paste* to import a database into FrontPage.

Figure 13.3 When you add a database file to your site, FrontPage automatically asks if you want to add a database connection to the database (top) and name it (bottom).

Figure 13.4 Click *Yes* when FrontPage asks if you want to create an *fpdb* folder in your Web site.

Figure 13.5 The imported database is placed inside the Web site's *fpdb* folder.

4. Click *Yes* when a FrontPage alert dialog box appears asking if you want to create an *fpdb* folder in your Web site (**Figure 13.4**). The folder will be created and the imported database placed inside (**Figure 13.5**). You can now extract information from the database through a database connection. For details, see *To create a database connection* on the next page.

IMPORTING DATABASES

Creating Database Connections

It's a subtle but crucial distinction: a database connection is not the same as a database. Instead the connection acts as a view, or portal, from a Web page to the information within the database. By using FrontPage to create and configure that connection, you can control exactly which pieces of the database your Web visitors see and use. As you follow the steps detailed in the rest of the chapter, remember that you're making a *connection* with a database, not creating the database itself.

To create a database connection

1. Make sure you know the pathname or URL for the database you want to use, whether it's already part of your Web site or on a remote server.

2. Open an existing Web page and click where you want the database to appear. You also can create a new page by choosing File > New > Page or Web ([Ctrl][N]) and then using the Task pane to open a blank page.

3. Once the page appears, choose Insert > Database > Results (**Figure 13.6**).

4. When the first screen of the Database Results Wizard appears (**Figure 13.7**), choose the connection you want to use: a sample connection with one of FrontPage's example databases, an existing connection, or a new connection. For more information on creating a new connection, see page 325.

Figure 13.6 To create a database connection in your Web page, choose Insert > Database > Results.

Figure 13.7 Use the first screen of the Database Results Wizard to choose a database connection.

Figure 13.8 Use the second screen of the Database Results Wizard to select a *Record source* using an existing field or by creating a *Custom query.*

Figure 13.9 If you choose *Record source*, use the drop-down menu to select the set of records you want to use.

Figure 13.10 Use the third screen of the Database Results Wizard to edit which fields will appear. The *More Options* button lets you filter and sort the results.

Figure 13.11 The Displayed Fields dialog box lets you add, remove, or rearrange the database fields shown.

5. Once you've made your choice, click *Next* and, after a moment, the second screen of the Database Results Wizard appears (**Figure 13.8**). Decide whether you want to select a *Record source* using the existing fields listed in the drop-down list or create a *Custom query.* (Custom queries use SQL statement syntax, which falls beyond the scope of this book.) If you choose *Record source*, use the drop-down menu to select the set of records you want to use (**Figure 13.9**).

6. Once you've made your choices, click *Next* and the third screen of the Database Results Wizard appears (**Figure 13.10**). By default, all of the record source's fields will be listed for display. If you want to exclude some fields, click *Edit List.*

7. When the Displayed Fields dialog box appears, use the *Remove* button to narrow the *Displayed fields* to only those you want users to see (**Figure 13.11**). The removed fields will be listed in the *Available fields* column. Use the *Move Up* and *Move Down* buttons to rearrange the order in which the fields will be displayed on your Web page. Click *OK* when you're done and you'll return to the wizard's third screen (**Figure 13.10**). If you want to sort or filter the fields more precisely, click *More Options.* For details, see *Filtering and sorting options* on page 328.

(continued)

CREATING DATABASE CONNECTIONS

8. Once you've made your choices, click *Next* and the fourth screen of the Database Results Wizard appears (**Figure 13.12**). Use the first formatting drop-down menu to choose whether to display the results as a table, list, or drop-down list. Depending on your choice, the dialog box will offer additional choices for formatting the results (**Figures 13.13** and **13.14**). Use the check boxes and drop-down menus to refine the appearance of the records and click *Next*.

Figure 13.12 Use the drop-down menu in the Database Results Wizard's fourth screen to format how the results are displayed.

Figure 13.13 If you choose a list format, use the checkboxes and *List options* drop-down menu to fine-tune how the results are displayed.

Figure 13.14 If you choose a drop-down menu format, use the dialog box's drop-down menus to fine-tune how the results are displayed.

Figure 13.15 Use the fifth screen of the Database Results Wizard to decide whether to split the results into smaller groups.

Figure 13.16 Once you've finished using the Database Results Wizard, FrontPage returns you to the now-formatted page.

Figure 13.17 When you save a page containing a database connection, FrontPage automatically assigns it an .asp suffix.

9. When the fifth screen of the Database Results Wizard appears (**Figure 13.15**), choose whether to *Display all records together* or *Split records into groups*. If you decide to split them, enter a number into the *records per group* text box.

10. Click *Finish* and you'll be returned to your page where placeholders for the database results (marked by << >>) will be displayed (**Figure 13.16**). The yellow areas mark the beginning and end of the database results and the explanatory text will not appear when the page is posted to the Web.

11. Save the page ((Ctrl)(S)) and when the Save As dialog box appears, FrontPage will have automatically given the file an .asp file suffix (**Figure 13.17**). ASP (Active Server Pages) files contain scripts linked to the server where the database resides. Click *Save* and the page will be saved as a database region.

(continued)

12. Click the Preview in Browser button in FrontPage's Standard toolbar (**Figure 13.18**), to get a more accurate sense of how the results will look to site visitors (**Figure 13.19**). To modify the results, see *To change a database connection* on page 331.

✔ Tips

- If you have only a handful of records to display, the *Split records into groups* choice will be dimmed in the wizard's fifth screen.

- When naming your database connection (step 4), it's helpful to include Conn in the name so it's always clear that this is the connection, rather than the database itself.

- If you want to display another set of records from this same database (or a different database), you'll need to create a second database connection by repeating steps 1–11.

Figure 13.18 To see how the database connection will appear, click the Preview in Browser button in the Standard toolbar.

Figure 13.19 The database connection as it appears from within a Web browser.

Figure 13.20 To establish a new connection, choose *Use a new database connection* and click *Create*.

Figure 13.21 When the Web Settings dialog box appears, click the *Database* tab, then click *Add*.

Figure 13.22 When the New Database Connection dialog box appears, name the connection, choose a type, and click *Browse* to find the database.

To create a new database connection

1. Click in the page where you want the database to appear and choose Insert > Database > Results (**Figure 13.6**).

2. When the Database Results Wizard appears (**Figure 13.20**), choose *Use a new database connection* and click *Create*.

3. When the Web Settings dialog box appears, click the *Database* tab, then click *Add* (**Figure 13.21**).

4. When the New Database Connection dialog box appears, type in a distinctive *Name* (**Figure 13.22**).

5. Use the *Type of connection* section to make a choice based on where the database you'll be using resides: a file-based database already on your Web site, data on a Web server, or data on a database server. For details on the choices, see *New Database Connection options* on page 327.

6. Click *Browse* to navigate your way to the database you want to use.

7. Once you find the database you're looking for, click *OK* to return to the New Database Connection dialog box, where the pathname for the database will be pasted into the text box.

(continued)

8. Click *OK* and the database connection will be listed in the Web Settings dialog box's *Database* tab (**Figure 13.23**). Click *OK* one more time, and you'll be returned to the first screen of the Database Results Wizard.

9. Click *Next* and, after a moment, the second screen of the Database Results Wizard will appear (**Figure 13.8**). To continue, see step 5 in *To create a database connection* on page 320.

✔ Tips

- If you choose *File or folder in current Web* in step 5 (**Figure 13.22**), when the Database Files In Current Web dialog box appears (**Figure 13.24**), you may need to use the *Files of type* drop-down menu (**Figure 13.25**) to find databases you've imported to your Web site.

- If you like, you can skip past the Database Results Wizard and create a new connection directly by choosing Tools > Web Settings and jumping to step 3 on page 325.

Figure 13.23 Established database connections are listed under the *Database* tab of the Web Settings dialog box.

Figure 13.24 When the Database Files In Current Web dialog box appears, use the *Files of type* drop-down menu to find a database you've imported.

Figure 13.25 The *Files of type* drop-down menu lists the database formats FrontPage supports.

Figure 13.26 Use the New Database Connection dialog box to set up a new connection to a database.

New Database Connection options

To reach the New Database Connection dialog box (**Figure 13.26**), choose Tools > Web Settings. When the Web Settings dialog box appears, click the *Database* tab, then click *Add* (**Figure 13.21**).

❶ **Name:** By default, FrontPage will have assigned the field a generic name, such as *Database1*. When you type in a distinctive name, it's helpful to put conn at the beginning to make it clear that this is the name of the database *connection*, not the database itself.

❷ **Type of connection:** Make your choice based on the kind of database you're connecting to and where it resides.

  File or folder in current Web: Use this choice to connect to a database stored within your Web site. FrontPage will automatically create a connection for Microsoft Access databases placed on your site. For other databases, make sure you import it in a format FrontPage supports. For details, see *Importing Databases* on page 318.

  System data source on web server: Use this choice to connect to a System Data Source Name on a Web server. The data can be a file-based database or a database management system.

  Network connection to database server: Use this choice to connect to a server dedicated to handling a large database, such as a Microsoft SQL Server.

  Custom definition: Use this choice to connect to a custom file or query designed to retrieve the necessary data. Use this option to edit the connection string when, for example, you're using a database that requires parameters that FrontPage can't set directly.

❸ **Advanced:** Click to set up user names, and passwords if Web users will be connecting to a password-protected database.

Filtering and sorting options

Use FrontPage's filtering options to limit the data that Web visitors see. Use the sorting options to fine-tune how the results are displayed.

To filter or sort the database results

1. To filter or sort the database more precisely, click *More Options* in the third screen of the Database Results Wizard (**Figure 13.10**).

2. When the *More Options* dialog box appears (**Figure 13.27**), click *Criteria* if you want to filter the database records or *Ordering* to sort the results.

3. When the Criteria dialog box appears (**Figure 13.28**), click *Add* to set up the filtering criteria.

4. When the Add Criteria dialog box appears (**Figure 13.29**), use the drop-down menus to select a *Field Name* and create a *Comparison* with the *Value*, then make a choice in the *And/Or* drop-down menu. Once you've set up the relationship, click *OK* and it will be added to the Criteria dialog box. Repeat until you've set up all your filtering criteria, then click *OK* (**Figure 13.30**).

Figure 13.27 To filter records, click *Criteria* in the More Options dialog box. To sort the results, click *Ordering*.

Figure 13.28 When the Criteria dialog box appears, click *Add* to set up the criteria for filtering records.

Figure 13.29 Use the drop-down menus to select a *Field Name*, set up a *Comparison* with the *Value*, and choose *And/Or*.

Figure 13.30 Once you've set all your filtering criteria using the *Add* button, click *OK*.

Figure 13.31 Use the Ordering dialog box to set which fields to sort and their sort order.

5. When the More Options dialog box reappears, click *Ordering* if you want to sort the database results.

6. When the Ordering dialog box appears, click listings in *Available fields* that you want to *Add* to the *Sort order* (**Figure 13.31**). To reverse the sort of any field, select it in the *Sort order list* and click *Change Sort*. Use the *Move Up* and *Move Down* buttons to rearrange the order in which the sorted fields will be displayed on your Web page. When you're done, click *OK* and you'll be returned to the More Options dialog box.

7. Click *OK* one more time, and you'll be returned to the third screen of the Database Results Wizard (**Figure 13.10**).

8. Click *Next* and, after a moment, the fourth screen of the Database Results Wizard will appear (**Figure 13.12**). To continue, see step 7 in *To create a database connection* on page 320.

FILTERING AND SORTING OPTIONS

Verifying a database connection

Make sure your database connection will work by first verifying it. If FrontPage verifies that the connection is correct, you're all set to publish your Web pages containing database connections. If FrontPage cannot verify the connection, probably because the database has been moved, you'll need to modify the connection. For details, see *To change a database connection* on page 331.

To verify a database connection

1. Choose Tools > Web Settings (**Figure 13.32**).

2. When the Web Settings dialog box appears, click the *Database* tab, choose an unverified connection (marked by a question mark in the *Status* column), and click *Verify* (top, **Figure 13.33**).

3. If FrontPage verifies the connection, the question mark will become a checkmark. If there's a problem, such as the database has been moved, the question mark will become a broken chain link (bottom, **Figure 13.33**). To fix a broken link, see *To change a database connection* on the next page.

Figure 13.32
To check or change your database settings, choose Tools > Web Settings.

Figure 13.33 Top: To check an unverified connection—marked by a question mark—click *Verify*. Bottom: Verified connections are marked by a checkmark, connections with problems by a broken chain.

Figure 13.34 To change a database connection, select it in the Web Settings dialog box's *Database* tab and click *Modify*.

Figure 13.35 Use the Database Connection Properties dialog box to change the connection or to find a database's new location.

Changing a database connection

If you move a database to another location, the connection to it will stop working. Fortunately, FrontPage makes it easy to change any database connection.

To change a database connection

1. Choose Tools > Web Settings (**Figure 13.32**).

2. When the Web Settings dialog box appears, click the *Database* tab, choose one of the database connections listed, and then click *Modify* (**Figure 13.34**).

3. When the Database Connection Properties dialog box appears (**Figure 13.35**), change the *Type of connection* or click *Browse* to find a database's new location.

4. Click *OK* and the changes will be applied to the database connection.

✔ Tip

■ The Database Connection Properties dialog box works identically to the New Database Connection dialog box (**Figure 13.26**). For details, see page 327.

CHANGING CONNECTIONS

To remove a database connection

1. Choose Tools > Web Settings (**Figure 13.32**).

2. When the Web Settings dialog box appears, click the *Database* tab, choose from the database connections listed, and then click *Remove*. The connection will be deleted.

3. Find any Web pages containing regions linked to the previously connected database and either delete the regions or connect them to another database by changing the connection. For details, see *To change a database connection* on the previous page.

Figure 13.36 To change a database's column values, right-click the database field and choose *Database Column Value Properties*.

Figure 13.37
Use the *Column to display* drop-down menu to choose another column.

Changing column values

If you want to change the columns displayed in a database connection, FrontPage offers a quick way to do it without running the Database Results Wizard again.

To change column values in a database

1. While in page view, right-click the database field and choose *Database Column Value Properties* from the shortcut menu ([Alt][Enter]) (**Figure 13.36**).

2. When the Database Column Value dialog box appears, use the *Column to display* drop-down menu to choose another column (**Figure 13.37**).

3. Click *OK* and the new column value will be pasted into the Web page.

BUILDING STYLE SHEETS AND DYNAMIC EFFECTS

14

Cascading Style Sheets, known as CSS, represent a leap forward for Web designers. Before CSS came along, you had much less control over the appearance and positioning of text in your Web pages. Now that version 4 and later Web browsers support CSS, it's much easier to lay out a Web page without constantly worrying about how it looks on different computer platforms.

CSS lets you apply a set of styles across your entire Web site, which means your pages will look more consistent. It also means a whole lot less work. Want to revise a headline style? Just make the change in your external style sheet. Bam, it's applied to the whole site. CSS is not without problems. The type formatting controls in CSS (known as CSS1) work fairly consistently in versions 4 or later of Internet Explorer and Netscape Navigator. The positioning controls (CSS2) are applied less consistently. However, this is not a major problem since a browser simply ignores—rather than mangles—any CSS2 code it can't interpret.

Using Dynamic HTML, which depends in part on CSS2, you can make text and graphics fly onto your page. If used judiciously, it can give a page a bit of dramatic snap. Sometimes mistakenly called text "animation," DHTML uses a completely different process than animated graphics, which are explained in *Adding and Editing Multimedia* on page 229.

Since FrontPage is designed to shield you, as much as possible, from coding by hand, this chapter just focuses on what you need to get rolling. Explaining all the ins and outs of style sheets and DHTML would take another whole book. If you want to get down to the nitty-gritty of both, check out Jason Cranford Teague's *DHTML and CSS for the World Wide Web, Second Edition: Visual QuickStart Guide* (2001, Peachpit Press).

BUILDING STYLE SHEETS AND DYNAMIC EFFECTS

Using Cascading Style Sheets

Style sheets come in three varieties: *external style sheets* control styles across multiple pages or an entire Web site, *embedded style sheets* control styles for individual pages, and *inline styles* control individual page elements. Put them all together and you have the coding rules that create Cascading Style Sheets.

With CSS you can define in one place exactly how you want all of your headings to appear on every page, right down to the size and color. At the same time, if you like, you can create a special heading style for a particular page—without disturbing your site-wide styles. That's the *cascading* part of CSS, which contains a set of definitions dictating which style takes precedence. In FrontPage, for example, if a single page contains inline styles, embedded styles, and a link to an external style sheet, the inline style comes first and the external style sheet last.

Inline styles are the least powerful of the three since their effect is confined to a single HTML element on a single page. For that reason, this chapter focuses on embedded and external style sheets.

Compared with embedded style sheets, external style sheets take a bit more work to set up. But because external style sheets can be applied site wide, they will save you hours of work in the long run. External style sheets offer another welcome bonus—faster downloads, since each page doesn't have to contain all the HTML formatting data.

To activate Cascading Style Sheets

1. Choose Tools > Page Options (**Figure 14.1**).

2. When the Page Options dialog box appears, click the *Compatibility* tab (**Figure 14.2**).

3. Use the *Browser versions* drop-down menu to select *4.0 browsers and later*.

4. In the *Available Technologies* section, make sure that *CSS 1.0 (formatting)* and *CSS 2.0 (positioning)* are checked (**Figure 14.3**). Click *OK* to close the dialog box and activate the Cascading Style Sheets feature.

To activate DHTML

1. Choose Tools > Page Options (**Figure 14.1**).

2. When the Page Options dialog box appears, click the *Compatibility* tab (**Figure 14.2**).

3. Use the *Browser versions* drop-down menu to select *4.0 browsers and later*.

4. In the *Available Technologies* section, make sure that *Dynamic HTML* is checked (**Figure 14.4**). Click *OK* and DHTML will be activated for use in your pages.

Figure 14.1 To activate CSS or DHTML, choose Tools > Page Options.

Figure 14.2 Click the Page Options dialog box's *Compatibility* tab to set which browser technologies your pages will use.

Figure 14.3 To activate CSS, make sure that *CSS 1.0 (formatting)* and *CSS 2.0 (positioning)* are checked in the *Available Technologies* section.

Figure 14.4 To activate DHTML, make sure that *Dynamic HTML* is checked in the *Available Technologies* section.

ACTIVATING CSS AND DHTML

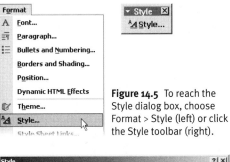

Figure 14.5 To reach the Style dialog box, choose Format > Style (left) or click the Style toolbar (right).

Figure 14.6 To create a new style, click *New* in the Style dialog box.

Figure 14.7 When the New Style dialog box appears, type a distinctive name into the *Name (selector)* text box and pick one of the *Format* drop-down menu items—*Font*, *Paragraph*, *Border*, *Numbering*, or *Position*.

Creating and Editing Embedded Style Sheets

An embedded style sheet can only be used for the single page in which it was created. To apply styles across multiple pages or an entire Web site, see *To create an external style sheet* on page 343. By the way, just in case you come across the term, embedded style sheets are sometimes called *internal* style sheets.

To create an embedded style sheet

1. Make sure you're in page view and choose Format > Style or click the Style toolbar if it is active (**Figure 14.5**).

2. When the Style dialog box appears (**Figure 14.6**), click *New*.

3. When the New Style dialog box appears, type a distinctive name into the *Name (selector)* text box and click *Format* (**Figure 14.7**).

4. Pick one of the *Format* drop-down menu items—*Font*, *Paragraph*, *Border*, *Numbering*, or *Position*—and use the dialog box that appears to choose properties for your new style. Once you've made one set of choices for, say, *Font*, you can use the *Format* drop-down menu to add *Border* properties.

(continued)

CREATING EMBEDDED STYLE SHEETS

5. Once you're done, inspect the results in the *Preview* area, and click *OK* (**Figure 14.8**). The new style—and any other HTML styles that you change—will be listed as a *User-defined style* in the Style dialog box (**Figure 14.9**).

6. If you want to create another new style, click *New* again and repeat steps 3–5. When you're done creating styles, click *OK* in the Style dialog box. If you want to see the CSS coding, select the affected page element in *Normal* view, then click the *HTML* tab (**Figure 14.10**).

✔ Tip

■ Use the Style dialog box's *List* drop-down menu (**Figure 14.6**) to toggle between views of *HTML tags* and *User-defined styles*. The *HTML tags* list shows all the HTML tags that also act as CSS rules. The *User-defined styles* list shows just the CSS rules you've created for the particular page.

Figure 14.8 Once you've defined your new style, inspect it in the *Preview* area, and then click *OK*.

Figure 14.9 A new or modified style will be listed as a *User-defined style* in the Style dialog box.

Figure 14.10 To see the CSS coding, select the edited page element in *Normal* view, then click the *HTML* tab.

Figure 14.11 To edit an embedded style, select it in the *Styles* list and click *Modify*.

Figure 14.12 The Modify Style dialog box works just like the New Style dialog box.

To edit an embedded style sheet

1. Make sure you're in page view and choose Format > Style or click the Style toolbar if it is active (**Figure 14.5**).

2. When the Style dialog box appears, use the *List* drop-down menu to find a standard HTML tag (*HTML tags*) or style you've already created (*User-defined styles*). Use the *Styles* list to select the style you want to change and click *Modify* (**Figure 14.11**).

3. When the Modify Style dialog box appears, the selected style will be listed in the *Name (selector)* text box. Click *Format* and choose the option you want to modify from the drop-down menu (**Figure 14.12**).

(continued)

4. When the dialog box related to your option appears, make your changes, and click *OK* (**Figure 14.13**). The Modify Style dialog box will reappear, with the changes reflected in the *Preview* and *Description* areas (**Figure 14.14**).

5. If you want to change other aspects of the style as well, use the Modify Style dialog box's *Format* drop-down menu to make additional choices. Once you're done, click *OK* in the Modify Style dialog box and you'll be returned to the Style dialog box (**Figure 14.9**).

6. If you want to change another style, select it in the *Styles* list and click *Modify*.

7. When you're done changing styles, click *OK* in the Style dialog box and the changes will be made within the page's HTML code.

Figure 14.13 When the dialog box related to your option appears, make your changes, and click *OK*.

Figure 14.14 Once you modify a style, you can inspect the changes in the Modify Style dialog box's *Preview* and *Description* areas.

Figure 14.15 When the Page Templates dialog box appears, click the *Style Sheets* tab and choose *Normal Style Sheet* or one of the style sheet templates.

Building External Style Sheets

Using external style sheets is a three-step process: First you create the sheet, then you build it or edit it by defining its styles, and finally you link your Web site or individual pages to the sheet.

Parts of the process are similar to working with embedded style sheets, but there are some key differences. For that reason, the entire process of creating, building, editing, and linking external style sheets is laid out here in detail.

To create an external style sheet

1. Choose File > New > Page or Web and when the Task pane appears, click *Page Templates.*

2. When the Page Templates dialog box appears, click the *Style Sheets* tab (**Figure 14.15**).

3. If you want to start from scratch with a blank style sheet, choose the *Normal Style Sheet.* Otherwise, choose one of the style sheet templates listed, which you can easily tweak later to suit your purposes by editing it

(continued)

4. Click *OK* and FrontPage will create a page, give it a .css suffix, and display the page in the main window. If it's a new style sheet, there's not much to see (**Figure 14.16**). If it's based on a template, it already will include definitions for a variety of HTML elements (**Figure 14.17**). In either case, save the page (Ctrl S). When the Save As dialog box appears, give the page a distinctive name, making sure to keep the .css suffix (**Figure 14.18**). You're now ready to build your new style sheet by defining styles for it. Or, if you've used a template for your style sheet, you're ready to modify the styles that already exist within it. For details, see *To build an external style sheet* on page 345 or *To edit an external style sheet* on page 347.

✔ Tips

- When creating a new style sheet, do not press Ctrl N or you'll bypass the New dialog box and wind up with a new HTML page, when what you want is a CSS page.

- While the Page Templates dialog box includes a text description of the various style sheet templates, the *Preview* area isn't available. Many of the templates, however, are based on FrontPage themes, which you can take a peek at by choosing Format > Theme to reach the Themes dialog box (**Figure 14.19**).

Figure 14.16 Until you add to it by defining styles, there's not much to see in a new external style sheet.

Figure 14.17 A template-based external style sheet gives you a head start by including definitions of a variety of HTML elements.

![Save As dialog box]

Figure 14.18 When saving and naming an external style sheet, be sure to keep the .css suffix.

![Themes dialog box]

Figure 14.19 You can preview some of the template-based style sheets in the Themes dialog box.

Figure 14.20 If you're starting from scratch, a new external style sheet will be completely blank.

Figure 14.21 Use the *Styles* list in the Style dialog box to select an HTML tag you want to modify.

Figure 14.22 After you've defined a style, the Style dialog box will include it in the *User-defined styles* list and offer a preview.

To build an external style sheet

1. Open the external style sheet, which will be completely blank (**Figure 14.20**).

2. Choose Format > Style or click the Style toolbar if it is active (**Figure 14.5**).

3. When the Style dialog box appears (**Figure 14.21**), select from the *Styles* list an HTML tag for which you want to create a style, and click *Modify*.

4. When the Modify Style dialog box appears, the HTML tag you selected will be listed in the *Name (selector)* text box (**Figure 14.12**). Click *Format*, then choose *Font, Paragraph, Border, Numbering,* or *Position* and use the related dialog box to modify the HTML tag. Your style changes will appear in the Modify Style dialog box's *Preview* and *Description* areas.

5. If you want to change other aspects of the HTML tag, use the *Format* drop-down menu to make additional choices. Once you're done, click *OK* in the Modify Style dialog box and you'll be returned to the Style dialog box where your new style will be listed in the *User-defined styles* (**Figure 14.22**).

6. To create styles for other HTML tags in your style sheet, use the Style dialog box's *List* drop-down menu to switch back to *HTML tags*. Repeat steps 3–5 until you've created styles for all the HTML tags you want.

(continued)

BUILDING EXTERNAL STYLE SHEETS

7. If you want to create some new custom styles, use the Style dialog box's *List* drop-down menu to switch to *User-defined styles* and then click *New* (**Figure 14.23**).

8. When the New Style dialog box appears, type a distinctive name for your custom style into the *Name (selector)* text box and click *Format* (**Figure 14.24**).

9. Choose *Font, Paragraph, Border, Numbering,* or *Position,* and use the related dialog boxes to define your new custom style. As you proceed, the style changes will appear in the New Style dialog box's *Preview* and *Description* areas.

10. Once you're done, click *OK* in the New Style dialog box and you'll be returned to the Style dialog box where your custom styles—along with the HTML tags you customized—will be listed in the *User-defined styles* (**Figure 14.25**).

11. Once you're satisfied with your custom styles, click *OK* and the changes will be added to your external style sheet (**Figure 14.26**). Save the page (⌃trl S) and you're ready to apply it to your Web site's pages. See *To link to external style sheets* on page 350.

Figure 14.23 To create a custom style in the Style dialog box, switch to *User-defined styles* and click *New*.

Figure 14.24 When creating a new style, give it a distinctive name and use the *Format* button's choices to define it.

Figure 14.25 The Style dialog box will list all your new styles as you define them in your external style sheet.

Figure 14.26 After you have defined your styles, the once-blank external style sheet will list all the additions that will be applied.

Figure 14.27 When the Style dialog box appears, select an item in the left-hand *Styles* list that you want to edit and click *Modify*.

Figure 14.28 Use the *Format* drop-down menu options to change aspects of the selected style.

Figure 14.29 Once you've made your changes, the Style dialog box will present a preview of the edited style.

To edit an external style sheet

1. Open the style sheet, and choose Format > Style or click the Style toolbar if it is active.

2. When the Style dialog box appears (**Figure 14.27**), select an item in the left-hand *Styles* list that you want to edit, and then click *Modify*.

3. When the Modify Style dialog box appears, the style you selected will be listed in the *Name (selector)* text box (**Figure 14.28**). Click *Format* and choose an option from the drop-down menu.

4. When the dialog box related to that option appears, make your changes, and then click *OK*. Continue clicking *Format* and choosing options from the drop-down menu until you've made all your changes.

5. Click *OK* and the changes will appear in the Style dialog box's preview windows, along with a *Description* listing the style's attributes (**Figure 14.29**).

6. If you want to change the style of another item, select it in the *Styles* list, click *Modify*, and repeat steps 3–5.

7. Once you've made all the style changes you want, click *OK* in the Style dialog box and the style sheet will list all your style changes.

EDITING EXTERNAL STYLE SHEETS

Specifying Multiple Fonts in External Style Sheets

Being able to specify multiple fonts in your styles is one of the best reasons for using external style sheets. In effect, you're telling the visitor's Web browser to use Font A and, if it can't find that on the visitor's computer, then use Font B, and if Font B's not present, then use Font C, and so on. That way if your Web visitor doesn't have the oh-so-cool font you've specified, at least they can see it in a font that is roughly similar.

For example, if your first-choice font family for H1 headings is a classic Oldstyle face, such as Bembo, then you'll want to specify similar looking but perhaps more common serif faces, such as Garamond and Caslon, as the second- and third-choice font families. As a backup plan for site visitors who have very few fonts on their computers, you also can include *generic* font family specifications so that their Web browsers will at least use a serif face. For a list of the most common font families found on computers, see **Table 14.1**. For a list of CSS's generic font specifications, see **Table 14.2**.

Unfortunately, FrontPage includes no way to specify multiple fonts without coding directly in the external style sheet. Fortunately, however, if you've already created an external style sheet it's pretty easy to add the multiple font specs.

Still, it's helpful to understand a little about how CSS styles are constructed (**Figure 14.30**). Each HTML element (known as a *selector* in CSS jargon) has at least one *property* and a *value* for that property. It's also possible for a selector to have several properties, and each property to have several values, such as multiple fonts.

Table 14.1

Most Common Font Families		
SERIF	WINDOWS	MACINTOSH
	Times	Times
	Times New Roman	Palatino
SANS SERIF	WINDOWS	MACINTOSH
	Arial	Geneva
		Helvetica

Table 14.2

CSS Generic Font Values	
CSS VALUE	SOME EXAMPLES
serif	Times, Garamond, Bodoni
sans serif	Arial, Helvetica, Geneva, Futura
monospace	Courier, Monaco, Letter Gothic
cursive (script)	Mistral, Park Avenue
fantasy (decorative)	Copperplate Gothic, VAG Round

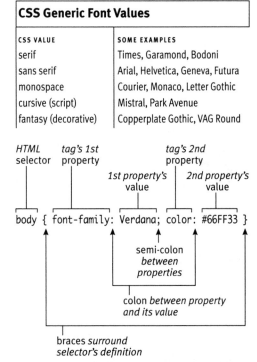

Figure 14.30 Each CSS style contains a *selector*, and at least one *property* and one *value*, which are set off by *braces*, *colons*, or *semi-colons*.

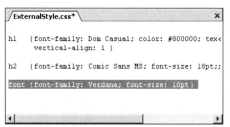

Figure 14.31 Find within the external style sheet the font definition to which you want to add multiple fonts. This example uses the *font* selector, but you also could specify multiple fonts for *h1*, *h2*, or any selector that accepts fonts.

```
ExternalStyle.css*                              ×
h1    { font-family: Dom Casual; color: #800000; tex
        vertical-align: 1 }

h2    { font-family: Comic Sans MS; font-size: 18pt;

font { font-family: Verdana; font-size: 10pt }
```

Figure 14.32 To list additional fonts, click between the font name and the semicolon.

```
ExternalStyle.css*                              ×
h1    {font-family: Dom Casual; color: #800000; text-align: left; font-si
        vertical-align: 1 }
h2    {font-family: Comic Sans MS; font-size: 18pt; letter-spacing: -1pt
font {font-family: Verdana, Arial, Helvetica, sans serif; font-size: 10pt
```

Figure 14.33 Separate each font you add with a comma and a blank space, then save the page (Ctrl S).

To specify multiple fonts

1. First create a style sheet following *To build an external style sheet* on page 345, then open it.

2. When the external style sheet opens, find the font definition to which you want to add multiple fonts (**Figure 14.31**).

3. Click your cursor at the end of the first font family listed (**Figure 14.32**), immediately in front of the semicolon.

4. Type a comma, a space, and the name of a second font family you want included in the definition. Continue adding font families, preceding each with a comma and space until you've added all the font families you want specified (**Figure 14.33**). Be sure to add a generic font specification as well.

5. Save the page ((Ctrl)(S)) and you're ready to apply it to your Web site's pages. See *To link to external style sheets* on the next page.

Linking to External Style Sheets

You can define an external style sheet to your heart's content, but you must link pages to that style sheet for its styles to be applied.

To link to external style sheets

1. Make sure you're in page view and open the page you want linked to the external style sheet (**Figure 14.34**).

2. Choose Format > Style Sheet Links (**Figure 14.35**).

3. When the Link Style Sheet dialog box appears (**Figure 14.36**), choose *Selected page(s)* if you want to apply the style sheet to only the current page. Choose *All pages* if you want to apply the external style sheet to your entire Web site. Click *Add*.

Figure 14.34 Open the page to which you want the external style sheet applied.

Figure 14.35 To link the page to the external style sheet, choose Format > Style Sheet Links.

Figure 14.36 Choose *Selected page(s)* if you want to apply the style sheet to only the current page. Choose *All pages* if you want to apply the external style sheet to your entire Web site. Click *Add* to find the style sheet.

Figure 14.37 Use the Select Style Sheet dialog box to navigate to the style sheet you want to use.

Figure 14.38 Once you've added the style sheet, click *OK* to apply it to the selected pages.

Figure 14.39 After applying the style sheet, the Web page from Figure 14.34 displays the new style.

4. When the Select Style Sheet dialog box appears, navigate to the style sheet you want to use, select it, and its URL or path-name will be pasted into the *URL* text box (**Figure 14.37**). Click *OK*.

5. The external style sheet will be listed in the Link Style Sheet dialog box (**Figure 14.38**). Click *OK* and the style sheet will be applied to the page(s) you selected (**Figure 14.39**).

To remove links to external style sheets

1. Open the page that's linked to the external style sheet.

2. Choose Format > Style Sheet Links (**Figure 14.35**).

3. When the Link Style Sheet dialog box appears, choose *Selected page(s)* if you want to remove the link only for the current page. Choose *All pages* if you want to remove all the Web site's links to the external style sheet. Select the style sheet in the *URL* window, and click *Remove* (**Figure 14.40**).

4. Click *OK* and the selected pages will lose the styles previously applied by the external style sheet.

Figure 14.40 To remove a style sheet link, select it and click *Remove*.

Figure 14.41 Select in the *Styles* list the user-defined style you want to remove and click *Delete*.

Figure 14.42 Once deleted, the customized *h1* disappears from the *User-defined styles* list.

Figure 14.43 Even though you deleted its *custom* style definition, a *generic* h1 tag remains part of your list of *HTML tags*.

Deleting Styles

Whether you're working with embedded styles or external style sheets, you can get rid of individual custom styles at any time. And if you've customized an HTML tag, such as H1, the same process will return the tag to its standard definition.

To delete custom styles

1. Make sure you're in page view and choose Format > Style or click the Style toolbar if it is active (**Figure 14.5**).

2. When the Style dialog box appears (**Figure 14.41**), select in the *Styles* list the user-defined style you want to delete and click *Delete*. The custom style will be removed from the Styles list (**Figure 14.42**).

✔ Tips

- Despite that word Delete, when it comes to standard HTML tags, this procedure is more like Undo. For example, in step 2 if you delete a custom version of a standard HTML tag, such as H1, it will disappear from the *User-defined styles* list. But it will still appear in the *HTML tags* list—just without the custom style it had previously (**Figure 14.43**).

- When you delete a custom style, it will be removed from the Styles list without any warning, so check the *Preview* area to make sure you've selected the style you really want to delete.

Using Dynamic HTML Effects

DHTML can be used to zip text around your pages, send graphics spiraling, and trigger events as visitors mouse around your site. The exact DHTML options available vary, depending on which elements you select on a page. In general, there are more DHTML options for text than there are for graphics. DHTML tags work with version 4 or later Microsoft Internet Explorer or Netscape Navigator browsers. Earlier browsers will simply show static—but correct—versions of your pages, which means browser compatibility is one less thing to worry about.

To apply dynamic effects

1. Make sure the DHTML Effects toolbar is visible by choosing Format > Dynamic HTML Effects (**Figure 14.44**). The toolbar will appear (**Figure 14.45**), and you can move it to a convenient spot on your screen.

2. Select the page element to which you want to apply DHTML (**Figure 14.46**).

3. Use the toolbar's *On* drop-down menu ❶ to select *when* the effect will be applied.

4. Use the toolbar's *Apply* drop-down menu ❷ to select *which* effect will be applied.

5. Depending on your choice in step 4, use the *<Choose Settings>* drop-down menu ❸ to further define the effect.

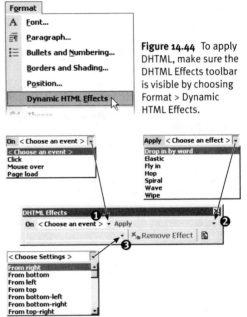

Figure 14.44 To apply DHTML, make sure the DHTML Effects toolbar is visible by choosing Format > Dynamic HTML Effects.

Figure 14.45 The drop-down menu choices in the DHTML Effects toolbar vary depending on which page element you select.

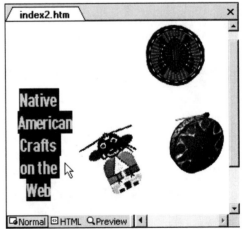

Figure 14.46 To apply an effect, first select a page element.

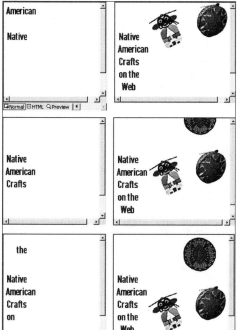

Figure 14.47 Use the *Preview* tab to see the final effect. In this example, *Drop in by word* was applied to the headline and *Fly in* to the graphic.

Figure 14.48 To cancel an effect, select the page element and click *Remove Effect* in the DHTML Effects toolbar.

6. If you want, select another page element and apply DHTML effects to it by repeating steps 3–5.

7. Once you're done setting the effects, click the *Preview* tab in FrontPage's main window to see how the effects look (**Figure 14.47**).

✔ Tip

- If you need to adjust the effect, click the *Normal* tab in FrontPage's main window, then click the toolbar and use the toolbar drop-down menus to change the settings. When you want to check the effect, be sure to click the *Preview* tab again.

To remove a dynamic effect

1. Select the page element whose effect you want to cancel.

2. Click on the DHTML Effects toolbar, then click *Remove Effect* (**Figure 14.48**). The effect will be canceled.

Using Page Transitions

This particular DHTML feature lets you create video-like transitions when a site visitor enters or leaves a page or your site. FrontPage includes more than 20 transition effects. While they are very cool, use page transitions only if you're creating a corporate intranet where you know for certain that *everyone* is using the Windows version of the Internet Explorer 4 or 5 browser. Page transitions don't work with other browsers, so be careful not to exclude those users.

Figure 14.49 To add page transitions, choose Format > Page Transition.

To add page transitions

1. Make sure you're in page view and the *Normal* tab is selected. Click anywhere in the page and choose Format > Page Transition (**Figure 14.49**).

2. When the Page Transitions dialog box appears (**Figure 14.50**), use the *Event* drop-down menu ❶ to select *when* the effect will be applied.

3. Use the *Transition effect* scrolling menu box ❷ to select *which* effect will be applied.

4. Enter a number in the *Duration (seconds)* text box ❸ to set *how long* the transition will take to complete.

5. Once you've made your selections, click *OK*. Click the *Preview* tab in FrontPage's main window to see how the transition looks.

Figure 14.50 Use the Page Transitions dialog box to select an *Event*, a *Transition effect*, and a *Duration*.

To remove page transitions

1. Make sure you're in page view and the *Normal* tab is selected. Click anywhere in the page and choose Format > Page Transition (**Figure 14.49**).

2. When the Page Transitions dialog box appears (**Figure 14.50**), use the *Transition effect* scrolling menu box to select *No Effect*, which is the first item in the list.

3. Click *OK* and the transition will be removed.

USING PAGE TRANSITIONS

PART 4

MANAGING AND PUBLISHING WEB SITES

MANAGING WEB SITE WORKFLOW

15

Like most publishing, Web publishing is usually a team sport. Writers create stories, editors proof copy and add headlines, artists produce graphics and illustrations, and designers lay it all out. Keeping track of who's doing what on a Web site can be a challenge. Sometimes even if you're doing it all yourself, it's easy to forget key tasks. FrontPage's tasks and reports views can be a big help in managing the workflow on the typical Web site with a zillion and one details.

You can use most of FrontPage's workflow features no matter how you're set up. Others, such as the system of checking Web files in and out (explained on page 379), will work only if your Web server has the FrontPage Server Extensions installed. For more on the extensions, see pages 385 and 417.

Creating Tasks

Essentially you have two choices in using FrontPage to create tasks: a close-focus, from-the-ground-up approach or a broader, top-down approach. Each has its place in the publishing process.

In the close-focus method, you would begin by linking specific files to a specific task, such as "create home page image maps." This works well when you already have a firm sense of exactly what work needs to be done. This is the process explained in *To link files to a task* on the next page, *To link files to a review* on page 369, *To assign a file* on page 374, and *To start a task* on page 384.

This files-based approach, however, may not be the best in every circumstance. Sometimes you may find it more helpful to begin by broadly defining the tasks and not associating them with any particular files. Only later would you create detailed tasks linked to specific files. In those cases, the broader, top-down approach works better, especially if you want to leave it to others to figure out the actual steps needed to accomplish the broader task. This more general approach is explained in *To create a task not linked to a file* on page 363, *To assign a task* on page 372, and *To mark a task completed* on page 383.

Figure 15.1 To link an open page to a task, choose File > New > Task.

Figure 15.2 Use the New Task dialog box to create and assign tasks.

To link files to a task

1. Open the page to which you want to assign a task and choose File > New > Task (**Figure 15.1**).

2. When the New Task dialog box appears (**Figure 15.2**), you'll notice that the current Web page will appear listed next to *Associated with* ❹.

3. Type a short description of the task or give it a name in the *Task name* text box ❶.

4. Use the option buttons to give the task a *Priority* ❷, though you can do that later if you prefer.

5. Type a name into the *Assigned to* text box or use the drop-down menu ❸ to pick from a list of previously used names. For details, see *To create a names master list* on page 371.

6. FrontPage will automatically supply the information in the middle of the dialog box ❺, so skip down to the *Description* area ❻ if you want to add any details about the task.

(continued)

CREATING TASKS

7. When you've finished (**Figure 15.3**), click *OK*. Repeat steps 2–6 to link other files with tasks if you wish.

8. Switch to the tasks view by clicking the Tasks icon in the Views Bar and the new task will appear in the Tasks list (**Figure 15.4**).

✔ Tips

■ To launch the files you've linked to a particular task, see *To start a task* on page 384.

■ If you want to link certain files to a category instead of a task, see *To categorize files* on page 367.

■ You don't have to assign a task when you create it. Instead you can do it any time. See *To assign a task* on page 372.

Figure 15.3 Once you've filled in the New Task dialog box, click *OK*.

Figure 15.4 Switch to the tasks view to see a list of tasks for building your Web site.

Figure 15.5 To create a task not linked to a particular file, choose Edit > Tasks > Add Task.

Figure 15.6 You also can create a task *not* linked to a file by right-clicking and choosing *Add Task* from the shortcut menu.

Figure 15.7 When the New Task dialog box appears, give it a name, priority, and, if you want, a description.

Figure 15.8 The new task will be added to the *Tasks* list with the *Associated With* column left blank.

To create a task not linked to a file

1. In any view, choose Edit > Tasks > Add Task (**Figure 15.5**). Or switch to the tasks view, right-click in the main window, and choose *Add Task* from the shortcut menu (**Figure 15.6**).

2. When the New Task dialog box appears (**Figure 15.7**), describe the task or give it a shorthand name in the *Task name* text box.

3. Use the option buttons to give the task a *Priority*.

4. Type a name into the *Assigned to* text box or use the drop-down menu to pick from a list of previously used names. For details, see *To create a names master list* on page 371.

5. FrontPage will automatically provide the information in the middle of the dialog box, so skip down to the *Description* area if you want to add any details about the task.

6. When you've finished, click *OK*. The new task will be added to the *Tasks* list with the *Associated With* column left blank (**Figure 15.8**). Repeat the steps to add as many tasks as you need.

✔ Tips

■ Unlike in **Figure 15.2**, you'll notice that in step 2 (**Figure 15.7**) the *Associated with* line says *(Is not associated)*. That tells you that the task you're creating or editing is a freestanding one that's not linked with any file.

■ You don't have to assign a task when you create it. Instead you can do it any time. See *To assign a task* on page 372.

CREATING TASKS

Organizing Files

FrontPage helps you organize your Web files with several labeling options. By labeling files by category, for example, you could create a Redesign category for all the files related to the upcoming redesign of your Web site. You can use whatever categories make sense: organizational categories, such as Production; product categories, such as New Widgets. The categories do not appear on the Web site itself, just in FrontPage's reports view.

FrontPage also includes another labeling choice, which it calls *review status*, for marking files that should be checked before they're published. By building your own master list of review procedures or mileposts, you can use the reports view to quickly see whether files and pages have been checked over by others on your Web site team. Before you begin labeling files by category or review status, it will speed your work if you first create a master list for each.

Figure 15.9 To create any master list for a file, right-click the file and choose *Page Properties* from the shortcut menu.

Figure 15.10 Use the buttons in the *Workgroup* tab to create master lists.

Figure 15.11 Use the Master Category List dialog box to add or remove file categories.

Figure 15.12 The new categories you create will be added to the *Available categories* list.

To create a categories master list

1. Right-click any open page and choose *Page Properties* from the shortcut menu (**Figure 15.9**).

2. Click the *Workgroup* tab in the dialog box that appears (**Figure 15.10**).

3. Click the *Categories* button to reach the Master Category List dialog box (**Figure 15.11**).

4. Type a category into the *New category* text box and click *Add*. The name will be added to the dialog box's existing list.

5. Repeat step 4 until you've added all the categories you want to the list.

6. Click *OK* and the categories will be added to the *Available categories* scrolling text box under the *Workgroup* tab (**Figure 15.12**). To label files by category, see *To categorize files* on page 367.

✔ Tips

■ To remove a category from the master list, select one in the dialog box's list, and click *Remove* (**Figure 15.11**). The category will be removed.

■ If you change your mind while changing categories in the master list, click *Reset* and the list will return to how it was before you opened it.

To create a review status master list

1. Right-click any file in the Folder List or listed in the main window and choose *Properties* from the shortcut menu (**Figure 15.13**).

2. Click the *Workgroup* tab in the dialog box that appears, then click the *Statuses* button (**Figure 15.14**).

3. When the Review Status Master List dialog box appears, type a category into the *New review status* text box and click *Add* (**Figure 15.15**). The new review procedure will be added to the dialog box's existing list.

4. Repeat step 3 until you've added all the review procedures you want to the list. Click *OK* and they will be available in any of FrontPage's review status drop-down menus. For details, see *To link files to a review* on page 369.

✔ Tips

■ To remove a review procedure from the master list, select one in the dialog box's list, and click *Remove* (**Figure 15.15**). The review procedure will be removed.

■ If you change your mind while adding or deleting review procedures, click *Reset* and the list will return to how it was before you opened it.

Figure 15.13
To create a review status master list, right-click any file in the Folder List or listed in the main window and choose *Properties*.

Figure 15.14 Click the *Statuses* button to build a review status master list.

Figure 15.15 Use the Review Status Master List dialog box to add or remove review procedures for files.

CREATING MASTER LISTS

Figure 15.16 To categorize files, choose Reports > Workflow > Categories in the Reporting toolbar.

Figure 15.17 In the Categories report, right-click the file you want categorized and choose *Properties*.

Figure 15.18 Check the categories you want applied to a file within the *Available categories* scrolling text box.

Figure 15.19 Multiple categories can be applied to a single file.

To categorize files

1. Choose View > Reports > Categories or choose Reports > Workflow > Categories if the Reporting toolbar is active (**Figure 15.16**).

2. When the Categories report appears, right-click the file you want categorized and choose *Properties* from the shortcut menu (**Figure 15.17**).

3. Click the *Workgroup* tab in the dialog box that appears, then, in the *Available categories* scrolling text box, check off the category boxes you want applied to the file (**Figure 15.18**). As you check boxes, the category will be added to the *Item(s) belong to these categories* text box.

4. Click *OK* and the chosen categories will be applied to the file (**Figure 15.19**).

✔ Tip

■ You can apply *multiple* categories to a *single* file.

CATEGORIZING FILES

367

To simultaneously categorize multiple files

1. Choose View > Reports > Categories or choose Reports > Workflow > Categories if the Reporting toolbar is active (**Figure 15.16**).

2. When the Categories report appears, press [Ctrl] as you select multiple files by clicking each in the list.

3. Right-click the selected files and choose *Properties* from the shortcut menu (**Figure 15.20**).

4. Click the *Workgroup* tab in the dialog box that appears (**Figure 15.10**), then, in the Available categories scrolling text box, check off the category boxes you want applied to the selected files (**Figure 15.18**).

5. Click *OK* and the categories will be applied to all the selected files (**Figure 15.21**).

Figure 15.20 To simultaneously categorize more than one file, right-click the selected files and choose *Properties* from the shortcut menu.

Figure 15.21 Multiple files can have the same categories applied to them simultaneously.

Figure 15.22 Choose Reports > Workflow > Review Status in the Reporting toolbar.

Figure 15.23 Click in the *Review Status* column of any file you want linked to a review, and a drop-down menu, with the first line blank, will appear.

Figure 15.24 Use the drop-down menu to link a review procedure to a file or type a new procedure into the text box.

Figure 15.25 Once a file's linked to a review procedure, the procedure will be listed in the Review Status report.

Figure 15.26 By creating a series of review procedures, you can quickly see the progress of work.

To link files to a review

1. Choose View > Reports > Review Status or choose Reports > Workflow > Review Status if the Reporting toolbar is active (**Figure 15.22**).

2. When the Review Status report appears, click in the *Review Status* column of any file you want linked to a review, and a drop-down menu, with the first line blank, will appear for the item (**Figure 15.23**).

3. Use the drop-down menu to link an existing review procedure to the file or type a new procedure into the text box (**Figure 15.24**).

4. Release the cursor and press [Enter] to link the file and the review step (**Figure 15.25**). Repeat until you've linked reviews to all the files you need (**Figure 15.26**).

✔ Tips

- Once a file has been reviewed, use the Review Status drop-down menu in step 3 to select the next necessary review. Or press [←Backspace] to clear the menu if all the necessary reviews of the file have been completed.

- Speed up the process by creating a master list of review procedures ahead of time. See page 366 for details.

- A file can only have one review status linked to it at a time, which makes sense if you think of the file as needing to clear a sequence of review hurdles: first this, then that, then the final OK.

LINKING FILES

To simultaneously link multiple files to a review

1. Choose View > Reports > Review Status or choose Reports > Workflow > Review Status if the Reporting toolbar is active (**Figure 15.22**).

2. When the Review Status report appears, press (Ctrl) as you select multiple files by clicking each in the list.

3. Right-click the selected files and choose *Properties* from the shortcut menu.

4. Click the *Workgroup* tab in the dialog box that appears and type a status name into the *Review status* text box or use the drop-down menu (**Figure 15.27**).

5. Click *OK* and the review status procedure will be assigned to all the selected files.

Figure 15.27 Use the *Review status* drop-down menu to apply a procedure to multiple files.

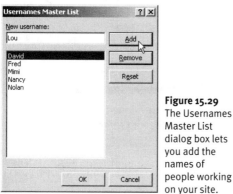

Figure 15.28 To create a names master list, click the *Names* button in the dialog box's *Workgroup* tab.

Figure 15.29
The Usernames Master List dialog box lets you add the names of people working on your site.

Figure 15.30
To remove a name from the master list, select it and click *Remove*.

Assigning Tasks

FrontPage lets you assign tasks to a specific person or workgroup. It also lets you assign particular files to a person or workgroup, for example, assigning all the image files to the art department. While it's common to assign a task as you create it, you also can assign it—or reassign it—later.

While FrontPage lets you create names for assignments one at a time, sometimes it's faster to go ahead and create a master list of people involved in a project. That way, any time you click an assignment drop-down menu, every name you need will appear.

To create a names master list

1. Right-click any file in the main window or in the Folder List and choose *Page Properties* from the shortcut menu (**Figure 15.9**).

2. Click the *Workgroup* tab in the dialog box that appears, then click the *Names* button (**Figure 15.28**).

3. When the Usernames Master List dialog box appears, type a name into the *New username* text box and click *Add* (**Figure 15.29**). The name will be added to the dialog box's existing list.

4. Repeat step 3 until you've added all the names you want to the list. Click *OK* and the added names will be available in any of FrontPage's name drop-down menus.

✔ Tips

- To remove a name from the master list, click a name in the dialog box, then click *Remove* (**Figure 15.30**). The name will be removed from the name drop-down menus.

- If you change your mind while changing names in the master list, click *Reset* and the list will return to how it was before.

ASSIGNING TASKS

371

To assign a task

1. Switch to the tasks view and click in the *Assigned To* column of the task you want to assign. A drop-down menu, with the first line blank, will appear for the item (**Figure 15.31**).

2. Use the drop-down menu to assign a name or type a new name into the text box.

3. Release the cursor and press (Enter) to apply the assignment (**Figure 15.32**).

✔ Tip

■ If you're in tasks view, you also can double-click the task and make your assignment changes in the Task Details dialog box (**Figure 15.33**).

Figure 15.31 To assign a task, click in the *Assigned To* column and a drop-down menu will appear.

Figure 15.32 Choose a name from the drop-down menu and press (Enter) to assign a task.

Figure 15.33 If you're in tasks view and want to change an assignment, double-click a task to jump straight to the Task Details dialog box.

Tasks		
Status	Task	Assigned To
● Not Started	edit image...	Mimi
● Not Started	Optimize g...	Mimi
◐ Completed	Finish Book!	Nolan
◐ Completed	Polish ho...	Nancy

Figure 15.34 To reassign a task, click in the *Assigned To* column of the task you want to reassign.

Tasks		
Status	Task	Assigned To
● Not Started	edit image...	Mimi
● Not Started	Optimize g...	Mimi ▼
◐ Completed	Finish Book!	Fred
◐ Completed	Polish ho...	Mimi
		Nancy
		Nolan

Figure 15.35 Use the drop-down menu to assign another name to the task or type a new name into the text box.

Tasks		
Status	Task	Assigned To
● Not Started	edit image...	Mimi
● Not Started	Optimize g...	Nancy
◐ Completed	Finish Book!	Nolan
◐ Completed	Polish ho...	Nancy

Figure 15.36 Press Enter to apply a reassignment in the Tasks list.

To reassign a task

1. Switch to the tasks view and click in the *Assigned To* column of the task you want to reassign (**Figure 15.34**). A drop-down menu will appear, listing everyone who has been assigned tasks so far.

2. Use the drop-down menu to assign another name to the task or type a new name into the text box (**Figure 15.35**).

3. Release the cursor and press Enter to apply the reassignment (**Figure 15.36**).

ASSIGNING TASKS

To assign a file

1. Choose View > Reports > Assigned To or choose Reports > Workflow > Assigned To if the Reporting toolbar is active (**Figure 15.37**).

2. When the Assigned To list appears, click in the *Assigned To* column of any file you want assigned, and a drop-down menu, with the first line blank, will appear for the item (**Figure 15.38**).

3. Use the drop-down menu to assign a name or type a new name into the text box.

4. Release the cursor and press (Enter) to apply the file assignment (**Figure 15.39**). Repeat until you've assigned all the files you need.

✔ Tip

■ By creating a master list of names, you can speed up the assignment process. See page 371 for details.

Figure 15.37 Choose Reports > Workflow > Assigned To in the Reporting toolbar.

Figure 15.38 Click in the *Assigned To* column and use the drop-down menu to assign a name or type a new name into the text box.

Figure 15.39 Press (Enter) to apply the assignment to the file.

Figure 15.40 To simultaneously assign multiple files, right-click the selected files and choose *Properties* from the shortcut menu.

updates.htm, sayhey.htm... Properties

General | Summary | Workgroup

Item(s) belong to these categories:

Available categories:
- [ ] Business
- [ ] Competition
- [ ] Expense Report
- [ ] Goals/Objectives

Categories...

Assigned to:

David
Lou
Mimi
Nancy
Nolan

Names...

Statuses...

[ ] Exclude this file when publishing the rest of the Web

OK | Cancel | Apply

Figure 15.41 Use the *Assigned to* text box or drop-down menu to apply a name to multiple files.

Assigned To		
Name	Title	Assigned To
updates.htm	Updates	Mimi
sayhey.htm	Tell us what you think ...	Mimi
test.avi	test.avi	Mimi
ExternalStyle...	ExternalStyle.css	Mimi

Figure 15.42 By simultaneously assigning multiple files, you can quickly tag who's responsible for what.

To simultaneously assign multiple files

1. Choose View > Reports > Assigned To or choose Reports > Workflow > Assigned To if the Reporting toolbar is active (**Figure 15.37**).

2. When the Assigned To list appears, press Ctrl as you select multiple files by clicking them in the Assigned To list.

3. Right-click the selected files and choose *Properties* from the shortcut menu (**Figure 15.40**).

4. Click the *Workgroup* tab in the dialog box that appears and type a name into the *Assigned to* text box or use the drop-down menu (**Figure 15.41**).

5. Click *OK* and the name will be assigned to all the selected files (**Figure 15.42**).

ASSIGNING FILES

Editing Tasks

As noted earlier, FrontPage lets you change many aspects of a task after you've created it. You can make multiple changes within the Task Details dialog box or change individual aspects directly within the Tasks list.

To make multiple changes to a task

1. Switch to tasks view, right-click the task you want to change, and choose *Edit Task* from the shortcut menu (**Figure 15.43**).

2. When the Task Details dialog box appears (**Figure 15.33**), use the *Task name* text box to rename the task.

3. Use the option buttons to give the task a new *Priority*.

4. Type a new name into the *Assigned to* text box or use the drop-down menu to pick from the other names listed.

5. Use the *Description* area to change any details about the task.

6. Click *OK* and the changes will be applied to the task.

✔ Tip

■ To quickly reach the Task Details dialog box (**Figure 15.33**), you also can just double-click the task in the Tasks List.

Figure 15.43 To edit a task, right-click it and choose *Edit Task* from the shortcut menu.

Figure 15.44 To change a task's name, click the item and when it becomes highlighted, type in a new name.

Figure 15.45 To change a task's description, click the item and when it becomes highlighted, type in a new description.

Figure 15.46 Press [Enter] to apply the change.

To change a task's name or description

1. Switch to the tasks view and click the task name or description you want to change.

2. When the item becomes highlighted, type in a new name (**Figure 15.44**) or description (**Figure 15.45**).

3. Press [Enter] and the change will be applied (**Figure 15.46**).

✔ Tip

- If a task is listed in the *Status* column as *Completed*, you cannot change its name. However, you can change its description.

To change a task's priority

1. Switch to the tasks view and click *once* in the *Priority* column on the task you want to change.

2. When the task becomes highlighted, click the item's priority once more. A drop-down menu will appear for the item.

3. Use the drop-down menu to change the item's priority (**Figure 15.47**). Press (Enter) and the new priority will be applied.

To sort tasks

1. Switch to tasks view by clicking the Tasks icon in the Views Bar (**Figure 15.48**).

2. Click any column label to sort the Tasks list by that column's value (**Figure 15.49**).

✔ Tip

- To reverse the sort order of any column, click the column label a second time (**Figure 15.50**).

Tasks			
Status	Task	Assigned To	Priority
● Not Started	edit image...	Fred	Medium ▾

High
Medium
Low

Figure 15.47 To change a task's priority, use the *Priority* column's drop-down menu.

Tasks

Figure 15.48 To sort tasks, switch to the tasks view.

Tasks		
Status	Task	Assigned To
● Not Started	Build order page	David
● Not Started	edit image map	Mimi
● Not Started	proof all copy	Nancy
● Not Started	update catalo...	Lou
◐ Completed	import fall images	Lou
◐ Completed	shrink logo	Mimi

Tasks		
Status	Task	Assigned To
● Not Started	Build order page	David
◐ Completed	import fall images	Lou
● Not Started	update catalo...	Lou
◐ Completed	shrink logo	Mimi
● Not Started	edit image map	Mimi
● Not Started	proof all copy	Nancy

Figure 15.49 Click the column labels to sort the Tasks list by, for example, *Status* (top) or *Assigned To* (bottom).

Tasks		
Status	Task	Assigned To
◐ Completed	import fall images	Lou
◐ Completed	shrink logo	Mimi
● Not Started	Build order page	David
● Not Started	edit image map	Mimi
● Not Started	proof all copy	Nancy
● Not Started	update catalo...	Lou

Figure 15.50 To reverse the sort order of any column, click the column label a second time.

Figure 15.51 To activate the checkout system, choose Tools > Web Settings.

Figure 15.52 Click the Web Settings dialog box's *General* tab and check *Use document check-in and check-out.*

Figure 15.53 When the alert dialog box appears, click *Yes.* The recalculating only takes a few seconds.

Using the Checkout System

FrontPage's checkout system offers a handy way to coordinate all the work being done on different files for your Web site. While a file is checked out, it cannot be changed by anyone else—a process known as source control. Others can read the last version of the file but cannot make any changes until the file is checked back in. When a file is checked back in, FrontPage saves any changes made to the file.

To activate the checkout system

1. Choose Tools > Web Settings (**Figure 15.51**).

2. When the Web Settings dialog box appears, click the *General* tab and check *Use document check-in and check-out* (**Figure 15.52**).

3. Click *OK* and when the alert dialog box appears, click *Yes* (**Figure 15.53**). Checkout control will be applied to the Web site.

To check out a file

1. While in folders or reports view (or with the Folder List visible), right-click the file you want to use, and choose *Check Out* from the shortcut menu (**Figure 15.54**).

2. A red checkmark will be placed next to the file, preventing anyone else from making changes to the file while it's checked out (**Figure 15.55**).

✔ Tip

■ If you try to check out a file that's already been checked out, a dialog box will give you the choice of opening the file in read-only status or canceling your request (**Figure 15.56**).

Figure 15.54 To check out a file, right-click it and choose *Check Out* from the shortcut menu.

Name	Title
✔ 🖻 addingDrawi...	Adding Drawings
✔ 🖻 addingImage...	Adding Images
✔ 🗎 animate.js	animate.js
✔ 🖻 chap_4.htm	Chap 4
• 🖻 chap_5.htm	Chap 5
• 🖻 confirmation....	Dear

Figure 15.55 Files in use are marked with a checkmark.

Microsoft FrontPage

addingImages.htm
The file is under source control and has read only attributes.

Do you want to check it out?

[Yes]   [No]   [Cancel]

Figure 15.56 If you try to open a file that's in use, an alert box lets you choose to see it in read-only mode or cancel your request.

Figure 15.57 Right-click on the file you want to check back in and choose *Check In* from the shortcut menu.

Figure 15.58 If you check out a file and want to check it back in without making any changes, right-click the file and choose *Undo Check Out*.

To check in a file

1. Make sure to first save your changes to the file you've checked out ([Ctrl][S]).

2. While in folders or reports view (or with the Folder List visible), right-click on the file you want to check back in and choose *Check In* from the shortcut menu (**Figure 15.57**). The file will now be available for others to check out and change, as denoted by the disappearance of the red check mark.

✔ Tip

■ Suppose you check out a file, make some changes, and then decide you don't want to make those changes after all. To check the file back in *without* saving those changes, right-click a file you've checked out and choose *Undo Check Out* from the shortcut menu (**Figure 15.58**). The file will be checked back in without being changed.

USING THE CHECKOUT SYSTEM

To see a list of checked out files

1. To quickly see which files are checked out and by whom, choose View > Reports > Checkout Status or choose Reports > Workflow > Checkout Status if the Reporting toolbar is active (**Figure 15.59**).

2. When the Checkout Status report appears, files *you* have checked out will be marked by a checkmark, while those checked out by others will be marked with a lock (**Figure 15.60**).

Figure 15.59 To see which files are checked out, choose Reports > Workflow > Checkout Status in the Reporting toolbar.

Name	Title	Checked Out By	Version
✓ order.htm	order.htm	Nolan	V1
✓ frameless...	Two Raven Trad...	Nolan	V1
✓ ravenba...	images/ravenban...	Nolan	V1
🔒 bullroar.gif	images/bullroar.gif	Nancy	V1
🔒 Sales Re...	Sales Reports.fp5	Nancy	V1
🔒 lonerave...	loneraven2.gif	Mimi	V1
🔒 newLone...	images/newLone...	Mimi	V1

Figure 15.60 In the Checkout Status report, files you're using show a checkmark. Files in use by others show a lock.

USING THE CHECKOUT SYSTEM

Figure 15.61 Once a task is finished, switch to tasks view, right-click the task, and choose *Mark Complete*.

Figure 15.62 To delete a task, right-click the task, and choose *Delete Task*.

Figure 15.63 When you try to delete a task, an alert dialog box will ask you to confirm your decision.

Completing Tasks

It's fine to assign, sort, and categorize tasks, but at some point you want to get them done. For general tasks not associated with any file, you can mark the task completed or delete it. For tasks with files linked to them, FrontPage offers another choice—Start Task—which launches the files tied to the task, even if they use another application. Once a file's ready to be published, see *To check or change a page's publishing status* on page 388.

To mark a task completed

◆ While in tasks view, right-click a task that's been finished and choose *Mark Complete* from the shortcut menu (**Figure 15.61**). The task's status will change to *Completed* and the task's bullet will turn green.

To delete a task

1. While in tasks view, right-click the task you want to delete and choose *Delete Task* from the shortcut menu (**Figure 15.62**).

2. When the Confirm Delete dialog box appears, click *Yes* (**Figure 15.63**). The task will be deleted, although any *files* associated with it will remain on your Web site.

COMPLETING TASKS

To start a task

◆ While in tasks view, right-click a task whose linked files you want to work on and choose *Start Task* from the shortcut menu (**Figure 15.64**). The files associated with the task will open and, if they use another application, that program also will be launched.

✔ Tip

■ You also can start a task by double-clicking it and, when the Task Details dialog box appears, clicking the *Start Task* button (**Figure 15.65**).

Figure 15.64 If files are linked to a task, right-click the task, choose *Start Task*, and the files will open.

Figure 15.65 You also can open a file linked to a task, by double-clicking it and clicking *Start Task* in the Task Details dialog box.

CHECKING AND PUBLISHING WEB SITES

Two crucial steps remain before you actually copy your local files over to a Web server. First, use FrontPage to analyze if any pages have problems, such as broken hyperlinks or slow-to-download files. Second, look at every page with a Web browser to check its general appearance.

When you're ready to publish, you'll need to have an Internet Service Provider (ISP) or Web Presence Provider (WPP) lined up to host your site, unless you're copying the files to an inhouse intranet. Your ISP's Web server does not need the FrontPage Server Extensions for your Web site's essential features to work properly. However, some of FrontPage's advanced bells and whistles will not be available unless the extensions are installed on the server. If your ISP still is using the FrontPage 2000-vintage extensions, your FrontPage 2002-generated pages will work fine, except for server-based features added since the 2000 version, such as Top Ten lists.

The FrontPage features that require the extensions to work include most of the custom form handlers and many of the components found in the Insert menu. The extensions, which act as translators between your Web site and the Web server, are on your FrontPage installation disc. They also can be downloaded for free from *www.microsoft.com/frontpage/*

Checking Your Site

FrontPage's reporting tools make it much easier and faster to get your site ready to publish. Instead of depending on your Web browser to find every problem, FrontPage provides a site summary of possible problems. The reports feature also lets you mark any pages on the site that you do not want published yet, avoiding the all-too-common problem of accidentally publishing pages prematurely. By the way, you'll find it easier to check your site using the Reporting toolbar (right, **Figure 16.1**). Activate it by choosing View > Toolbars > Reporting.

To check and fix your site

1. Choose View > Reports > Site Summary (left, **Figure 16.1**). Or if the Reporting toolbar is activated, choose *Site Summary* from the drop-down menu (right, **Figure 16.1**).

2. When the Site Summary appears in FrontPage's main window, it will list general site information and any problems (**Figure 16.2**).

3. If the summary lists problems, such as *Broken hyperlinks*, double-click that line in the report to see a list of the problem pages.

4. To fix an individual page in the list, double-click it and the appropriate dialog box will appear, allowing you to fix the problem (**Figure 16.3**).

5. Repeat steps 2–4 until you've fixed all the problems.

Figure 16.1 To check your Web site for problems, choose View > Reports > Site Summary (left) or use the Reporting toolbar (right).

Figure 16.2 The Site Summary report provides a detailed overview of your site's problems. Double-click any line for details.

Figure 16.3 Double-click a listing in the Broken Hyperlinks report and the Edit Hyperlink dialog box will appear, enabling you to fix the link.

Figure 16.4 To examine a particular problem, use the Reporting toolbar to choose Reports > Problems and pick the relevant command in the submenu.

Figure 16.5 To see hidden folders, check *Show hidden files and folders* under the *Advanced* tab.

✔ Tips

- To return to the Site Summary after you've double-clicked to an individual problem report, click the Reporting toolbar and use the drop-down menu to select Site Summary.

- If you want to check for a particular problem, such as broken links, use the Reporting toolbar to choose Reports > Problems and pick the relevant command in the submenu (**Figure 16.4**).

- By default, any files placed inside hidden folders (those preceded by an underscore, such as the *_private* folder) will not appear in the Site Summary or problem reports. To have those files show up in reports, choose Tools > Web Settings, then click the *Advanced* tab, and check *Show hidden files and folders* (**Figure 16.5**).

Marking pages to publish

Running a quick check of the publishing status of your site's pages gives you a chance to mark pages that are not yet ready for public viewing. It also enables you to switch pages you previously marked *Don't Publish* to *Publish* if you have finished working on them. Running the review doesn't do anything to actually prepare the pages for publication. It's just meant to help keep you from accidentally publishing pages prematurely by highlighting which pages are set to be published.

To check or change a page's publishing status

1. Choose View > Reports > Workflow > Publish Status or choose Reports > Workflow > Publish Status if the Reporting toolbar is active (**Figure 16.6**).

2. FrontPage's main window will switch to the reports view and show the publishing status of all your site's files (**Figure 16.7**). If you spot pages whose status you want to switch, click in the page's *Publish* column and use the drop-down menu to change its status (**Figure 16.8**).

Figure 16.6 Choose Reports > Workflow > Publish Status in the Reporting toolbar.

Name	Title	Publish	Modif ▲
animate.js	animate.js	Publish	9/13/
chap_4.htm	Chap 4	Publish	9/15/
chap_5.htm	Chap 5	Publish	9/17/
confirmation.htm	Dear	Don't Publish	9/15/
contentsframe.htm	this is new sideframe	Don't Publish	9/15/
creatingSite.htm	Create Sites	Don't Publish	9/15/

Figure 16.7 The Publish Status report shows which Web pages are and aren't marked for publishing.

Name	Title	Publish	Modif ▲
animate.js	animate.js	Publish	9/13/
chap_4.htm	Chap 4	Don't Publish	9/15/
chap_5.htm	Chap 5	Publish	9/17/

Figure 16.8 Use the Publish column's drop-down menu to change a page's status.

Figure 16.9 To change the publishing status of several pages, right-click them in the Publish Status list or Folder List and choose *Properties* from the shortcut menu.

Figure 16.10 Check (or uncheck) the *Exclude this file* box to change the publishing status of the selected pages.

✔ Tip

- To change more than one page at a time, press Ctrl as you click pages in the Publish Status list or Folder List, then right-click the selected pages, and choose *Properties* from the shortcut menu (**Figure 16.9**). When the page's Properties dialog box appears, click the *Workgroup* tab and check (or uncheck) *Exclude this file when publishing the rest of the Web* at the bottom of the dialog box (**Figure 16.10**). Click *OK* and the status changes will be applied.

MARKING PAGES TO PUBLISH

Hiding pages from browsers

Some pages, such as your external style sheets, need to be on your Web server, but you may not want them visible to users. FrontPage creates a private folder for every Web site, which Web browsers won't detect. By placing files and subfolders inside the private folder, you can post files without having the world see them. The underscore at the beginning of the folder name is what hides the folder. You can create additional hidden folders if you like by putting an underscore at the beginning of the new folder's name, such as _Inhouse.

To hide pages

1. Switch to folders view and activate the Folder List.

2. Click the file(s) you want hidden and drag it to the _private folder in the Folder List (**Figure 16.11**). The file will be hidden from Web browsers, yet accessible for your Web server.

Figure 16.11 To hide pages from browsers, drag them into the _private folder in the Folder List.

Figure 16.12 To add meta tags to a page, first choose File > Properties.

Figure 16.13 Click *Add* under the *Custom* tab to create a new meta tag.

Figure 16.14 Use the User Meta Variable dialog box to add keywords to your meta tags.

Adding Meta Tags for Search Engines

Meta tags are bits of HTML coding, which among many uses, help search engines, such as Yahoo!, Alta Vista, and Excite, create directories to the World Wide Web. FrontPage makes it easy to add meta tags to attract the attention of search engines or keep them out of your site. Adding keyword meta tags makes it easier for search engines to categorize your site. The robot meta tags used on page 393 keep the same engines from indexing your site or following all its links, something you may want to do for an experimental site or one intended just for friends and family. The robot tag won't block every search engine, but it will keep out the vast majority.

To help search engines index your site

1. With your Web site open, choose File > Properties (**Figure 16.12**).

2. When the Page Properties dialog box appears, click the *Custom* tab, then click *Add* in the *User variables* section (**Figure 16.13**).

3. When the User Meta Variable dialog box appears, type keywords into the *Name* text box, then type the actual keywords that summarize your site's topics—each separated by a comma and a single space—into the *Value* text box (**Figure 16.14**).

(continued)

4. Click *OK* to close the User Meta Variable dialog box and the keywords will be listed in the Page Properties dialog box (**Figure 16.15**).

5. If you want to change the keywords, select that line in the *User variables* list and click *Modify*. To delete the keywords entirely, click *Remove*.

6. Once you're satisfied with the keyword changes, click *OK*. The keywords will be added to your site's meta tags.

✔ Tips

■ If you want to inspect the normally invisible meta tag keywords, click the *HTML* tab at the bottom of the main window and you'll find the keywords in the section above <title> (**Figure 16.16**).

■ Always use multiple keywords to create broad *and* narrow descriptions of your site. That way people using a search engine will pick up your site in a general category search but also find it when looking for a particular product or service.

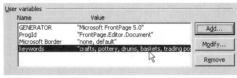

Figure 16.15 New meta tags are added to the Page Properties dialog box.

Figure 16.16 To see the normally invisible meta tag keywords, click the *HTML* tab.

Figure 16.17 To block search engines from indexing your site, type robots into the *Name* text box, and noindex, nofollow into the *Value* text box.

Figure 16.18 Click the *HTML* tab to see the robot-blocking meta tags.

To keep out search engines

1. With your Web site open, choose File > Properties (**Figure 16.12**).

2. When the Page Properties dialog box appears, click the *Custom* tab, then click *Add* in the *User variables* section (**Figure 16.13**).

3. When the User Meta Variable dialog box appears, type robots into the *Name* text box, then type noindex, nofollow into the *Value* text box (**Figure 16.17**).

4. Click *OK* to close the User Meta Variable dialog box and return to the Page Properties dialog box. Click *OK* and the meta tags will be added to your site's HTML coding (**Figure 16.18**).

Publishing to the Web

After you've fixed your Web pages and marked which ones should be published, you should preview them in several Web browsers. Use Internet Explorer *and* Netscape Navigator (in several versions of each) to check each page's appearance and links, since each browser interprets HTML code a bit differently. Make a point of also checking your pages on a Macintosh, particularly since PC-created images can look a bit washed out on Mac-driven monitors, which run a tad brighter than PC-driven monitors. Depending on how the pages look and behave, you may need to readjust some of your pages to avoid cross-platform problems. For details on which Web technologies work with various browsers, see *Setting Web Browser Compatibility* on page 416.

Once you've fixed any problems found in the browsers, you're finally ready to copy your Web site files from your local hard drive to the Web server you'll be using. Before you start, you'll need to know the server address that you'll be copying your files to, plus a user name and password to gain access to the server. Check with the Web server's administrator if you need help.

By the way, if you want to find a Web Presence Provider that uses FrontPage Server Extensions on its Web servers, the publishing process includes a step for locating one.

Figure 16.19 To start the publishing process, choose File > Publish Web.

Figure 16.20 Type a URL or local file path into the *Enter publish destination* text window or click *Browse* (top). Once you enter a destination, click *OK* (bottom).

Figure 16.21 Click *OK* to create a FrontPage web for the publishing destination.

To set the publish destination and options

1. Open the Web site you want to publish and choose File > Publish Web (**Figure 16.19**).

2. When the Publish Destination dialog box appears, type a URL or local file path into the *Enter publish destination* text window or click *Browse* to navigate to a folder on the Web or an internal server (top, **Figure 16.20**). Once you have entered the destination, click *OK* (bottom, **Figure 16.20**).

3. An alert dialog box will appear if the destination does not already contain a FrontPage web (**Figure 16.21**). Click *OK* and the web will be created. Depending on where the destination file resides, you also may need to enter a user name and password.

(continued)

SETTING THE PUBLISHING DESTINATION

4. When the Publish Web dialog box appears (**Figure 16.22**), click the *Options* button to reach the Options dialog box.

5. When the Options dialog box appears, the *Publish* tab will already be selected (**Figure 16.23**). Choose whether you want to publish *Changed pages only* or *All pages, overwriting any already on destination*. The *Changes* option button by default is set for the first choice, which compares the files in your local Web site (*source*) and the published one (*destination*). If you want to keep a record of what files are published, check *Log changes during publish*.

6. Click *OK* and the Publish Web dialog box will reappear with the local Web site listed on the left and the nearly empty destination site on the right (**Figure 16.24**). You are ready to go, so see *To publish your site* on page 401.

✔ Tips

■ You can only publish to destinations listed in the Publish Destination dialog box's drop-down menu (**Figure 16.20**). If the destination you need is not listed, see *To add a publishing destination* on page 397. To switch to another destination already listed in the Publish Destination dialog box's drop-down menu, see *To change a publishing destination* on page 400.

■ If you select the *Use source file time-stamps* option button in the Options dialog box (**Figure 16.23**), the most recent local files will be uploaded to the destination Web site. While that sounds good, be aware that it can cause problems if more than one person is updating the site, since the most recent files may not be the correct files.

Figure 16.22 Click the *Options* button to reach the Options dialog box.

Figure 16.23 Use the Options dialog box's *Publish* tab to set how differences between the local and destination Web sites are handled.

Figure 16.24 Once you set the publish destination, the Publish Web dialog box will display the files and folders of the local and destination Web sites.

Figure 16.25 To add or change a publishing destination, first choose File > Publish Web.

Figure 16.26 When the Publish Web dialog box appears, click *Change*.

Figure 16.27 Use the *Browse* button to navigate to the publishing destination you want to add.

Figure 16.28 When the New Publish Location dialog box appears, navigate to a folder on your own hard drive, a local network, or Web site.

To add a publishing destination

1. Open the Web site you want to publish and choose File > Publish Web (**Figure 16.25**).

2. When the Publish Web dialog box appears, click *Change* (**Figure 16.26**).

3. When the Publish Destination dialog box appears, click *Browse* (**Figure 16.27**).

4. When the New Publish Location dialog box appears, navigate to a folder on your own hard drive, a local network, or Web site (**Figure 16.28**). Skip to step 8 unless you need to create a new folder.

(continued)

5. Click the Create New Folder icon in the New Publish Location dialog box (**Figure 16.29**).

6. When the New Folder dialog box appears, give the folder a *Name*, use the *Folder Contains* drop-down menu to select *Web*, and click *OK* (**Figure 16.30**).

7. Select the type of Web you want to use in the Add Network Place Wizard dialog box and click *OK* (**Figure 16.31**). When the New Publish Location dialog box reappears, click *Open* (**Figure 16.32**).

Figure 16.29 If you need a new folder, click the Create New Folder icon in the New Publish Location dialog box.

Figure 16.30 Give the new folder a *Name*, select *Web* in the *Folder Contains* drop-down menu, and click *OK*.

Figure 16.31 Select the type of Web you want to use and click *OK*.

Figure 16.32 When the New Publish Location dialog box reappears, click *Open*.

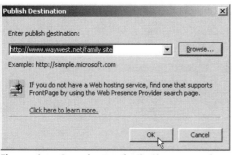

Figure 16.33 Once the new destination appears in the Publish Destination dialog box, click *OK*.

Figure 16.34 After you add a new publishing destination, its URL or file path name will appear in the top text window of the Publish Web dialog box.

8. The new destination will be listed in the Publish Destination dialog box (**Figure 16.33**). Click *OK* and the new destination will appear near the top of the Publish Web dialog box and in the right window's folder list (**Figure 16.34**). You're now ready to publish your Web site. See *To publish your site* on page 401.

✔ Tips

■ Depending on how your Internet connection's configured, you may need to connect to your Web server before clicking the *Browse* button in the Publish Destination dialog box (**Figure 16.27**).

■ An alert dialog box will appear if the destination does not already contain a FrontPage web (**Figure 16.21**). Click *OK* and the web will be created.

To change a publishing destination

1. Open the Web site you want to publish and choose File > Publish Web (**Figure 16.25**).

2. When the Publish Web dialog box appears, click *Change* (**Figure 16.26**).

3. When the Publish Destination dialog box appears, use the drop-down menu to select another predefined destination (**Figure 16.35**). (If the destination is not listed in the drop-down menu, see *To add a publishing destination* on page 397.)

4. Click *OK* to close the Publish Destination dialog box. The destination will now be listed in the Publish Web dialog box.

Figure 16.35 Use the Publish Destination dialog box's drop-down menu to select another predefined publishing destination.

Figure 16.36 Once the Publish Web dialog box displays your local Web site's folders and a destination site, you're ready to click *Publish*.

Figure 16.37 When the Enter Network Password dialog box appears, enter the *User Name* and *Password* assigned to you by the server's administrator.

Figure 16.38 Once FrontPage connects to the server, it will list the local pages that will be uploaded.

Figure 16.39 After another pause, FrontPage will begin copying your Web pages to the Web server.

To publish your site

1. Once you have set the destination and options for your Web site, open the Web site and choose File > Publish Web (**Figure 16.25**). For more information on setting the destination and options, see page 395.

2. When the Publish Web dialog box appears, check *Include subwebs* if you want to also publish any subwebs within your Web site (**Figure 16.36**). Click *Publish* and FrontPage will use your default Internet access connection to connect to your Web server. For more information on the Publish Web dialog box, see *Publish Web options* on page 404.

3. Type in the user name and password the Web server administrator assigned you when the Enter Network Password dialog box appears (**Figure 16.37**).

4. There will be a brief pause as FrontPage compiles a list of the pages that need to be uploaded to the Web server (**Figure 16.38**). After another pause (the length will depend on how many new pages you're uploading and your connection speed), FrontPage will begin copying your Web pages to the Web server (**Figure 16.39**).

(continued)

5. Once FrontPage completes the transfer, it will offer you the choice of seeing the now-published site, seeing a log of the files published, or closing the dialog box by clicking *Done* (**Figure 16.40**). The first two choices will launch your Web browser to display the site or the log (**Figure16.41**). Clicking *Done* returns you to the Publish Web dialog box, where you can see that the files from the local site (on the left) have been copied to the Web site (on the right) (**Figure 16.42**).

Figure 16.40 Once FrontPage completes the transfer, you can choose to see the now-published site, a log of the files published, or return to FrontPage's main window.

Figure 16.41 Use the optional Publish Log to check which local Web site's folders and files were uploaded to the destination site, and at what time.

Figure 16.42 After you publish your site, the Publish Web dialog box displays what's on the local and destination Web sites.

Publishing Web Structure ? X

(?) FrontPage has detected that changes you have made to the navigation structure conflict with changes another author has made to the Web you are publishing to. What do you want to do?

○ Do not replace the navigation structure of the destination web

○ Replace the navigational structure of the destination web

● Let FrontPage merge the changes

If you let FrontPage merge the changes, it will publish the navigation structure but only replace another author's change if yours is more recent.

Continue   Cancel

Figure 16.43 When you update a site, FrontPage will alert you if the update will change the site's navigation structure.

Publish Web (Alt+P)

Figure 16.44 Once you publish a site, you can publish further changes just by clicking the Publish Web button.

Publishing FrontPage Components X

(!) The following pages in your web site contain dynamic FrontPage components, such as a Search Form or a FrontPage form handler. They will not work unless they are published to a web server running the FrontPage Server Extensions or SharePoint Team Services from Microsoft.

sayhey.htm
survey.htm

To enable these components, publish your web site to a server running the latest version of the FrontPage Server Extensions or SharePoint Team Services from Microsoft.

Continue   Cancel

Figure 16.45 If your server lacks FrontPage Server Extensions, a dialog box will alert you.

✔ Tips

■ Depending on how your Internet connection's configured, you may need to connect to your Web server before clicking the *Publish* button in the Publish Web dialog box. Once you're done uploading your site to the server, disconnect from the Internet if you're using a dial-up connection.

■ If you choose to overwrite pages already on the Web site, FrontPage will alert you if that will change the site's navigation structure (**Figure 16.43**). You'll have the choice of leaving the structure as is, replacing it with your changes, or merging both versions by using only the newest pages.

■ After the first time you publish your Web site and assuming your Publish Web dialog box settings remain the same, you can just click the Publish Web button whenever you need to update your site on the Web server (**Figure 16.44**). The site will be published without opening any dialog boxes, so if you need to change any publishing settings, use the File > Publish Web command instead.

■ FrontPage helps you avoid posting pages that won't work on your Web server. If your server doesn't have the necessary FrontPage Server Extensions, a dialog box will alert you if any of your pages require those extensions (**Figure 16.45**).

Publish Web options

To reach the Publish Web dialog box (**Figure 16.46**), choose File > Publish Web.

❶ **Publish from:** This is the file path name for your local Web site. To set it, see *To publish your site* on page 401.

❷ **Publish to:** This is the URL or file path name for your destination Web site, which is the site to which you want to publish pages. See *To set the publish destination and options* on page 395.

❸ **Change:** Click to change the destination Web site. See *To add a publishing destination* on page 397 and *To change a publishing destination* on page 400.

❹ **Local site's folders and files:** Beneath the path name for your local site are listed all the local site's folders and files. By clicking the column labels (*Name, Status, Modified,* etc.), you can sort the files based on that column. Click the chosen column again to reverse the sort order.

❺ **Destination site's folders and files:** Beneath the URL or path name for your destination site are listed all the folders and files already published to that site. By clicking the column labels (*Name, Modified, Author,* etc.), you can sort the files based on that column. Click the chosen column again to reverse the sort order.

❻ **Up one level:** Click the folder icon to move one level higher in the hierarchy of the local or destination site folders.

❼ **X icon:** Click to delete selected files or folders from the local or destination site lists.

Figure 16.46 Use the expanded Publish Web dialog box to control which pages are published.

➑ Status: This column, which only appears in the local Web site list, helps you know which local files have already been published to the destination Web site. Files marked *Publish* have been created or changed since you last published the site. They also are marked with a green checkmark in the *Name* column. Files marked *Up to date* already have been copied to the Web site.

➒ Include subwebs: It's sometimes convenient when publishing larger Web sites to create subwebs—smaller webs within the main web for natural subdivisions such as sales or personnel. Whether you include or exclude subwebs in a posting will depend on whether each subdivision is responsible for publishing its own subweb's materials.

➓ Hide: Click to hide the destination Web site's list of files, leaving only the local file list visible. A Show button will then appear for re-expanding the Publish Web dialog box.

⑪ Options: Click to reach the dialog box controlling various publishing options. For more information, see page 396.

⑫ Publish: Click to publish local files to the destination Web site. Depending on how your Internet connection's configured, you may need to connect to your Web server before clicking the *Publish* button.

PART 5

APPENDIX
& INDEX

INSTALLING & CONFIGURING FRONTPAGE

It's tempting to install FrontPage and immediately start building your Web site. But take a minute to configure how FrontPage handles HTML codes, and you'll be assured that your Web site will be compatible with the Web browsers people use when they visit your site. If you just want to build Web pages and don't need to run a Web server on your local machine, then FrontPage 2002 works fine with Windows 98 or later. If you plan on installing a FrontPage-enabled Web server on your local computer—essential if you want to check most of the program's Web Components before publishing them to a remote Web server—you will need to be running Windows NT 4.0 with Service Pack 6 or later. Installing a local Web server, by the way, falls beyond the scope of this book.

What you'll need before starting

◆ A PC equipped with the equivalent of an Intel Pentium or Celeron chip.

◆ At least 32 MB of RAM (memory); 128 MB if you are running Windows 2000 Professional.

◆ At least 175 MB of free space on your hard drive (more to install some of the clip art included on the CD).

◆ A 56Kbps modem for dial-up Internet connections. Office networks typically have much faster, hardwired Internet connections, so you'll have plenty of speed there.

◆ A color monitor capable of displaying at least 256 colors.

◆ A CD-ROM drive for installing FrontPage.

Installing FrontPage

If you need to save hard drive space and do not have enough room for FrontPage's standard version, see *To install a custom version of FrontPage* on page 412.

To install the standard version of FrontPage

1. Turn off all programs, including any anti-virus program you have running in the background.

2. Put the FrontPage 2002 or Office XP CD in your disc drive. Once the CD launches, the *User information* screen will appear (**Figure A.1**). Enter your *User name*, *Initials*, and the 25-character *Product Key*, which you'll find on the back of the CD's jewel case. When you're done, click *Next*.

3. When the *End-User License Agreement* screen appears (**Figure A.2**), check *I accept the terms in the License Agreement* and click *Next*.

4. Depending on whether you are upgrading FrontPage or installing it for the first time, the next screen will say *Upgrade Now* or *Install Now* and be set to install FrontPage in your main programs file (**Figure A.3**). In most cases, you should just click *Next* and the standard version of FrontPage will be installed. If you want to change the installation location, click *Browse* and navigate to where you want the program installed. You also can select one of three other installation configurations: *Typical*, *Complete*, or *Custom*, and click *Next*. For more information on these options, see *To install a custom version of FrontPage* on page 412.

Figure A.1 Begin by entering the 25-character *Product Key* found on the back of the CD jewel case.

Figure A.2 Check the *I accept the terms in the License Agreement* box and click *Next*.

Figure A.3 Depending on whether you are upgrading FrontPage or installing it for the first time, choose *Upgrade Now* or *Install Now* to install the standard version of FrontPage.

Figure A.4 Double-check that the components you need are listed, then click *Install*.

Figure A.5 Once the installation begins, a progress bar appears.

Figure A.6 When the installer asks you to restart your computer, click *Yes*.

5. The next screen will list what will be installed (or first removed if you are upgrading from an earlier version of FrontPage) (**Figure A.4**). Click *Install* and the standard version of FrontPage will be installed (**Figure A.5**).

6. When the installer asks you to restart your computer, click *Yes* (**Figure A.6**). Once your computer restarts, see *To activate FrontPage* on page 415.

✔ Tip

■ If you're upgrading from FrontPage 98, you don't need to do anything differently. The installer will detect the earlier version and leave it in place. However, your original Start menu shortcut to FrontPage 98 will be replaced by a FrontPage 2002 shortcut. If you want to keep using the FrontPage 98 program on the computer, you'll need to create a new shortcut to FrontPage 98.

To install a custom version of FrontPage

1. Follow steps 1–3 in *To install the standard version of FrontPage* on page 410. When the installer asks you to *choose an install type*, select *Typical, Complete* or *Custom,* then click *Browse* and navigate to where you want the program installed (**Figure A.7**). Finally, click *Next.*

2. When the *Features to install* screen appears (**Figure A.8**), you'll need to decide which parts of FrontPage to install—and which to leave out. To reach any subitems, click on the + to expand items in the list. To collapse the list, click the –.

3. Click the drop-down menu of any item to select your installation option for that item (**Figure A.9**). For details on your choices, see **Table A.1**.

4. Once you've made all your choices, click *Next* and then *Install.* FrontPage will install your choices (**Figure A.5**).

5. When the installer asks you to restart your computer, click *Yes* (**Figure A.6**). Once the computer restarts, see *To activate FrontPage* on page 415.

Figure A.7 To install a custom version of FrontPage, select *Typical, Complete* or *Custom,* then click *Browse* and navigate to where you want the program installed.

Figure A.8 When the *Features to install* screen appears, you'll need to decide which parts of FrontPage to install.

Table A.1

Custom Installation Choices

ICON	TEXT	EXPLANATION
🖻	Run from My Computer	Installs item & default subitems
🖻	Run all from My Computer	Installs item & all subitems
⊗	Run from CD	Runs item if CD in player
⊗	Run all from CD	Runs item & all subitems if CD in player
✕	Not Available	Will not be installed
🖭	Installed on First Use	If item ever used, asks for CD & installs

Figure A.9 Use the drop-down menu of any item to select an installation option for that item.

Figure A.10 Use the *Space Required* and *Space Available* figures at the bottom of the *Features to install* screen to gauge if you'll have enough hard drive space for all your choices.

Figure A.11 Click any item to expand it and see which subitems will be installed.

✔ Tips

■ It can seem a bit confusing but the + and – in step 2 simply expand or collapse your *view* and have nothing to do with which items will or won't be installed. Instead, you must use each item's drop-down menu (as described in step 3) to set which items are installed.

■ As you select items to install in step 3, use the *Space Required* and *Space Available* figures at the bottom of the *Features to install* screen to gauge if you'll have enough hard drive space for all your choices (**Figure A.10**).

■ The standard (default) installation does not install all the subitems under each item. Click to expand an item if you want to see which subitems will be installed (**Figure A.11**).

■ If you change your mind on what items you need, you can go back and add or remove FrontPage components later on. For details, see *To update, repair, or uninstall FrontPage* on the next page.

To update, repair, or uninstall FrontPage

1. Turn off all programs, including any anti-virus program you have running in the background.

2. Put the FrontPage or Office XP disc into your CD-ROM drive. Once the CD launches, the *Maintenance Mode Options* screen will appear (**Figure A.12**).

3. Click *Add or Remove Features* to do exactly that, *Repair FrontPage* if you want to reinstall FrontPage's default installation, or *Uninstall FrontPage* to uninstall the program.

4. If you choose *Add or Remove Features* in step 2, the *Features to install* screen will appear (**Figure A.13**). Select the items you want to add or remove, then click *Update*. For details on adding or removing FrontPage features, see steps 2–3 of *To install a custom version of FrontPage* on page 412.

5. Continue clicking *Next* until you're done, then click *OK* to exit the installation. Be sure to restart your computer before continuing.

Figure A.12 To update, repair, or uninstall FrontPage, reinsert the program disc into your CD drive and make your choice.

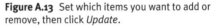

Figure A.13 Set which items you want to add or remove, then click *Update*.

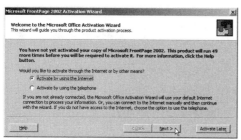

Figure A.14 When FrontPage asks whether you want to activate, click *Next*.

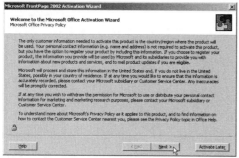

Figure A.15 Microsoft's privacy policy requires extra work to avoid sharing your information.

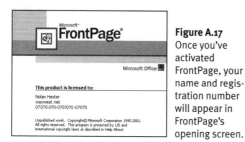

Figure A.16 Only the *Country/Region* field is required before clicking *Next*.

To activate FrontPage

1. The first time you start up FrontPage after installing it, you'll be asked whether you want to activate the program (**Figure A.14**). Click *Next* to do so.

2. The next screen explains Microsoft's privacy policy (**Figure A.15**). Known as an opt-out policy, the policy says Microsoft is free to "distribute your personal contact information for marketing and marketing research purposes" unless you contact the Microsoft Customer Service Center. Click *Next* (and if you want, make a note to contact the service center to opt out of having your information shared with marketers).

3. In the *Customer Information* screen, you are required only to provide a country or region (**Figure A.16**). The rest of the information is optional, so it's your choice whether to provide it. When you are done, click *Next* and the Activation Wizard will use your default Internet setup to dial a local telephone number and send the information to Microsoft.

4. Once the information is transmitted, click *OK* and you're done. The next time you launch FrontPage, your name and registration number appear in the program's opening screen (**Figure A.17**). Now you're ready to set the defaults for how FrontPage will code your pages, which controls how they'll appear in various Web browsers. See *Setting Web Browser Compatibility* on the next page.

Figure A.17 Once you've activated FrontPage, your name and registration number will appear in FrontPage's opening screen.

Setting Web Browser Compatibility

If every Web browser rendered HTML the same way, creating Web pages would be so simple. In that perfect world, you wouldn't need to remember how different HTML tags look in Internet Explorer vs. Netscape Navigator or which tags work in old or new browsers. Until that day comes, FrontPage offers a decent compromise. You decide which browsers you want to code for and FrontPage automatically generates the proper HTML. Sure, you still have to decide whether to code for the broadest group of browsers—and forego CSS and DHTML—or use the new tags and risk excluding some folks. But at least you won't have to worry about which tags work with which browsers.

Figure A.18 To set browser compatibility and how FrontPage handles HTML code, choose Tools > Page Options.

Figure A.19 Use the *Compatibility* tab to set which browsers you want to code for, and FrontPage will automatically generate the proper HTML.

To set browser compatibility

1. Choose Tools > Page Options (**Figure A.18**).

2. When the Page Options dialog box appears, click the *Compatibility* tab (**Figure A.19**).

3. Use the *Browsers* drop-down menu to choose which Web browsers you'll be coding for. Your choice will check or uncheck boxes in the *Available Technologies* section, indicating which technologies you'll be able to use with that choice.

4. Use the *Browser versions* drop-down menu to choose which versions you'll be coding for. This choice will further narrow the number of checked boxes in the *Available Technologies* section, indicating which technologies you'll be able to use with that choice.

5. By default, the *Servers* menu is set to *Custom*. Leave it alone unless you are absolutely sure exactly which server software will be used on your Web server.

6. Check or uncheck *Enabled with Microsoft FrontPage Server Extensions*. Again, your choice will affect the items turned on or off in the *Available Technologies* section. For more on FrontPage Server Extensions, see page 385.

7. Once you're done making your choices, click *OK*, and FrontPage will base its HTML code on those choices. If you change your mind, you can change the settings any time, though only pages coded after that point will reflect your changes.

Setting HTML Coding Preferences

You don't need to mess with this unless you intend to tweak FrontPage's HTML coding directly. However, if you plan on jumping into your code now and then, these settings let you wrap the code the way you want and color the various coding tags just how you want them.

To set HTML code preferences

1. If you have a Web page with the HTML already set just how you want it, open it in FrontPage ((Ctrl)(O)). Otherwise, skip to step 2.

2. Choose Tools > Page Options (**Figure A.18**).

3. When the Page Options dialog box appears, click the *HTML Source* tab (**Figure A.20**).

4. In the *General* section, choose *Reformat using the rules below* ❶.

5. If you opened a page in step 1, click *Base on current page* ❷ in the *Formatting* section. Otherwise, check any or all of the three *Formatting* boxes ❸ to set how you want the HTML to appear. Use the text boxes and arrows for *Indent* ❹ and *Right margin* ❺ to set how you want those items to appear in HTML.

Figure A.20 Use the *HTML Source* tab to set how you want the HTML to appear when you switch to FrontPage's *HTML* view.

Figure A.21 Use the *Color Coding* tab to set the colors used in your HTML and script tags.

6. Now, click the *Color Coding* tab within the Page Options dialog box to set the colors used in your HTML.

7. When the *Color Coding* tab appears (**Figure A.21**), use the drop-down menus to change any of the default colors. For details on using the color drop-down menus, see step 4 on page 150.

8. Once you're done setting the *HTML Source* and *Color Coding* tabs, click *OK*. The changes will be applied to your HTML coding.

✔ Tip

■ If you change your mind setting items in the *HTML Source* tab, click *Reset* to return to the original settings.

SETTING HTML CODING PREFERENCES

INDEX

INDEX

New from Peachpit Press!

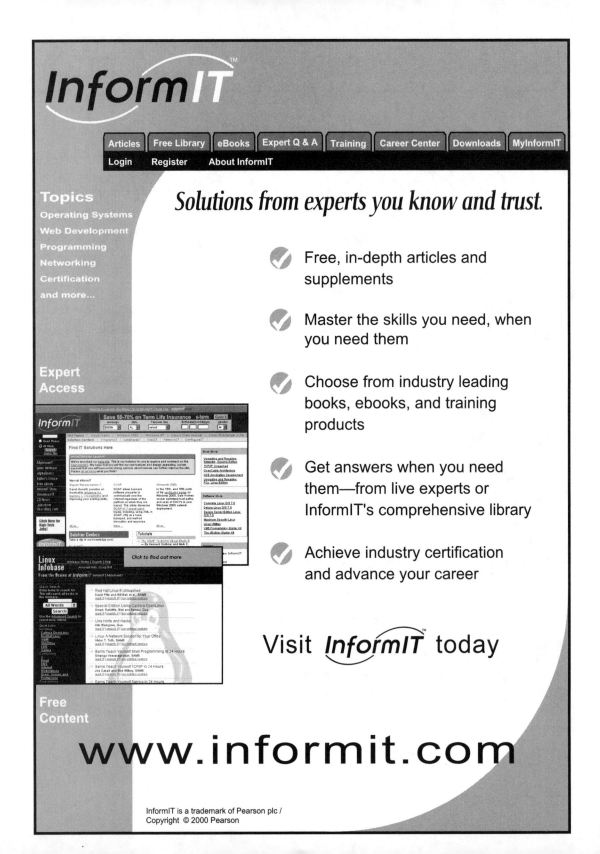